Last documents:
– *The Road of Time*, Philippe Guillemant;
– *Vaccination: The Great Illusion*, Bickel.

Original title: *Géopolitique des cryptomonnaies.*

Talma Studios
231, rue Saint-Honoré
75001 Paris – France
www.talmastudios.com
info@talmastudios.com

Cover pictures:
– NASA Blue Marble of the Earth's Eastern Hemisphere
– ID 88696100 © Nils Ackermann | Dreamstime.com
– ID 107725361 © Jiri Hera | Dreamstime.com

ISBN : 979-10-96132-62-1   EAN : 9791096132621
© All rights reserved

Nancy Gomez – Patrick Pasin

Geopolitics of Cryptocurrencies

"Bitcoin is the Foundation Stone of the Monetary Revolution of the 21st Century."

Translated from French

Introduction

What could be the possible link between Muammar Gaddafi, Benedict XVI, North Korea, Iran and Russia in a book devoted to cryptocurrencies and the financial revolution in progress?

"We came, we saw, he died."
Thus, paraphrasing Julius Caesar's famous phrase "Veni, vidi, vici," then US Secretary of State Hillary Clinton comments on the death of Muammar Gaddafi in October 2011 following the military intervention in Libya that took place between 19 March and 31 October 2011. Under the auspices of the United Nations, its official mission is to implement Security Council Resolution 1973, the objective of which is "to take all necessary measures, notwithstanding paragraph 9 of resolution 1970 (2011), to protect civilians and civilian populated areas under threat of attack in the Libyan Arab Jamahiriya."

Organized by France, the United Kingdom, the United States, Canada and NATO, the result of this military intervention went beyond the declared purpose of the Resolution 1973, leading to the destruction of the Libyan State. Moreover, Europe has yet to finish paying the price for the chaos it has helped to establish in this country, once one of the richest on the continent.

However, information contained in the emails of the former Democratic candidate declassified by the State Department on December 31, 2015 tells a story quite different than the official version[1]: thanks

---
1. *Hillary Emails Reveal True Motive for Libya Intervention*, Brad Hoff, *Foreign Policy Journal*, 01/06/2016.

Introduction

to his stocks of gold and silver (more than 140 tons of each metal, valued at a few billion dollars), Muammar Gaddafi was preparing the creation of a single currency for Africa. For the former French-speaking colonies, it would have constituted an alternative to the CFA franc and favored their economic independence, to the detriment of the interests of France and, more generally, of the United Kingdom and the European Union, but also of the United States, by ultimately reducing the role of the dollar. It is for this monetary priority, which would push then President Nicolas Sarkozy to carry out military actions in Libya, according to Hillary Clinton's correspondence. One is therefore led to believe that a currency is worth the chaos, death, desolation and destruction of a country.

The Pope goes away, business resumes
1 January 2013: Fabio Tonacci publishes in *La Repubblica* an article entitled: *Vatican, stop at cards and ATMs. Payment services suspended.*[2] In summary, in a sovereign state, it is no longer possible to withdraw money from ATMs or pay with the cards of US giants Visa and Mastercard. This is, of course, an economic disaster for the Vatican.

The decision is officially due to the absence of authorization from the Italian central bank given to Deutsche Bank Italia, supplier of payment terminals for bank cards in the Vatican. This reason seems questionable, all the more so as the suspension begins to last weeks long.

February 11: Benedict XVI announces, to the surprise of the whole world, that he renounces to "the ministry of Bishop of Rome, Successor of Saint Peter, entrusted to me by the Cardinals on 19 April 2005, in such a way, that as from 28 February 2013, at 8:00 p.m., the See of Rome, the See of Saint Peter, will be vacant and a Conclave to elect the new Supreme Pontiff will have to be convoked by those whose competence it is."[3] Therefore, there will be no Pope as of

---

2. *Vaticano, stop a carte e bancomat – Sospesi i servizi di pagamento*, **Fabio Tonacci,** *La Repubblica*, **01/03/2013.**
3. *Declaratio*, **Benedictus PP XVI, Libreria Editrice Vaticana, 02/10/2013.**

March 1, less than three weeks from the date of his announcement. It is an almost unprecedented event in two millennia of papal history, for Celestine V can be considered the only Roman pope to have resigned on his own initiative—he formalized his renunciation on December 13, 1294.

Benedict XVI, aware of the importance of the decision he is announcing, justifies his decision by stating that "in order to govern the Barque of Saint Peter and proclaim the Gospel, both strength of mind and body are necessary, strength which in the last few months, has deteriorated in me to the extent that I have had to recognize my incapacity to adequately fulfill the ministry entrusted to me."[4]

12 February: the following day, the Vatican's disconnection from the payment system, which had lasted several weeks, is suspended. As a result, all services are restored and business resumes.

Given the simultaneity of events and even if the resignation is explained by reasons of "vigor"—not even "health"—it makes sense to wonder if the disconnection of the financial system was not a means of pressure to push the Pope to resign.

However, where would this pressure come from? There are not too many countries with sufficient weight over global financial and banking institutions to make such a decision; in fact, there is only one: the United States. Would they have acted to prevent Benedict XVI from continuing his great reconciliation project with the Patriarch of Moscow aimed at Euro-Russian geopolitical integration? It is not the purpose of this book to dwell on facts that are only interpretative, so we will not go any further in this direction. Nevertheless, there is no doubt that the organization of the current international financial system can constitute a threat against a (small) state as effective as a military intervention, while being more discreet and less costly.

Iran, on the front line

Moreover, the Vatican is not the only State to be financially sidelined. In February 2002, the US Senate Banking Committee unanimously approves a law prohibiting SWIFT from serving Iranian banks subject

---
4. *Declaratio*, Benedictus PP XVI, Libreria Editrice Vaticana, 02/10/2013.

Introduction

to sanctions. As a result, they are all disconnected from the system in March, including the central bank, and can therefore no longer carry out any international banking transactions. One can imagine the consequences, all the more so as assets are frozen, to the tune of approximately 32 billion dollars[5], according to the director of the central bank of Iran, Valiollah Seif, and remain partly frozen.

January 2016, however, Iranian banks are reintegrated, after the signing of the nuclear agreement.

North Korea, inevitably
In March 2017, SWIFT announces in a press release that it has disconnected the last banks in the north of the peninsula connected to its system: "The North Korean banks that were still connected to the network no longer meet SWIFT's membership criteria. As a result, these entities will no longer have access to SWIFT's financial messaging system."

Officially, this decision is taken "because North Korea is currently receiving increased international attention."

Russia too?
At the height of the sanctions imposed by the United States and Europe against Russia following "Russia's direct and indirect military intervention in Ukraine, including the annexation of Crimea"[6], there are calls for Russian financial institutions to be disconnected from the SWIFT network, including that of the European Parliament, which: "(…) calls for the EU to consider excluding Russia from civil nuclear cooperation and the SWIFT system."

This would be a very severe blow to Russia, which would probably see its banking system collapse, at least in part. Moreover, some Duma deputies announced that such a decision would be considered a declaration of war.

---

5. *Where are Iran's billions in frozen assets, and how soon will it get them back?*, **Matt Pearce**, *Los Angeles Times*, 01/20/2016.
6. Joint Motion for a Resolution (2014/2841(RSP)), European Parliament, 09/17/2014.

In the end, the threat was not put into effect; in any case, it would have posed an almost insurmountable problem for Europeans: by disconnecting Russia from SWIFT, no more international transfers would have been possible; how then could they pay for the energy that reaches full gas pipelines from Russia? It is surprising that MEPs did not think about this before threatening.

Realizing the risk that such a situation could eventually represent, the Deputy Finance Minister, Alexeï Moïseïev, declares in August 2014 that his ministry and the Central Bank are preparing the creation of a SWIFT equivalent in Russia.

However, overnight, Russian users of Visa and MasterCard credit cards find themselves without their means of payment, as a result of the immediate sanctions applied against their country. This situation temporarily creates enormous problems for which Russia has to find solutions. In particular, it develops the Mir card payment system, introduced in December 2015, which enables its banks to replace Visa and MasterCard.

"Allow me to issue and control the money of a nation, and I care not who makes its laws!"[7]

Cryptocurrencies, notably the main one, bitcoin, have so far escaped the monopoly of banks and governments of fiat money. They still represent a drop in the ocean of international finance. Some even predict their imminent disappearance, drawing a parallel with the Tulip crisis in 18th century Holland, considered the first speculative crash in history. Is that so sure?

Perhaps there will be a collapse in the value of bitcoin, on which speculation has been falling since 2017, but we don't believe cryptocurrencies are going to disappear anytime soon, since they offer powerful solutions, as well as other benefits, including geopolitical ones.

However, we will refrain from saying that Benedict XVI or Muammar Gaddafi would still be in office if they had had a sovereign

---

[7]. Quote attributed to Mayer Amshel Rothschild (1744-1812), the founder of the banking dynasty.

cryptocurrency, or that Iran's economic situation today would be one of particular prosperity. However, the unexpected emergence of cryptocurrencies, now a global phenomenon, and the advantages they represent over the current financial system can only raise the question of their large-scale development in the public sphere.

Thus, it is now possible that they constitute one of the solutions to an increasingly global and multipolar world, but also increasingly unequal and destructive. Could they even contribute to world independence and peace? And to the creation of new sources of wealth while many economies stagnate, despite the needs of populations? These are some of the questions to which *Geopolitics of Cryptocurrencies* wishes to provide answers, prospective scenarios and avenues for reflection.

We will begin with a general overview, and then present the decisions and actions of many countries on all continents, before considering, in the last chapter, scenarios for the creation of cryptocurrencies between states.

Chapter 1

General Overview of Cryptocurrencies

Concepts and definitions

A **cryptocurrency** (or "**altcoin**") is a digital currency secured by a complex encryption system. It is therefore not simply an electronic means of payment but a currency, in the sense that it can be used to make payments for the purchase of goods or services, either in an expanded or restricted manner within a community. In most cases, it is also a financial asset, subject to the law of supply and demand, and therefore open to speculation.

Unlike traditional currencies, the first cryptocurrencies are not issued by central banks or financial institutions, but created *ex nihilo* by individuals and private entities, who intervene at all stages of their management and set the rules of their governance. They make them known through the disclosure of white papers—forms of manifesto of intent—to explain the objectives of the project and its operation, including the technological bases used. Indeed, a cryptocurrency relies on the powerful technology of the **blockchain**, which constitutes a rupture and a revolution in the organization and the processing of information, just as central computers, PCs, the Internet and mobile networks did before it.

"A blockchain is a digitized, decentralized, public ledger of all cryptocurrency transactions. Constantly growing as 'completed' blocks (the most recent transactions) are recorded and added to it in chronological order, it allows market participants to keep track of digital currency transactions without central recordkeeping. Each node (a computer connected to the network) gets a copy of the blockchain, which is downloaded automatically.

Originally developed as the accounting method for the virtual currency bitcoin, blockchains—which use what's known as

Chapter 1

distributed ledger technology (DLT)—are appearing in a variety of commercial applications today. Currently, the technology is primarily used to verify transactions, within digital currencies though it is possible to digitize, code and insert practically any document into the blockchain. Doing so creates an indelible record that cannot be changed; furthermore, the record's authenticity can be verified by the entire community using the blockchain instead of a single centralized authority."[8]

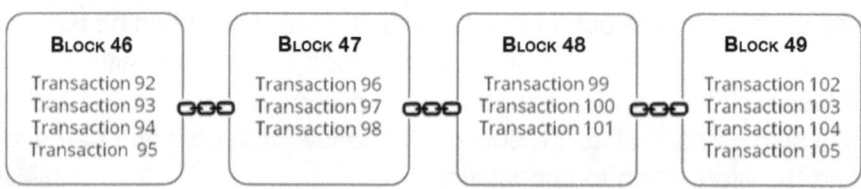

"The information being kept in the blockchain network is transparent in so far as the common data base is simultaneously available to all computers incorporated in the network. The records preserved therein are publicly available and easily checked. The blockchain network may not be broken up since the change of even one unit of information requires replacement of information in the entire network."[9]

In short, a blockchain is a large public register, anonymous and unforgeable. Some blockchains are public, others are private. Their use is not limited to money creation, but offers almost unlimited opportunities in banking and finance, insurance, logistics, health, land registration, humanitarian affairs, etc. Indeed, the latest generations of blockchains make it possible to insert **Smart Contracts**, IT protocols that facilitate, control and execute the negotiation and/or execution of a contract, in order to benefit from security greater than traditional contractual clauses and to reduce transaction costs.

---

8. Blockchain. www.investopedia.com/terms/b/blockchain.asp.
9. *The information network based on the blockchain technology was built up in the Republic of Belarus*, press release of the National Bank of the Republic of Belarus, 07/19/2017.

General Overview of Cryptocurrencies

The Blockchain Against Hunger

As we have indicated, the technology that supports cryptocurrencies can be used for multiple purposes. Here is one of the most significant examples. On 30 May 2017, the World Food Program (WFP), the UN agency fighting hunger, published the following information on its website[10]:

"(…) In Jordan's Azraq camp, 10,000 refugees are now able to pay for their food by means of entitlements recorded on a blockchain-based computing platform. This was developed by WFP as part of a pilot known as 'Building Blocks'."

Robert Opp, WFP's Director of Innovation and Change Management, explains that "blockchain technology allows us to step up the fight against hunger. Through blockchain, we aim to cut payment costs, better protect beneficiary data, control financial risks, and respond more rapidly in the wake of emergencies. Using blockchain can be a qualitative leap—not only for WFP, but for the entire humanitarian community."

Here is how this innovation works:

"WFP's system relies on biometric registration data from the United Nations High Commissioner for Refugees (UNHCR) and uses biometric technology for authentication purposes. Refugees purchase food from local supermarkets in the camp by using a scan of their eye instead of cash, vouchers or e-cards.

The conflict in Syria has forced close to five million people to flee abroad in search of safety. In neighboring Jordan alone, WFP provides much-needed assistance to more than half a million Syrians.

The pilot aims to create a platform that the wider humanitarian community could use. Depending on the results of the pilot, WFP will look at expanding the use of blockchain technology to areas such as digital identity management and supply chain operations.

---

10. *Blockchain Against Hunger: Harnessing Technology In Support Of Syrian Refugees*, World Food Program, 05/30/2017.

Chapter 1

> WFP believes that twenty-first century developments in mobile technology, biometrics and solutions such as blockchain, have the potential to transform the lives of people in need across the world and address the roots of hunger."
> Thus, bitcoin could disappear, certainly not the blockchain.

The blockchain appears in 2008, with the creation of the bitcoin, the main and first cryptocurrency, followed, since then, by more than one thousand five hundred others, including the ether, the litecoin, the dash, the ripple, etc. There are mainly five ways to obtain it:

- purchase them from an online exchange platform or via vending machines. Payment can be made in cash, or even with another cryptocurrency;

- subscribe to an **ICO** (Initial Coin Offering), a fundraising tool based on cryptocurrencies. The emitting company creates "**tokens**" (digital tokens) in exchange for bitcoins, ethers, etc. Tokens are not dividend-paying shares and their purchase offers no specific guarantee to the investor: they only represent the hope of a medium or short term gain, when it is not a fraud or a scam. In the context of an ICO intended for the creation of a currency, subscribers receive a quantity of tokens according to their investment;

- benefit from an **airdrop**, i.e. free distribution of the cryptocurrency by the creators;

- participate in its exploitation by **mining**;

- receive it as a payment for a service or the sale of a good.

To possess cryptocurrencies requires depositing them in a **wallet** installed on a computer or mobile phone. It is possible to have several portfolios on different platforms, especially if one acquires various cryptocurrencies, because not all are available on each exchange.

When the wallet is open, you get an **address** and a **private key**. Only the address can be communicated; transmitting your private key is like giving away or losing your wallet. Transfers are made from portfolio to portfolio. Once validated, there is no turning back: the transaction is final and cannot be duplicated. It takes ten minutes for the transaction to be known throughout the blockchain bitcoin, less time for other cryptocurrencies.

Mining appears for the creation and recording of an encrypted currency. Contrary to what the name suggests, it is not a question of "mining" a deposit, but rather of solving complex mathematical equations for the creation and recording of a block, each of them corresponding to one or more transactions. Mining therefore refers to creating a block (also called a **"node"**), validating it and linking it to the other blocks that make up the blockchain.

The **miner** brings his computer skills and equipment to provide the necessary computing power. To mine cryptocurrencies, a computer with a good graphics card is generally sufficient, except for bitcoin: it requires such particular computing resources that specific computer hardware, the **miners**, was created and is offered for sale.

Mining is generally remunerated by the allocation of units or fractions of the mined cryptocurrency.

Encrypted currencies are called "mined" when the creation of the currency requires the intervention of a miner; otherwise, they are called "validated" or "pre-mined."

Mining uses the **"hash"** or **hash function**, which consists of applying to each block an additional unique mathematical function of equal importance. Each block creation in the chain contains the hash of the previous block, making it impossible to go back. The development of the chain is one-way. Thus secured, it is difficult for a sole miner with diversion intentions to intervene on the channel.

In the case of bitcoin mining, "the difficulty is adjusted every 2016 blocks based on the time it took to find the previous 2016 blocks. At the desired rate of one block each 10 minutes, 2016 blocks would take exactly two weeks to find. If the previous 2016 blocks took more than two weeks to find, the difficulty is reduced. If they took less than two weeks, the difficulty is increased. The change in difficulty is in

Chapter 1

proportion to the amount of time over or under the two weeks the previous 2016 blocks took to find."[11] This is also why mining requires heavy investments in terms of equipment and energy resources.

As a result, miners are grouping together to increase their computing power by forming **pools of miners** or **mining farms**, the largest of which own up to several tens of thousands of networked mining machines and computers. This resource-intensive activity has developed other services such as cloud mining, which sells computing capacity in exchange for a fraction of the cryptocurrencies generated.

Currently, all computers in the blockchain network process every piece of information. The transaction is therefore slow and energy consuming. By way of comparison, Visa makes up to 1,667 transactions per second, while ethereum (the blockchain that supports ether, among other things) generates twenty and bitcoin only seven! To accelerate the process and reduce the energy footprint without sacrificing safety, new developments are underway, as blockchain is still in its infancy.

Fred Ehrsam, co-founder of the platform Coinbase, says: "We are birthing into existence systems which transcend us. In the same way democracy and capitalism as systems determine so much of the emergent behavior around us; blockchains will do the same with even greater reach. These systems are organisms, which take on lives of their own and are more concerned with perpetuating themselves than the individuals who comprise them. As technology stretches these systems to their limits, the implications become more pronounced. So we'd be wise to carefully consider the structure of these systems while we can. Like any new powerful technology, blockchains are a tool that can go in many different directions. Used well, we can create a world with greater prosperity and freedom. Used poorly, we can create systems which lead us to places we didn't intend to go."[12]

---

11. Difficulty. https://en.bitcoin.it/wiki/Difficulty
12. *Blockchain Governance: Programming Our Future*, Fred Ehrsam, Medium.com, 11/27/2017.

PoW or PoS?

These two acronyms are inherent to blockchains and cryptocurrencies. The first means **Proof of Work** and the second is **Proof of Stake**. "Proof of stake (PoS) is a type of algorithm by which a cryptocurrency blockchain network aims to achieve distributed consensus. In PoS-based cryptocurrencies, the creator of the next block is chosen via various combinations of random selection and wealth or age (i.e., the stake). In contrast, the algorithm of proof-of-work-based cryptocurrencies such as bitcoin uses mining; that is, the solving of computationally intensive puzzles to validate transactions and create new blocks."[1]

New cryptocurrencies use a hybrid method to benefit from the advantages of both systems.

---

1. Proof of Stake. https://en.wikipedia.org/wiki/Proof-of-stake

Cryptographic Hash Function

"A cryptographic hash function is a special class of hash function that has certain properties which make it suitable for use in cryptography. It is a mathematical algorithm that maps data of arbitrary size to a bit string of a fixed size (a hash) and is designed to be a one-way function, that is, a function which is infeasible to invert."[13] The SHA-256 (Secure Hash Algorithm), derived from the SHA-2, defined by the NSA (National Security Agency), is used for the cryptography of currencies, including the mining and creation of addresses.

"Pedagogical illustration of the principle of hashing functions: greatly reducing an image resolution will reduce a file size, but the resulting condensate is still sufficient to quickly tell two images apart in most cases."[14]

---

13. Cryptographic Hash Function. https://en.wikipedia.org/wiki/Cryptographic_hash_function
14. Author: Unique Nitrogen (own work) [CC BY-SA 4.0 (https://creativecommons.org/licenses/by-sa/4.0)], via Wikimedia Commons.

The NSA at the Origin of the Principle of Cryptocurrencies?

On June 18, 1996, thus in the last century, i.e. an eternity in Internet matters, three authors of the Cryptology Division published a study[15], which already presents the problem of future cryptocurrencies. Here are the first paragraphs of the introduction: "With the onset of the Information Age, our nation is becoming increasingly dependent upon network communications. Computer-based technology is significantly impacting our ability to access, store, and distribute information. Among the most important uses of this technology is *electronic commerce*: performing financial transactions via electronic information exchanged over telecommunications lines. A key requirement for electronic commerce is the development of secure and efficient electronic payment systems. The need for security is highlighted by the rise of the Internet, which promises to be a leading medium for future electronic commerce.

Electronic payment systems come in many forms including digital checks, debit cards, credit cards, and stored value cards. The usual security features for such systems are *privacy* (protection from eavesdropping), *authenticity* (provides user identification and message integrity), and *nonrepudiation* (prevention of later denying having performed a transaction).

The type of electronic payment system focused on in this paper is *electronic cash*. As the name implies, electronic cash is an attempt to construct an electronic payment system modeled after our paper cash system. Paper cash has such features as being: portable (easily carried), recognizable (as legal tender) hence readily acceptable, transferable (without involvement of the financial network), untraceable (no record of where money is spent), anonymous (no record of who spent the money) and has the ability to make "change." The designers of electronic cash focused on preserving the features of untraceability and anonymity. Thus,

---

15. *How To Make a Mint: The Cryptography of Anonymous Electronic Cash*, Laurie Law, Susan Sabett, Jerry Solinas, National Security Agency Office of Information Security Research and Technology, Cryptology Division, 06/18/1996.

electronic cash is defined to be an electronic payment system that provides, in addition to the above security features, the properties of user anonymity and payment untraceability.

In general, electronic cash schemes achieve these security goals via *digital signatures*. They can be considered the digital analog to a handwritten signature. Digital signatures are based on *public key cryptography*. In such a cryptosystem, each user has a secret key and a public key. The secret key is used to create a digital signature and the public key is needed to verify the digital signature. To tell who has signed the information (also called the message), one must be certain one knows who owns a given public key. This is the problem of key management, and its solution requires some kind of authentication infrastructure. In addition, the system must have adequate network and physical security to safeguard the secrecy of the secret keys.

This report has surveyed the academic literature for cryptographic techniques for implementing secure electronic cash systems. Several innovative payment schemes providing user anonymity and payment untraceability have been found. Although no particular payment system has been thoroughly analyzed, the cryptography itself appears to be sound and to deliver the promised anonymity. (...)"

Thirteen years before the creation of bitcoin, this report from the NSA's Cryptology Division already carries all the foundations of future cryptocurrencies.

Moreover, since the creator(s) of bitcoin are still unknown to this day, despite all available means of control and surveillance, some do not hesitate to consider that it is the invention of secret services, such as Natalya Kasperskaya, co-founder of Kaspersky Labs and president of Infowatch, who says: "Bitcoin is a project of American intelligence agencies, which was designed to provide quick funding for US, British and Canadian intelligence activities in different countries. [The technology] is 'privatized,' just like the Internet, GPS and TOR. In fact, it is dollar 2.0. Its rate is controlled by the owners of exchanges."[16]

---

16. *Bitcoin is a 'Project of US Intelligence,' Kaspersky Lab Co-Founder Claims*, Sputnik International, 01/19/2018.

Main cryptocurrencies

They can be classified by function: structuring currency, social currency, e-commerce currency, anonymous currency, experimental currency, local currency, etc. The classification according to the technology on which a currency is based makes it easier to understand the stakes. Similarly, the organization that governs blockchain depends on the nature of the encrypted currency. If technology and governance are open, closed or semi-open, the objectives are different: adding the word "coin" is not enough to make it a real "alternative currency" (AltCoin). The idea is also to keep in mind who the "owners" of governance are so as to not make a mistake and adhere in full knowledge to the project posted. The notion of public or private currency is added to the nature of the function: for example, bitcoin is a currency open by its technology and public by its governance; ripple is a semi-closed currency due to its technology and private by its governance; the AmazonCoin is a currency closed by its technology and private by its governance.

It is impossible to certify the number of cryptocurrencies issued to date, even if it is admitted that there are already 1,300, or even 1,500, in circulation. Coinmarketcap.com, however, classes 1,526, but only the top 1,160 are a little significant. There is no immediate reason why the creative process should stop.

Bitcoin is by far the most important and best known, along with ether, ripple, litecoin, monero, etc. Among the multitude that we haven't presented, there is even one created especially for marijuana enthusiasts, which has, legally, its own website and Twitter account!

As with currencies, each cryptocurrency has its own code: BTC (bitcoin), ETH (ether), XRP (ripple), LTC (litecoin), etc.

We will present in a synthetic way and in chronological order the best known and most widely used ones, no matter the origin of their creator(s), which are all of international scope.

2009
Bitcoin (BTC or XBT)

It is the first digital currency to historically decentralize money. Bitcoin is the technological and ideological standard of encrypted currencies. Announced in 2008, the source code of the system was published on January 3, 2009 by a person under the pseudonym Satoshi Nakamoto. It echoes the financial crisis of 2008, which seriously undermines the confidence to be placed in banking institutions and trusted third parties, which the bitcoin protocol does not need, where every transaction is recorded in a public digital accounting book and shared with all. The transactions are anonymous but visible by all, because the users of the bitcoin community have a complete copy of all exchanges validated.

The paradigm shift that bitcoin proposes continues to question society, states and banks, by demonstrating that a currency without a single center can change its environment and give "a new lease of life to 19th century utopians such as Proudhon, Robert Owen and Ernest Solvay, who saw money as a tool for social transformation."[17] It does not mean, however, that the system presents neither limits nor dangers, in particular because of its grey areas. On the other hand, what is certain is that the maximum quantity of bitcoins that can be emitted is 21 million units, a figure that is not likely to be reached before 2140.

As the use of bitcoin expands and the pace of trading increases, new currencies such as Bitcoin Cash and Bitcoin Gold are being introduced. Although they share almost the same name, they are not "bitcoin" but more recent currencies, resulting from a schism or **"hard fork"** that comes from a different operation decided by the association of miners and companies wishing to develop the initial Blockchain Bitcoin project differently. Several cryptocurrencies present the same situation.

---

[17]. *La Chine, puissance dominante du bitcoin, la crypto-monnaie libertaire*, Bertrand Hartemann, Asialyst, 09/12/2017.

General Overview of Cryptocurrencies

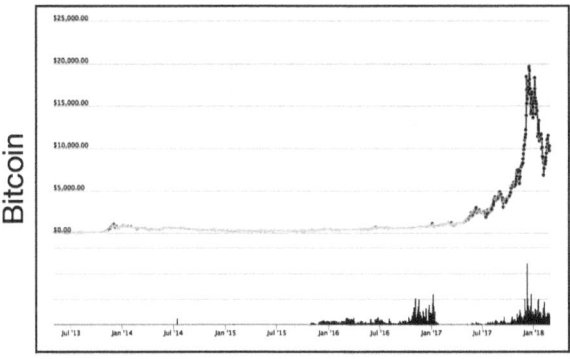

Source: Coingecko.com

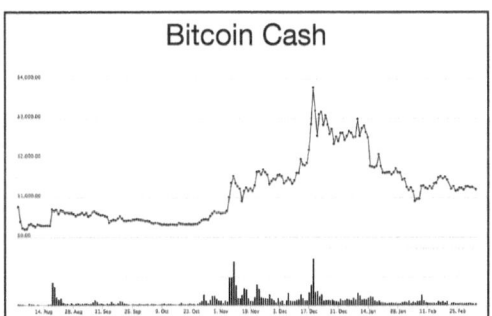

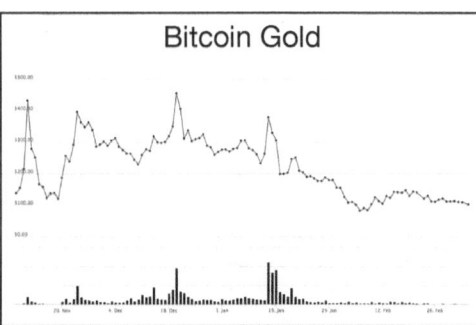

2011

The Litecoin (LTC)

Its creator, Charles Lee, former Google employee, develops his own code from the principle and source code of bitcoin. His concept is to market litecoin as a complementary currency to bitcoin, as silver is to gold.

It is planned to reach 84 million units, four times more than bitcoin. One of the most popular cryptocurrencies, litecoin challenges bitcoin in terms of mining, operations processing and increased storage capacity, with much lower transaction costs, "close to zero." It is therefore particularly intended for daily transactions, especially as it allows instant payments. The litecoin is therefore positioned as a global open source micro-payment network, fully decentralized and without central authority.

Chapter 1

In order to avoid conflicts of interest and improve the governance of the network, Charles Lee decides on December 20, 2017 to sell all of his litecoins, but he continues to develop the project.

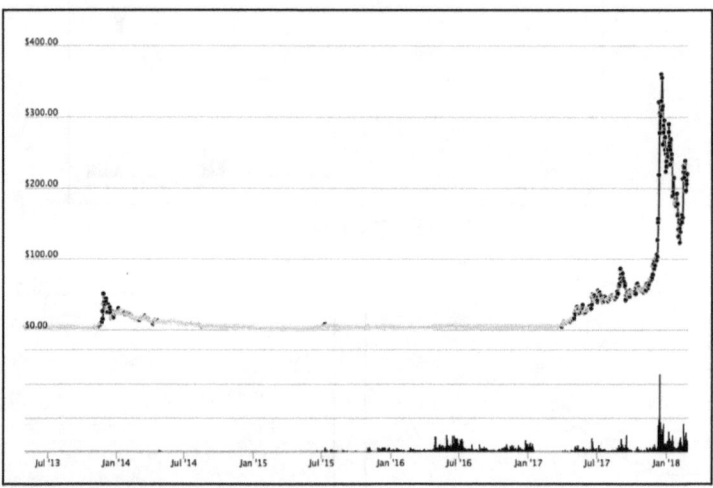

Source: Coingecko.com

2012
The Ripple (XRP)

Ripple, a company founded in 2004 by Ryan Fooger in Vancouver, is taken over in 2011 by programmer Jed McCaleb (creator of Stellar Lumens, eDonkey and Mt. Gox, which we will talk about later) and investor Chris Larsen who then developed the "Open Coin" project. The Ripple or Ripple Net protocol is therefore launched in 2012 to enable "secure, instantly and nearly free global financial transactions of any size with no chargebacks."

It functions as an asset exchange network accepting fiduciary currencies, cryptocurrencies, raw materials, etc., which makes it a solution of choice for banks. In October 2017, the company announces that it has entered into partnerships with a hundred financial institutions, but this causes the rejection on the part of defenders of individual freedoms and alternative encrypted currencies. Indeed, the ripple is also a pre-mined cryptocurrency, whose governance is private. It is also controversial given the amount of units that the leaders have reserved for themselves.

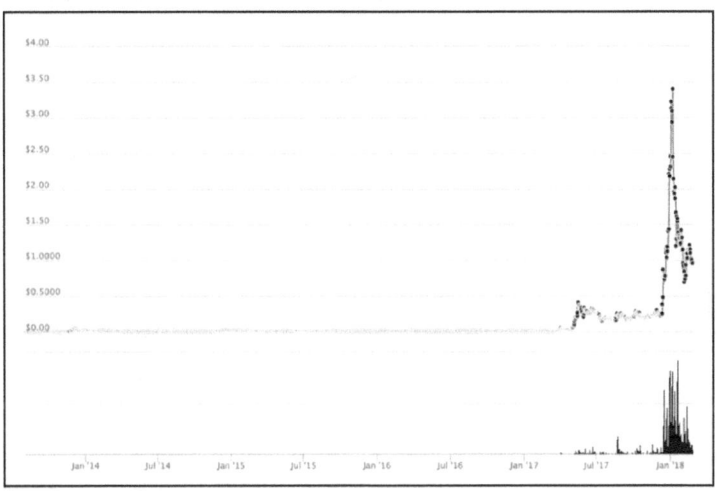

Source: Coingecko.com

2013
The DogeCoin (DOGE)
Billy Markus (IBM engineer, USA) and Jackson Palmer (Adobe Marketing, Australia) begin their adventure by parodying the development of cryptocurrencies with a doge meme, represented by a Shiba Inu, a dog breed native to Japan, which they would later use as their dogecoin logo. They are encouraged by the Front Range Community College to make it a reality.

Their project is based on the luckycoin, used in video games and itself backed by the litecoin.

Dogecoin has one of the largest communities of motivated and involved developers regarding projects that go beyond the objectives of a cryptocurrency, including fundraising operations, which aided Jamaica's bobsleigh team to participate in the 2014 Winter Olympics, a project in Kenya with Doge4Water, the Nascar stock-car race, etc.

Chapter 1

The dogecoin's priority is micro-payments. Also, in order to maintain a very low price, the initial issue volume is set at 100 billion units, in increments of five million dogecoins per year. Transaction blocks and security keys can be processed in less than a minute, compared to about ten for bitcoin.

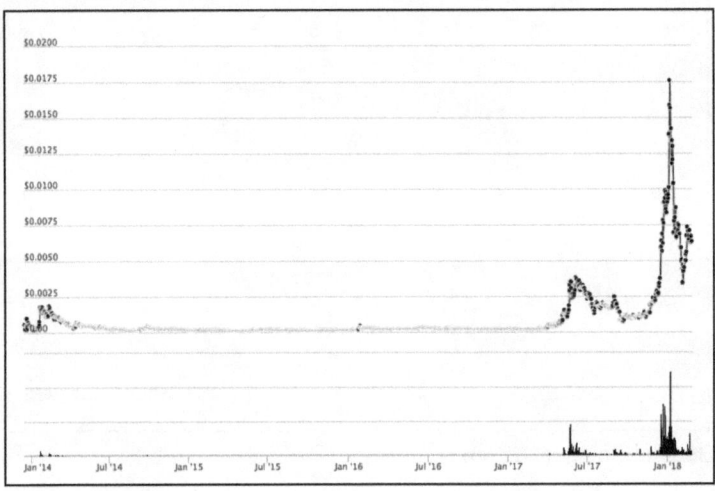

Source: Coingecko.com

2014
1) The Dash (DASH)

The darkcoin renamed "dash" in 2015, for obvious marketing reasons (a mix of "digital" and "cash") starts from the basic bitcoin code. The idea is to develop a currency worth "digital cash" and as fast as cash. The transactions are anonymous and the confirmation time is less than 2.5 minutes.

Its creator, Evan Duffield, published a press release on June 26, 2017, which reads as follows: "We are building a world-wide financial network capable of putting every individual's money under his/her direct control without intermediaries. We are building Dash Evolution because we believe it's needed and offers value to society. We are not building it to get rich. Since we do not have short-term profit motives, we shouldn't rush an unfinished product to market."[18]

---
18. *Hong Kong | Research and Planning*, Evan Duffield, Hackernoon, 06/25/2017.

General Overview of Cryptocurrencies

This cryptocurrency integrates anonymity functions that are not available with bitcoin and allows an instant transfer of funds. It is one of the few large cryptocurrencies whose governance system and budget are entirely decentralized.

Be careful not to confuse dash and dashcoin, also launched in 2014, a totally different cryptocurrency, whose technology is based on CryptoNote, like the monero below. In terms of value and use, the two cryptocurrencies are without comparison, the dashcoin not even reaching a total capitalization of $700,000. There are still other variations of cryptocurrencies using some form of the word "Dash," as is the case for a lot of cryptocurrencies, therefore it is better to be careful when one decides to invest (or to mine) in this domain.

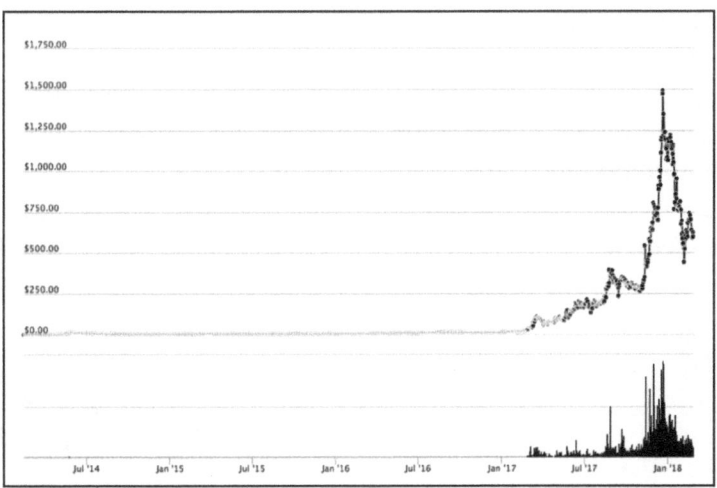

Source: Coingecko.com

2) The Monero (XMR)

"Monero" means "coin" in Esperanto. It is backed by a public and anonymous blockchain system (CryptoNote), unlike the bitcoin network, which works with pseudonyms. The departure address, transaction amount and arrival address are hidden. For each transaction, single-use public stealth keys are used, consisting of a public send key to protect the transmission and a public view key to view the transaction. The amount can be shared with third parties, should the sender authorize it. To ensure complete anonymity, the sender uses a Ring Signature, an encrypted signature in a circle, the amount of which is hidden by the Ring Confidential Transactions (Ring CT) function. The principle consists in mixing the operation with false transactions created for this purpose and other real ones, in order to counter potential attacks.

The responsibility and commitment of this community is to not compromise privacy and to give individuals back control over their personal information. New technological developments are regularly announced, primarily to make trade faster.

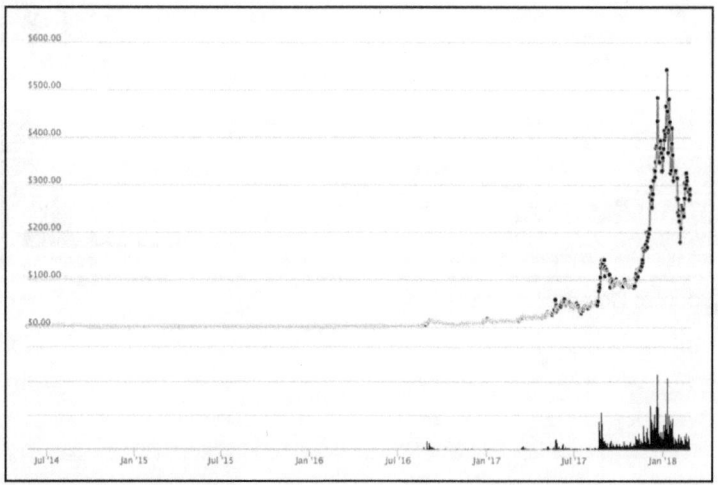

Source: Coingecko.com

A Solar and Orbital Cryptocurrency

At around 400th place in terms of capitalization, SolarCoin (SLR) is included in our presentation because, in addition to its environmental commitment, its model may provide states with solutions like the geopolitical scenarios that we present in Chapter 3.

Launched in January 2014 by the SolarCoin Foundation, this currency aims to stimulate solar energy production by companies and citizens by rewarding them with 1 SLR for each MWh produced. To take advantage of this, it is necessary to provide two PoW (proof of work): the one which is common to the system of cryptocurrencies and a second, original one, which is a certificate of production of MWh verified by a third party.

The distribution of solarcoins is scheduled to last forty years and reach a production of 97,500 TWh of solar electricity. To date, of the 97.5 billion solarcoins planned, 4,177,668.60 have been distributed in 58 countries on five continents:

Source: www.solarcoin.org

The SolarCoin Foundation partnered in September 2016 with Cloud Constellation, "a space-based data storage company scheduled to launch a network of data storage satellites to provide high-speed global cloud storage satellites as a space-based data center designed for the secure transfer and storage of sensitive information."[19] The deployment is scheduled for the end of 2018, making solarcoin "the first orbital currency."

---

19. SolarCoin. www.wikipedia.org/wiki/SolarCoin.

Chapter 1

Solarcoin is also recognized by the International Renewable Energy Agency (Irena), which has more than 150 member states. It is the first cryptocurrency to receive such a privilege from an international institution.

The solarcoin principle could also be used for many other environmental projects

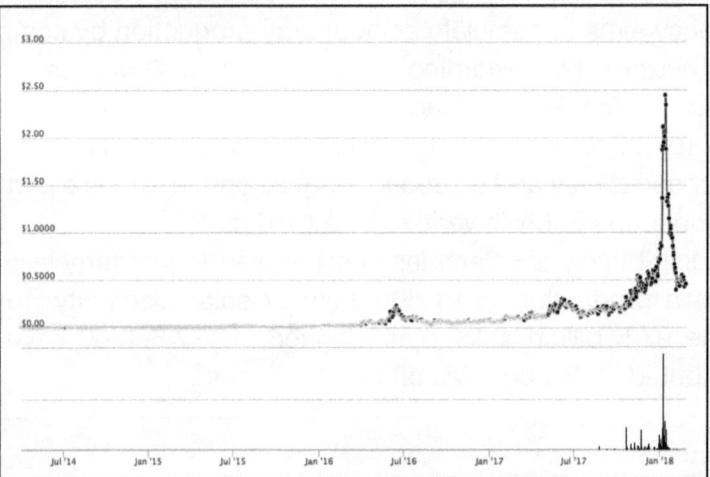

Source: Coingecko.com

2015
1) The Ether (ETH)

It is the first currency based on the second generation of the blockchain technology, the Ethereum, which includes the creation of Smart Contracts. It was launched in July 2015 by the Russo-Canadian Vitalik Buterin—he was nineteen when he published his white paper in December 2013.

A piracy in 2016, which allowed its authors to steal part of the funds raised to finance the project, led to the creation of two separate blockchains and cryptocurrencies: ether (ETH) and an unofficial version called the "classical ether" (ETC).

Ether is today positioned as the second cryptocurrency in terms of total capitalization, after bitcoin; ETC is far behind.

One of the original features of Ethereum's protocol is its ability to revolutionize the role of traditional trusted third parties (notaries, lawyers, etc.) in asset-bearing transactions. Smart Contracts, while efficient and fast, settle classic operations in a few seconds with the guarantee of flawless execution.

Since its creation, Vitalik Buterin's company has experienced rapid growth thanks to its hundreds of decentralized applications (DApps or Apps): while the Bitcoin Blockchain is intended solely for currencies, Ethereum allows developers to create all types of applications in all fields, such as digital signature, copyright or royalty management, crowdfunding platforms, stock market delivery, social media, online games, electric car recharge management, etc.

In May 2017 the Enterprise Ethereum Alliance was created, with more than 100 members, including institutions and large companies such as Toyota, Samsung, Microsoft, Intel, J.P. Morgan, ING, MasterCard, etc.

Chapter 1

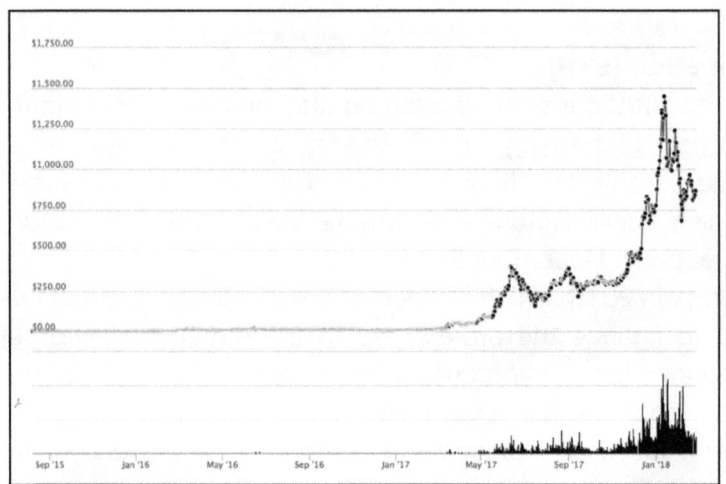

Source: Coingecko.com

2) The Tether

Launched in November 2015, the project relies on Tether, a company incorporated in Hong Kong and present in the United States, and close links with the world's main exchange, Bitfinex, also based in Hong Kong—it carries out up to 40% of global transactions on bitcoin. Originally positioned on the Bitcoin Blockchain, the tether joined the litecoin system in June 2017.

While it only ranks between 15th and 20th in the classification of cryptocurrencies by total capitalization, the main reason why we present it is that it offers an (almost) unique feature in the world of cryptocurrencies: according to its creators, each tether issued corresponds to one US dollar in reserve. With just over $2.2 billion in circulation, that means they have over $2.2 billion in reserve. However, at the end of January 2018, serious doubts started to appear about the reality of these assets—we will discuss this again below.

The primary objective of tether is to facilitate transactions between exchanges, which is why the parity is set at 1 tether = 1 dollar.

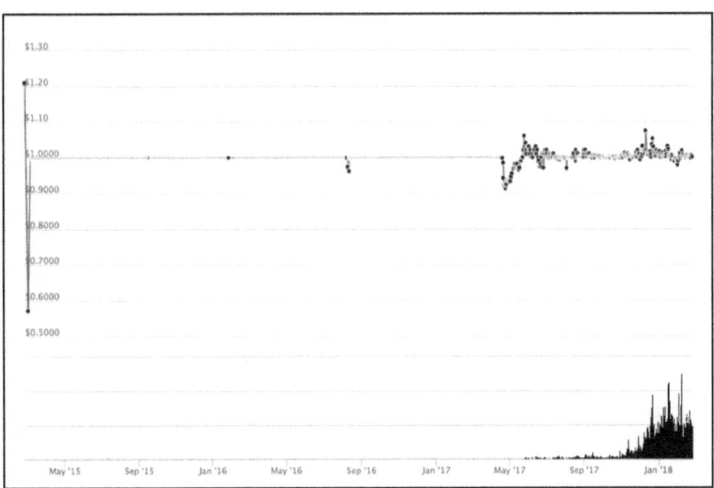

Source: Coingecko.com

Chapter 1

2016
The Neo (NEO, ANS or ANC)

Called "Chinese Ethereum," neo is both a decentralized blockchain technology and a cryptocurrency. The story begins in February 2014 under the name AntShares (ANS), the first open source blockchain developed in China.

Da Hongfei, its founder, describes Neo as an "open network for a public economy," which is a compromise between a decentralized exchange technology (DEX) and a Smart Contract solution that is 100% compatible with banking regulations and national laws, by reintroducing the trusted third party authorized to validate transactions. The ambition is to integrate all economic and exchanges on the same protocol where the declaration of identity, the authorization of both parties and the validation of transactions is mandatory. The system can process up to ten thousand transactions per second.

As for the cryptocurrency, 100 million neos have been created, of which 65 million are in circulation.

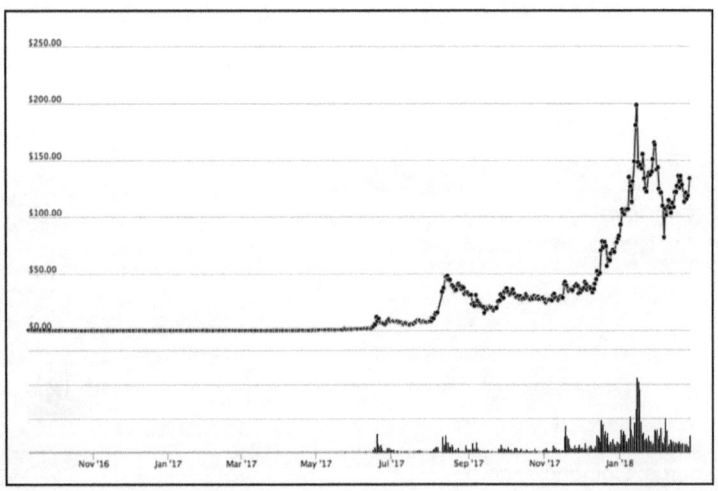

Source: Coingecko.com

2017
The Iota (IOTA or MIOTA)

Created in 2015 by David Sonstebo, Sergey Ivancheglo, Dominik Schiener and Serguei Popov, but definitively open to the public after two years of testing, Iota presents several particularities, which make it a new revolution in the realm of blockchain: whereas the ether is turned towards Smart Contracts, it is linked to connected objects or Internet of Things (IoT).

Its technology, Tangle, using the concept of "Directed Acyclic Graph" (DAG), different from the blockchain, offers free transactions, a fast confirmation time and an unlimited number of simultaneous transactions.

Supervised by the IOTA Foundation based in Berlin, the system is offered in partnership with various multinationals involved in the Internet of Things (Volkswagen, Deutsche Telekom, Microsoft, Samsung, Fujitsu,...), allowing them applications beyond digital currency, such as securing digital data, developing electric vehicle charging networks, electronic voting, etc.

Iota is pre-mined at 2,779,530,283 units, which means there is no mining and there will be no new issuance. Its capitalization places it among the top ten cryptocurrencies.

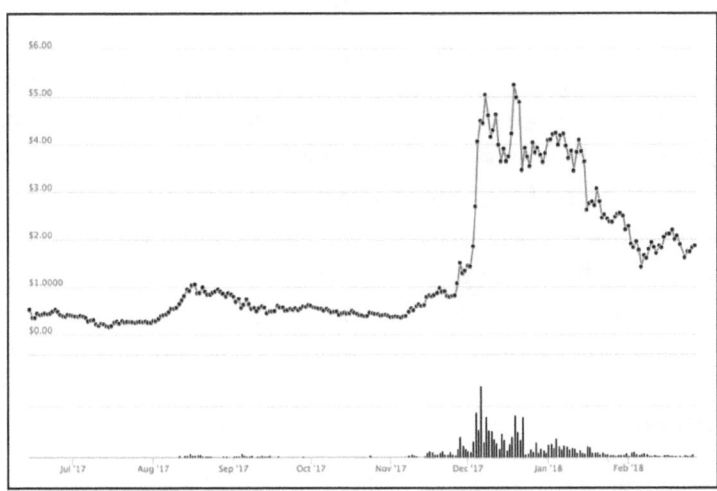

Source: Coingecko.com

GAFA's Cryptocurrencies

It seems logical that the four giants of the web—Google, Apple, Facebook and Amazon—would have been interested in cryptocurrencies; for the moment, they have, however, missed this revolution.

Google
No announcement has been made by the company to create a cryptocurrency, which does not mean that it is not studying the subject.

Apple
The company turned to payment methods and created the ApplePay system, which is by no means a cryptocurrency.

Facebook
The social network giant has been interested in payment services for a few years, but without major initiative and projects, and nothing particular in the field of cryptocurrencies has been developed.

However, the subject still appears to be a mission that Mark Zuckerberg has for Facebook in 2018, declaring about cryptography and cryptocurrencies that "they come with the risk of being harder to control. I'm interested to go deeper and study the positive and negative aspects of these technologies, and how best to use them in our services."[20]

Is it surprising that the notion of "control" is so present in his short text, which is the opposite of the very principle of cryptocurrencies? On January 30, the company announces that it is now banning all advertising for cryptocurrencies and ICO. To better introduce its own later?

---

20. *Mark Zuckerberg's personal challenge for 2018: Fix Facebook*, Michelle Castillo, CNBC, 01/04/2018.

Amazon

Launched in May 2013, the Amazon Coin is worth a cent and only allows you to purchase software for Kindle, Kindle Fire and Android devices from an application or the Amazon Appstore.

In reality, it is similar to a coupon or a gift voucher valid on Amazon.com: the Amazon Coin does not have the attributes of a currency, its main function being rather to reinforce its community through a feeling of belonging while proposing alternative solutions of payment and loyalty. The Amazon Coin should therefore be classified in the category of permission marketing, which allows more personal data to be obtained with the customer's consent, and can therefore not be considered as a cryptocurrency.

Chapter 1

Here is a table of about twenty of these cryptocurrencies, as of December 20, 2017, classified in alphabetical order and presenting the number of units issued, the dollar rate, their capitalization, i.e. the unit price in dollars multiplied by the number of units issued, as well as the average number of transactions per hour:

General Overview of Cryptocurrencies

(12/20/17)	Supply	Price (USD)	Marketcap (USD)	Transactions avg. per hour
Auroracoin (AUR)	15,699,286	1.46	22,908,103	26
Bitcoin (BTC)	16,740,136	17,295.8	289,534,428,769	16,682
Bitcoin Cash (BCH)	16,853,192	3,208.47	54,073,019,516	4,241
Bitcoin Gold (BTG)	16,803,588	371.62	6,244,544,339	336
Blackcoin (BLK)	76,558,064	0.568	43,447,153	98
Dash (DASH)	7,765,747	1,285.74	9,984,695,743	701
Dogecoin (DOGE)	112,359,106,384	0.0055	621,601,777	1,223
Ethereum (ETH)	96,455,281	816.66	78,770,716,050	43,854
Ethereum Classic (ETC)	98,758,749	40.28	3,978,004,368	2,207
Feathercoin (FTC)	176,733,190	0.441	77,998,446	43
Litecoin (LTC)	54,389,058	330.86	17,995,223,786	5,963
Megacoin (MEC)	36,464,050	0.069	2,530,998	3
Monero (XMR)	15,501,165	408.1	6,326,009,370	406
Namecoin (NMC)	14,567,757	4.27	62,202,427	14
Novacoin (NVC)	2,037,813	8.21	16,731,177	9
Peercoin (PPC)	24,524,669	6.13	150,286,294	49
Quarkcoin (QRK)	253,410,498	0.015	3,717,606	8
Reddcoin (RDD)	28,699,565	0.003	86,316,677	154
Vertcoin (VTC)	42,120,850	8.7	366,512,785	275
Zcash (ZEC)	2,875,100	599.02	1,722,234,469	535

Source: BitInfoCharts.com

Chapter 1

If we take capitalizations over $5 billion on January 1, 2018, twelve days later, we get the following table, with eighteen currencies:

Symbol	Name	Price USD	Supply	Marketcap USD
BTC	Bitcoin	13,817	16,775,462	220,312,641,500
XRP	Ripple	2.02	38,739,144,847	73,159,871,770
ETH	Ether	743	96,703,227	71,379,299,630
BCH	Bitcoin Cash	2,349	16,887,750	38,832,048,390
XOT	IOT	1,382	21,000,000	27,579,037,340
ADA	Cardano	0.7	25,927,070,538	17,372,332,400
IGNIS	IGNIS	15.25	1,000,000,000	14,490,952,200
BCC	Bitcash	403	6,191,512	14,169,587,690
LTC	Litecoin	224	54,567,733	12,111,896,117
YBC	YbCoin	3,993	3,020,627	11,464,938,271
DSH	Dashcoin	624	17,574,970	10,416,964,270
SPOTS	Spots	10.75	1,000,000,000	10,214,190,750
MIOTA	IOTA	3.45	2,779,530,283	9,596,427,563
XEM	NEM	1.07	8,999,999,999	8,900,234,100
DASH	DigitalCash	1,025	7,787,993	7,737,359,482
XLM	Stellar Lumens	0.43	17,858,969,367	7,270,796,524
ALP	Alpcoin	1.38	4,084,224,205	5,363,806,126
XMR	Monero	330	15,546,731	5,108,461,207
	Total of the market capitalization (USD)			565,480,845,330

Source: CryptoCoinCharts.info

We find that bitcoin loses $70 billion in capitalization over the twelve days and ether loses $7 billion, leading to ripple becoming the second largest capitalization.

CryptoCoinCharts also offers a graph, which allows one to visualize the purchasing volume of the various cryptocurrencies. Thus, on 1 January, the number of transactions in ethers and ripples was fairly close to that of bitcoin. The comparison, on the other hand, is incomparable for transactions in value, given the price of bitcoin.

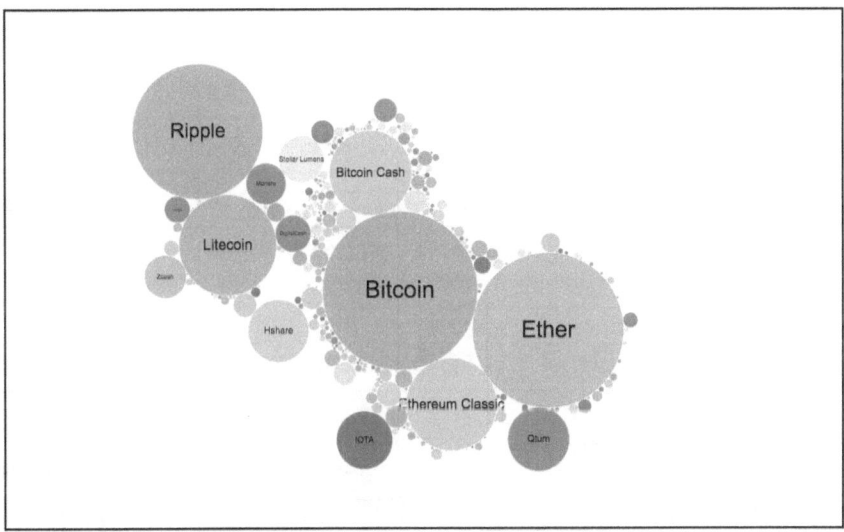

Source: CryptoCoinCharts.info

Highly speculative values
The tables above show that the capitalization of the main cryptocurrencies reaches sums that can appear delirious for goods that have no other existence than virtual. Thus, as of December 20, 2017, the capitalization of bitcoin is approaching $300 billion and that of ethereum is moving towards $80 billion.

Ten days later, on January 1, 2018, the capitalization of bitcoin drops to $220 billion and that of ether is now *only* $71 billion.

The situation on February 10 is even worse: while on January 1, there are still eighteen currencies whose capitalization exceeds $5 billion,

Chapter 1

there are only fourteen forty days later. As for the total capitalization of the top eighteen, it goes from $565.5 billion to $378.5 billion, a drop of $187 billion and 33% in one month and ten days:

Symbol	Name	Price USD	Supply	Marketcap USD
BTC	Bitcoin	8,835	16,856,075	146,801,676,888
ETH	Ether	875	97,524,814	85,164,759,700
XRP	Ripple	1.08	39,009,215,838	42,157,767,053
BCH	Bitcoin Cash	1,275	16,959,675	21,477,891,531
BCC	Bitcash	1,281	9,217,556	11,640,164,762
ADA	Cardano	0.40	25,927,070,538	10,328,136,913
LTC	Litecoin	161	55,152,333	8,806,654,901
XLM	Stellar Lumens	0.41	18,432,206,941	7,485,430,229
NEO	Neo	126	65,000,000	7,331,461,823
EOS	EOS	1.98	659,643,398	6,132,112,476
MIOTA	IOTA	0.62	2,779,530,283	5,494,805,726
XEM	NEM	0.62	8,999,999,999	5,184,186,507
DASH	DigitalCash	650	7,875,512	5,070,219,057
XMR	Monero	256	15,704,812	4,009,971,660
LSK	Lisk	28.97	117,913,528	3,267,920,410
TRX	Tron	0.05	65,748,192,475	3,229,513,222
NET	Netcoin	3.20	787,126,712	2,485,528,549
ETC	Ethereum Classic	24.52	99,750,666	2,450,979,498
	Total of the market capitalization			378,519,180,905

Source: CryptoCoinCharts.info

Who knows how much the total capitalization will be when you read this book? The phenomenon is common to cryptocurrencies and does not only affect bitcoin. CNBC explains, for example, on January 18, 2018 "Ripple's XRP coin has fallen 74 percent from an all-time high of $3.84 hit on Jan. 4, erasing $44 billion from the holdings of Chris Larsen, co-founder and executive chairman of Ripple. (…) At XRP's peak on Jan. 4, Larsen was worth $59.9 billion. That made him one of the five richest people in the U.S. and wealthier than Google's founders, based on *Forbes*' rich list."[21] Now, at the current price, he is worth only $15 billion. Here is the evolution of capitalization for the currencies shown in the tables on 1 January and 10 February (the fall would be even greater if the data in the table were taken on 20 December):

Name	Market capitalization (USD)		Evolution (in %)
	01/01/18	02/10/18	
Bitcoin	220,312,641,500	146,801,676,888	-33,4
Ripple	73,159,871,770	42,157,767,053	-42,4
Ether	71,379,299,630	85,164,759,700	19,3
Bitcoin Cash	38,832,048,390	21,477,891,531	-44,7
Cardano	17,372,332,400	10,328,136,913	-40,5
Bitcash	14,169,587,690	11,640,164,762	-17,9
Litecoin	12,111,896,117	8,806,654,901	-27,3
IOTA	9,596,427,563	5,494,805,726	-42,7
NEM	8,900,234,100	5,184,186,507	-41,8
DigitalCash	7,737,359,482	5,070,219,057	-34,5
Monero	5,108,461,207	4,009,971,660	-21,5

The only currency that appreciates is ether; the others fall sharply in forty days.

---

21. *Ripple co-founder loses $44 billion on paper during cryptocurrency crash*, Evelyn Cheng, CNBC, 01/17/2018.

Bitcoin, a Ponzi scheme?

"A Ponzi scheme is a fraudulent investment operation where the operator generates returns for older investors through revenue paid by new investors, rather than from legitimate business activities or profit of financial trading. Operators of Ponzi schemes can be either individuals or corporations, and grab the attention of new investors by offering short-term returns that are either abnormally high or unusually consistent.

Companies that engage in Ponzi schemes focus all of their energy into attracting new clients to make investments. Ponzi schemes rely on a constant flow of new investments to continue to provide returns to older investors. When this flow runs out, the scheme falls apart.

The scheme is named after Charles Ponzi, who became notorious for using the technique in the 1920s."[22]

Perhaps the most famous case is Bernard Madoff, whose fraud is around $65 billion. Arrested in December 2008, he was sentenced to 150 years in prison in June 2009.

In principle, bitcoin does not exactly match the criteria of a Ponzi scheme for the following main reasons:
- there is no dividend or remuneration paid to investors;
- there is no centralized organization that diverts money to the top of a possible pyramid;
- Bitcoin can continue to operate even if no new participants join the system. While this can have an impact on prices, it keeps value as long as it is accepted as a means of payment.

This does not mean, however, that there is no fraud and no Ponzi scheme in the world of cryptocurrencies. For example, the BitConnect platform, which created its BitConnect Coin (BCC), is suspected by many experts of being a Ponzi scheme because it announces that it offers a 1% daily profit to those who lend their BCC.[23] No investment for the public can guarantee such a return.

Here is what can be read on the English version of Wikipedia: "OneCoin is a Ponzi scheme promoted as a cryptocoin with a private blockchain. It is promoted by offshore companies OneCoin Ltd (Dubai) and OneLife Network Ltd (Belize), both led by Bulgarian Ruja Ignatova. OneCoin has been described as a Ponzi scheme,

---

22. Source: Wikipedia.
23. *BitConnect is a Ponzi scheme, ethereum and litecoin founders warn*, Mix, TheNextWeb.com, 12/2017.

both because of how it has been set up and because of many of the people who are central to OneCoin having previously been involved in other such schemes."

In the spring of 2016, Chinese police investigated OneCoin before arresting its members and seizing the equivalent of about $30 million.

Italy, in turn, becomes concerned about the OneCoin case in December 2016 through the Competition and Market Authority (AGCM), which, in a press release issued on 27 February 2017, orders the cessation of all activities related to this cryptocurrency.[24]

Then it is the German, Indian, Bulgarian, Scandinavian, etc. authorities who carry out seizures, arrests, or in the least warnings and bans.

On June 16, 2017, Ruja Ignatova declares that OneCoin has a legal license to practice issued by the Vietnamese government. In fact, the document turns out to be a forgery.[25]

Some platforms do not hesitate to mislead the public, like BitKRX in South Korea, which falsely uses the acronym KRX for Korea Exchange, i.e. the Seoul Stock Exchange, in order to make people believe that its operations were created by the stock exchange authorities!

Mid-December, the Korean authorities also intervene in the Mining Max case, a mining company with its headquarters in Las Vegas and facilities in Seoul. Twenty-one people, including the president, currently on the run and wanted by Interpol, "are accused of embezzling about $250 million from 18,000 investors in 54 countries, including the United States, South Korea, China and Japan."[26] The system typically corresponds to a Ponzi scheme, as you have to pay to become an affiliate and have others sign up to receive rewards.

We can therefore only recommend caution to those who want to invest in cryptocurrencies, in whatever form, including ICOs, which can prove to be completely based on hot air.

---

24. *Vendite piramidali: Antitrust sospende la promozione della criptomoneta OneCoin da parte di One Life*, ACGM, 02/27/2017.
25. *OneCoin Vietnamese regulatory document forged, govt says*, Behind MLM, 06/21/2017.
26. Yonhap News Agency, in *Multimillion Dollar Cryptocurrency Scam By Mining Max Busted In South Korea*, Himanshu Goenka, *International Business Times*, 12/20/2017.

Chapter 1

What can I buy with bitcoin?

The answer is now easy: almost everything, at least in countries where it is not prohibited. This ranges from public services to commercial websites, from donations to NGOs to luxury goods; the list continues to grow on the one hand and on the other hand to extend to other cryptocurrencies.

For example, riding the wave, the sports car dealer MoonLambos displays on its website the following slogan: "The premier destination for exotic supercars that deals exclusively in cryptocurrency." Thus, happy bitcoin owners can buy their Lamborghini, Ferrari or Aston Martin at a cost of 10 to 50 units.

On the side of advocacy, many NGOs now accept donations in bitcoin along with other cryptocurrencies; the Bulgarian crowdfunding platform Bithope has even specialized in financing its campaigns with this new means of payment. Increasingly more exchanges like Coinbase, for example, do not charge transaction fees for donations to NGOs, which is not the case with other sites, e.g. Paypal, which takes its commission on each transaction. The IRS, the U.S. tax department, also considers donations paid in bitcoin to be tax deductible.[27]

---

27. *Transforming the Social Sector: Bitcoin and Blockchain for Good*, Paul Lamb, *Huffington Post*, 09/19/2017.

Exchanges

All one needs to buy and sell cryptocurrencies is a computer and an Internet connection or a smartphone that can connect to these specialized digital platforms. All work with bitcoin and its competitors, sometimes up to more than two hundred and fifty of them, but they do not necessarily accept all currencies as means of payment.

There are dozens of exchanges around the world, sometimes covering several countries or geographical areas. Here is a non-exhaustive list in the top three countries in terms of volumes: Coincheck, Bitflyer, Zaif, SBI Virtual Currencies in Japan; Coinbase/GDAX, Poloniex, Gemini, Kraken in the United States; Bithumb, Korbit, Coinis in South Korea.

Many exchanges have developed specific features that distinguish them from their competitors. For example Localbitcoins.com, founded in Finland in 2012, allows sales between individuals from all over the world, according to the classified ad principle. Payments are left to the convenience of the parties, and when the transaction is completed, the cryptocurrencies are transferred to the acquirer's account or to a portfolio of his choice.

The CryptoCoinCharts.info site indexes 125 platforms classified by the volume of exchanges of cryptocurrencies in US$ value. Here is the table of the first twenty as of January 1, 2018 at 6 pm (Paris time):

Chapter 1

	Trading Pairs	24h Volume USD	24h Volume BTC
Bitfinex	16	1,904,413,059	148,261
Coinone	6	1,106,359,760	86,132
Bittrex	264	676,203,574	52,643
Poloniex	97	659,521,002	51,345
Coinbase GDAX	10	647,883,945	40,439
Bitstamp	11	622,306,596	48,447
HitBTC	245	474,942,334	36,975
Kraken	47	434,136,209	33,798
ACX	6	260,024,161	20,243
Gemini	3	171,467,134	13,349
Bithumb	11	160,323,711	12,481
CEX.IO	25	158,743,134	12,358
Quoine	24	136,767,908	10,648
bitFlyer	3	106,718,829	8,308
Korbit	4	104,323,750	8,122
Binance	7	91,092,887	7,092
Liqui	167	70,629,389	5,499
EXMO	39	70,336,779	5,476
YoBit	698	67,976,254	5,292
BTC-e / WEX	26	58,229,339	4,533

As the system is not centralized, there can be significant differences in the price of bitcoin, depending on the country, as shown in this table:

General Overview of Cryptocurrencies

Exchanges	Prices in USD
Bithumb (South Korea)	17,641.55
Bitstamp (Luxemburg)	13,311.71
GDAX (USA)	13,270.00
Golix (Zimbabwe)	19,810.1 – 21,000

(Bitcoin prices on Japanese platforms have not been listed since they are denominated in yen, and the exchange rate would distort the comparison.)

In general, prices in South Korea are higher than anywhere else, with the exception of Zimbabwe, for specific reasons, which we explain below.

The role of exchanges in pricing

Cryptomarket prices differ between exchanges, which contribute to their fixation. Sometimes, their practices generate suspicions, as illustrated by the case presented by Himanshu Goenka in *International Business Times*[28]:

"Bitcoin Cash was created as Bitcoin fork Aug. 1, and Coinbase said it had "been monitoring the Bitcoin Cash network over the last few months" before deciding to "enable full support including the ability to buy, sell, send and receive. (...)

Early Tuesday, the price of BCH was hovering below the $2,200 mark and did not stray far from there through the day. But in the run-up to the announcement, it began moving upward and seemed to settle at about the $3,100 level, before suddenly spiking to a high of about $8,500 (which could have been an error of some sort). For about an hour, the unusual spike led to Coinbase suspending BCH trade, and the price chart now shows a peak of just over $3,400 shortly before midnight. The price again settled around the $3,100 level, an almost 40 percent rise in less than 24 hours.

---

28. *Bitcoin Price Crashes After Coinbase Starts Bitcoin Cash Trading*, Himanshu Goenka, *International Business Times*, 12/19/2017.

On the other hand, the price of bitcoin, which had been over $19,000 early Tuesday, was seeing weakness during the day's trade, and crashed sharply to $15,000 following the announcement. It has since clawed its way back to over $17,000, but the sudden fall of over 20 percent, combined with the rise in BCH price, and the fact that Coinbase did not notify its users in advance, left the trading exchange open to accusations of insider trading."

It defends itself by explaining that its employees have been banned from trading on the BCH for weeks, which has not reassured many people, because, seen from the outside, it can resemble price manipulation, as it (sometimes) happens with the stock exchange.

The "market capitalization" data indicated on the platforms can also mislead the investor: it is calculated by multiplying the price by the number of units issued. However, it does not always correspond to the actual number in circulation, which can generate a major discrepancy. We will see this below with the example of Iceland and its auroracoin, which, even before the beginning of distribution by airdrop, ranked third among cryptocurrencies, just behind bitcoin and ripple, with a capitalization exceeding $1 billion. Everything quickly went back to normal with the fall of the price, but it is better to be vigilant with the data presented, especially since they come, most of the time, from exchanges whose profits come from transactions.

Pay attention to the electricity bill!
Looking at bitcoin's price, how large its latest fluctuations may be, mining may seem like an exciting thing to start since this activity is paid in bitcoin. However, there is a key point that must be taken into account before starting: electricity consumption. Running the algorithm to mine bitcoin requires a lot of calculations, therefore energy.

For example, a crowdfunding project that appeared on the Indiegogo platform before it was suspended consisted in "building one of the largest mining farms." The authors, from Tajikistan according to their information, wanted to raise $10 million in order to buy the necessary mining equipment (including more than 2,000 Antminer S9) to generate eighteen bitcoins in twenty-four hours, or just over 500 in a month. As they indicate, the preliminary calculation of electricity consumption amounts to 5,500 kW/h and 3,960,000 kW/month, for a monthly bill of $80,000! Admittedly, the bitcoin of that time was still advantageous, provided, however, that it succeeded in mining the quantity planned.

The specialized site Digiconomist.net has created the Bitcoin Energy Consumption Index, which presents data linking electricity consumption and bitcoin mining. Here are some for the year 2017:

Description	Values
Bitcoin's current estimated annual electricity consumption* (TWh)	36.68
Implied Watts per GH/s	0.273
Electricity consumed per transaction (KWh)	304.00
Bitcoin's electricity consumption as a percentage of the world's electricity consumption	0.16%
Annual carbon footprint (kt of CO2)	17,972
Carbon footprint per transaction (kg of CO2)	148.86

* 1 TWh (terawatt hour) = one billion kWh
1 GH/s = one billion hashes per second
1 kt (kiloton) = 1,000 tons

The figure of 36.68 TWh may not be very significant for the reader, but it represents an annual consumption higher than that of countries such as Hungary, Denmark, Ireland, Peru, Algeria, etc. If bitcoin were a country, it would rank around 60th in electricity consumption, more than 150 countries would consume less than it. Not to mention that the table is only for bitcoin and leaves out all other cryptocurrencies, however less greedy in energy.

Chapter 1

Electricity consumption by country compared to the one used to mine bitcoins

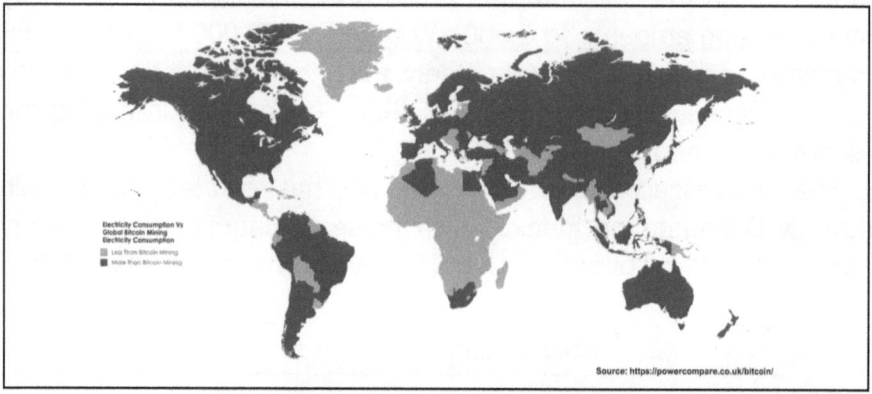

In clear, countries consuming less energy than the "country" bitcoin

In the end, about 0.16% of the world's annual electricity consumption is used to mine bitcoins, resulting in a huge carbon footprint.

In comparison, all data centers would consume more than 3% of the world's electricity, with a forecast of 6% by 2020, and annual inquiries on Google alone would burn as much electricity as Laos, around 4 MWh.[29] As for the three million ATMs installed worldwide, they would use around 6 MWh/year.

Consequently, countries wishing to develop a cryptocurrency mining activity must first benefit from abundant and cheap energy resources, which excludes a large number of them—this remark should however be put into perspective in light of the current bitcoin price. Indeed, even if studies show that producing a bitcoin costs between $60 and $400 of electricity depending on the country and energy source, this becomes marginal at the prices reached early 2018: $400 represents less than 3% of the price of $14,000.

All the more so as the volume of calculations continued to increase over the years, not only has the sociology of the bitcoin miner changed, but also the structures and their strategy. The largest

---
29. *Une recherche Google, c'est combien de CO_2 ?*, ConsoGlobe, 11/18/2016.

mining companies now have well over 100,000 machines working in continuous operation. They are therefore able to seek the best operating conditions on the planet. This is illustrated by this passage from an Investopedia article:

"Over the years, bitcoin miners have cut back on energy costs by moving production to China, a country which reportedly accounts for 60% of bitcoin production operations. A majority of Chinese bitcoin mines are situated in its Sichuan province, where hydropower dominates.

Iceland, which provides naturally cooling Arctic air for overheated systems and uses geothermal energy, is also a prominent venue for bitcoin mining operations. Chinese miners have not provided estimates for bitcoin production costs. But Genesis mining, which shifted its mines from China to Iceland, estimated that it cost $60 for the company to produce a single bitcoin."[30]

This is a new form of competition between states, to which we will return. Meanwhile, sustainable projects are beginning to emerge. For example, a mining company in Manitoba, which mines with 30 miners over an area of about 6,000 m^2, uses the heat generated to grow vegetables and maintain a pond of 800 fish, whose treated waters are rich in nitrates and serve as fertilizers for plants.[31]

Geopolitics of vending machines

Cryptocurrencies can be purchased on exchanges but also in specialized vending machines, often a simpler process. Some models also allow you to sell them and receive immediate payment.

The ATM Radar Corner[32] website provides several data, maps and graphs concerning the installation of these devices in the world. At the end of December 2017, there were 2,002 spread over 61 countries:

---

30. *Do Bitcoin Mining Energy Costs Influence Its Price?*, Rakesh Sharma, Investopedia, 11/26/2017.
31. *How this greenhouse and fish farm operation is fuelled by bitcoin mining*, Samantha Samson, CBC News, 01/04/2018.
32. www.coinatmradar.com provides a lot of interesting information, including the location of the closest ATMs to where you are, with the coordinates, the type of operations performed, the fees, etc.

Chapter 1

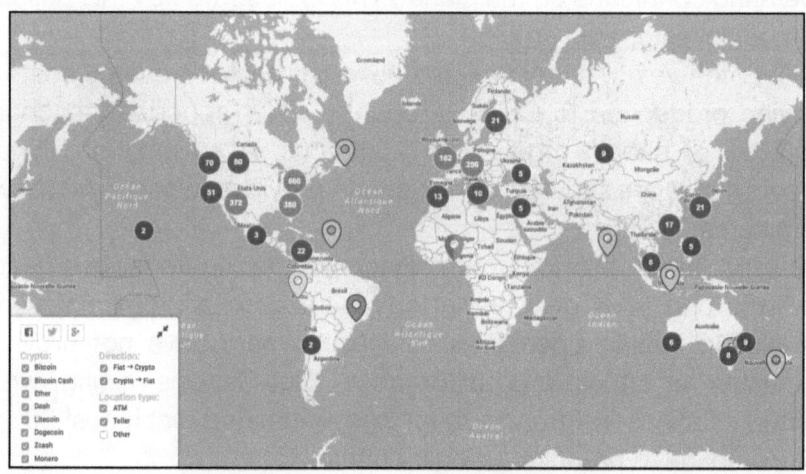

North America has the most, followed by Europe, Asia, Oceania and South America; Africa does not have any yet:

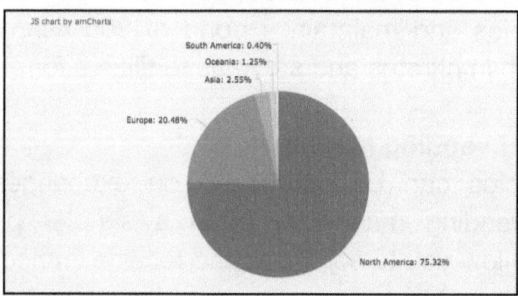

Bitcoin ATMs by Country (12/2017)			
United States	1 286	10	Hong Kong
Canada	325	9	Slovenia
United Kingdom	105	7	Taiwan
Austria	93	7	Panama
Spain	38	6	Greece
Australia	23	6	Dominican Rep.
Switzerland	22	5	Romania
Czech Rep.	21	4	Vietnam
Finland	21	4	Philippines
Italy	17	4	Macao
Netherlands	14	4	Kosovo
Slovakia	12	4	Serbia
Mexico	12	4	Belgium
Japan	12	4	Croatia
Russia	10	4	Poland

* Only countries with at least four distributors are shown. Thus, the table does not include those with a single machine installed such as China, Indonesia, Brazil, Chile, Peru, France, Sweden, Portugal, Ukraine, Saudi Arabia, etc., or those with two or three machines, such as South Korea, Singapore, Israel, Norway, Denmark, Estonia, Hungary, Bulgaria, Colombia, Kazakhstan.

Chapter 1

All vending machine process the bitcoin, but other cryptocurrencies can also be purchased:

ATMs dealing with :	In number	In %
Bitcoin	2,002	100.0%
Litecoin	664	33.1%
Ether	289	14.4%
Dash	156	7.8%
Bitcoin Cash	107	5.3%
Zcash	10	0.5%
Dogecoin	4	0.2%
Monero	1	0.1%

* Source: Coin ATM Radar (12/28/2017)

Still according to the website Coin ATM Radar at the end of 2017:
- although there are many manufacturers of cryptocurrency vending machines, the top three have manufactured more than 75% of all machines currently installed;
- during the last seven days of 2017, an average of almost four ATMs are installed every day. Here is the installation curve of the park, the first machines appearing at the end of 2013:

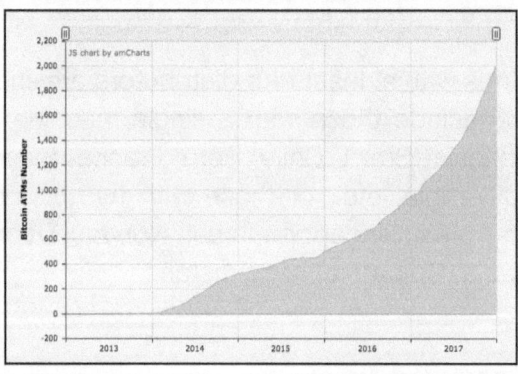

There are wide geographical disparities in the number of vending machines installed, but also in costs, as shown by two installations in progress: 15% in Nigeria versus 0.1% in Barbados.

The overall average provides a commission of 9.36%. The purchasing costs are higher, at 10.29%, while the sale costs are 6.65% (reminder: not all vending machines allow cryptocurrencies to be sold, which is why the average cost is not equal to the sum of the two divided by two).

Update: As of 15 February 2018, Coin ATM Radar had 2,248 ATMs, or 10% more in one month, located in 63 countries.

Attacks against exchanges
With the vertiginous rise in the price of bitcoin and other cryptocurrencies, it was inevitable that hacking attempts would multiply. In the case of a decentralized system where information is distributed over the entire network, direct blockchain hacking is by nature impossible. On the other hand, the so-called "51% attack" is possible: "If an entity controls more than 50% of the total network power, it may then exclude transactions and/or modify the order of transactions over the course of the attack. Indeed, as long as the attacker has more than 50% of the network's computing power, he can secretly build a longer chain than the one produced by the rest of the network. Once made public (...), the chain of the attacker then replaces the chain of the honest miners."[33]

Apart from this particular case, hackers focus instead on security weaknesses and code failures on the exchanges and mobile applications (digital wallets), thus out of the blockchain system: "There have been at least three dozen heists of cryptocurrency exchanges since 2011; many of the hacked exchanges later shut down. More than 980,000 bitcoins have been stolen, which today would be worth about $4 billion. Few have been recovered. Burned investors have been left at the mercy of exchanges as to whether

---

33. *Qu'est-ce qu'une attaque des 51% ?*, Jean-Luc, Bitcoin.fr, 10/30/2016.

Chapter 1

they will receive any compensation."[34] Most of them haven't recovered anything and won't ever recover anything.

Here are some of the main attacks in decreasing chronological order:

- 20 December 2017: the EtherDelta platform announces that it has suffered a DNS attack on its server. At least 308 ethers (about $267,000) are stolen along with the equivalent of hundreds of thousands of dollars in tokens;

- December 19, 2017: the South Korean exchange Youbit (formerly Yapizon) announces the termination of its activities following a new computer attack: 17% of its assets have reportedly been stolen. It has already suffered an attack in April, which cost it over 3,800 bitcoins, or about $35 million at the time. The company states on its website that its customers can already recuperate 75% of their assets; the balance will depend on the results of the liquidation. According to South Korea's Internet and Security Agency (KISA), which is conducting the investigation, hackers working for North Korea initiated the first theft. No information has yet been provided for the second;

- December 6: the Slovenian NiceHash exchange is hacked and 4,700 bitcoins are stolen, equivalent to $80 million;

- November 21: The company behind the digital currency tether says nearly $31 million of its tokens were stolen two days earlier;

- July: CoinDash, an Israeli exchange, reports that $7 million has been stolen from investors after its website was attacked and an ICO's contact address was changed;[35]

- August 2, 2016: Bitfinex, based in Hong Kong and one of the three largest exchanges in the world and the number one in dollar transactions, was robbed of approximately 120,000 bitcoins for a value of $65 million at that time;

- June 17, 2016: After raising approximately the equivalent of $150 million in ethers to fund the Ethereum, the Decentralized Autonomous

---

34. *Cryptocurrency Exchanges Are Increasingly Roiled by Hackings and Chaos*, Reuters, 09/29/2017.
35. *Millions 'stolen' in NiceHash Bitcoin heist*, Dave Lee, BBC, 12/08/2017.

Organization (DAO) is robbed of 3.7 million ether totaling nearly $80 million;

- December 2014: Bitstamp is robbed of 18,866 bitcoins, or approximately $5.2 million (the unit price is $279)[36];
- February 28, 2014: Mt. Gox, the world's leading exchange, based in Japan, declares bankruptcy. According to its CEO, Mark Karpelès, the equivalent of nearly $460 million in bitcoin is stolen by hackers, making this the biggest embezzlement in the history of cryptocurrencies.

To this list should be added the announcement that was given at a press conference on 26 January 2018, by the Japanese platform Coincheck, presented as the largest exchange in volume, with 32% of world trade. It reports that it has been the victim of a theft of 500 million nem units, equivalent to $530 million or €430 million. The company announces by press release on 28 January that it would reimburse its 260,000 victim customers with its capital. To date, it is the largest theft in the history of cryptocurrencies, even larger than Mt. Gox.

Beware, danger!
However tempting it may be to speculate on cryptocurrencies, as it may seem like easy money, this is false, and we do not recommend it, unless you can afford to lose the money invested or know that you will not need it. Indeed, we do not know who is behind some of them or how they are actually governed. So, who can say that exchanges are not manipulating quotations or that, all of a sudden, a large number of bitcoins and other currencies will not end up on the market, causing prices to collapse? Similarly, is it legitimate to fuel speculation on the ripple or some other digital currency, so that a handful of individuals receive indecent fortunes that do not really enrich the community?

Moreover, while we finish writing this book, a scandal so huge is beginning to emerge, that it could have repercussions on the entire

---

36. *Details of $5 Million Bitstamp Hack Revealed*, Stan Higgins, CoinDesk, 07/01/2015.

sphere of private cryptocurrencies. Thus, Bloomberg announces on January 29 that the team managing tether has received subpoenas from the U.S. Commodity Futures Trading Commission in December.[37] As indicated above, tether issuers state on their website (www.tether.to) that each unit issued is guaranteed by a unit of currency, with a parity of 1 tether = 1 US dollar. With $2.2 billion in circulation, that arithmetically means they have the equivalent of $2.2 billion in cash. But nothing is less certain.

And, even worse for the definitive credibility of private cryptocurrencies, since tether is linked to Bitfinex, one of the main exchanges in the world, it could mean that tether is not only a $2.2 billion scam, but that, in addition, Bitfinex manipulated bitcoin prices by buying them in large quantities and paying for them by issuing tethers. Even more suspicious is the fact that the audit of Tether's accounts announced in September 2017 was abandoned in January, for a reason that cannot fool anyone: "Given the excruciatingly detailed procedures Friedman was undertaking for the relatively simple balance sheet of Tether, it became clear that an audit would be unattainable in a reasonable timeframe."

These revelations contributed to a drop in the price of bitcoin—it plunged to $6,653 on February 5, one-third of the ceiling price of $19,458 on December 17, 2017, although there was a rebound in the following days.

Beware, thieves!
In the world of cryptocurrencies, one should not only be wary of their issuer, exchanges and price manipulation, but also theft. Indeed, cyber security companies have already identified several malwares. For example, Kaspersky Lab communicates in November 2017 about Crypto Shuffler, a virus that steals e-wallet content: "It exploits users' lack of attention. It gets assets by infiltrating its victims' computers and by then copying and

---

37. *Regulators Subpoena Crypto Exchange Bitfinex, Tether*, Matthew Leising, Bloomberg, 01/31/2018.

pasting the payee's identification code, substituting its own contact information."[38]

With the values that cryptocurrencies now represent, it is inevitable that this kind of malware will multiply, and vigilance must be total.

There is another risk to note: when you buy cryptocurrencies, you do not know the identity of their owners. However, contrary to what is often stated, anonymity is not always absolute (we explain this below). You may find yourself in a situation where it is later discovered that your seller is a drug dealer or a terrorist. Even if you are unaware of this and are acting in good faith, it is difficult for the time being to know what the legal consequences would be, either possible confiscation of your purchase or even ban of your entry into certain countries.

---

[38]. *Un virus voleur de bitcoins découvert par Kaspersky Lab*, Sputnik News, 11/02/2017.

Chapter 1

The CoinHive Threat
"Monetize Your Business With Your Users' CPU Power"

According to its founders, "Coinhive offers a JavaScript miner for the Monero Blockchain that you can embed in your website. Your users run the miner directly in their browser and mine XMR for you in turn for an ad-free experience, in-game currency or whatever incentives you can come up with."[39] The monero was chosen for technical reasons related to its Cryptonight algorithm.

This is an interesting alternative to advertising, especially since the installation of the function on a site is simple and only takes a few moments. The problem is that, most of the time, the user is not aware that as long as he remains connected, his processor is used without his knowledge to mine moneros. The consequences are: 1) the computer operates at a slower speed; 2) an increased energy consumption, and hence a higher electricity bill, and your battery's duration decreases, which can lessen your autonomy when traveling.

In addition, CoinHive can be installed by hackers, who will then use their victims' processors without them noticing. In October 2017, the security specialist Check Point cites this application as the sixth most used malware.[40] "Troy Mursch from Bad Packets Report recently conducted an investigation, in which he found that the ongoing cryptojacking trend has infected nearly 50,000 websites. According to his report, 48,953 websites are running cryptocurrency mining malware." An anti-virus, however, may block it, as shows our personal experience:

39. Https://coinhive.com.
40. *Cryptocurrency Mining Presents New Threat to Business, says Check Point*, Check Point 11/13/2017.

General Overview of Cryptocurrencies

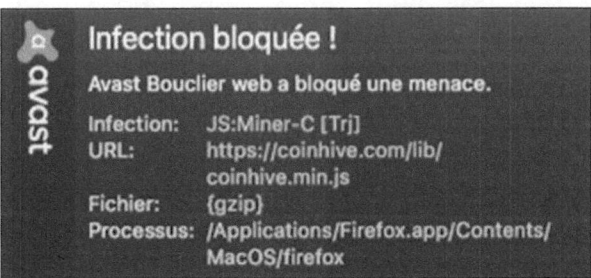

Nevertheless, advertisements broadcasted by YouTube have been hacked to mine monero without the knowledge of Internet users, once again due to Coinhive, also found in Google Chrome extensions and applications for Android. Even if telephones do not offer a great deal of computing power, it is a problem for users, especially as they do not know its origin. So if you see it appear somewhere on your computer, you will now know what it is. But this will also mean that it is probably time to update your anti-virus or install one. Otherwise, you will be contributing to the enrichment of miners sometimes from another continent.

Moreover, private individuals are not the only targets of pirates, as companies have also been victims of "cryptojacking," i.e. mining on their computers and servers without their knowledge. The British insurer Aviva and Tesla are among the last known examples.[41]

---

41. *The Cryptojacking Epidemic*, RedLock CSI Team, 02/20/2018.

Chapter 1

When the United States misses out on the deal of the century
In October 2013, the Department of Justice closes Silk Road, a darknet site that sells drugs and other prohibited products to over 100,000 customers. Its creator, Ross Ulbricht, alias Dread Pirate Roberts, is arrested, and two lots of 29,655 and 144,336 bitcoins are seized on his computer.

They are sold at an auction in 2014 and 2015, but as Ulbricht challenges the legality of the procedure in court, among other reasons because two FBI investigators stole some of his bitcoins for their own account, the Justice Department waits before communicating the amount of the sales.

Two years later, the founder of Silk Road drops his legal action. The Manhattan attorney's office then confirms by press release dated September 29, 2017 that the authorities can definitively seize the proceeds of the sales of the confiscated assets, and that the second lot has generated the sum of $48,238,116.[42] This corresponds to 144,336 bitcoins, at a unit price of $334.20 — it is very far from recent prices.

If the authorities had waited until late September 2017 to sell the second lot, when the price was $4,400, it would have generated $635 million in revenue, almost $600 million more than the amount obtained. While waiting until the end of December, when the price seemed to (momentarily) stabilize around $14,400, almost $2.1 billion would have gone into the federal government's coffers.

The 29,655 bitcoin lot was also auctioned off at the end of June 2014. The first operation of this kind, as *Fortune* reports, "this auction is essentially a test run for the government on how to handle future auctions of bitcoin, or other digital-only assets."[43]

Spread over a twelve-hour period, it generates sixty-three bids per forty-five registered bidders and yields $17.2 million, at a unit price of $580, which is higher than what the second lot sold for the following year.

---

42. *Acting Manhattan U.S. Attorney Announces Forfeiture Of $48 Million From Sale Of Silk Road Bitcoins*, Department of Justice, U.S. Attorney's Office, Southern District of New York, 09/29/2017.
43. *U.S. launches sale of $17.2 million of bitcoin seized in raid*, Laura Lorenzetti, Fortune, 206/27/2014.

General Overview of Cryptocurrencies

It remains to be seen to whom the funds will be allocated, as *Fortune* indicates: "The U.S. Attorney's office did not specify if the proceeds from the seizure will go to the agencies, including the FBI and IRS, that helped bring down Silk Road, or if the money will instead go to the U.S. Treasury."[44]

It is sure that with a little patience, there would have been much more to distribute. But who could have predicted such a development in 2013, 2014 or 2015?

	Quantities	Real revenues	At a price of $4,400	At a price of $14,400
Lot 1	29,655	17,200,000	130,482,000	427,032,000
Lot 2	144,336	48,238,116	635,078,400	2,078,438,400
Totals	173,991	65,438,116	765,560,400	2,505,470,400

Learning from one's mistakes

In a counterfeit drug case in Utah, the authorities seize the accused's assets, including 513 bitcoins (BTC) and 512 bitcoins cash (BCH). At the time of the event, in December 2016, the value of the portfolio was less than $500,000. But, given the volatility and soaring prices, the prosecutor's office asks the court to sell these assets without delay, according to Federal Rules of Civil Procedures, which provide that the government has the option to sell any property subject to forfeiture prior to the final forfeiture order if, among other reasons, it is "perishable or at risk of deterioration, decay, or injury by being detained in custody pending the action."[45]

This is not exactly the case for the cryptocurrencies, but in December 2017 the judge agrees to the sale, which generates about

---

44. *The Feds Just Collected $48 Million from Seized Bitcoins*, Jeff John Roberts, *Fortune*, 10/02/2017.
45. *US Government Selling bitcoins Seized From Dark Web Seller*, A.J. Dellinger, *International Business Times*, 12/16/2017.

$8.5 million at current prices, instead of the valuation of $500,000 at the time of the seizure. Pending the completion of the procedures, the sum will be held by the Treasury.

Finland and Bulgaria's turn
Bloomberg announces on 20 February 2018 that the Finnish authorities are in possession of two thousand bitcoins confiscated after dozens of raids that have been going on since 2016. As that they are part of the euro zone, they cannot consider them as currency, and therefore follow the recommendations of the Treasury to auction off, considering it best to avoid "commercial exchanges, which can be untrustworthy and opaque."[46] At the current rate, this represents the equivalent of more than $20 million.

In May 2017, Bulgaria puts an end to a system of tax frauds operating in several countries of the region with the complicity of customs officers. The Southeast European Law Enforcement Center (Selec), which contributed to the operation, explains on 17 May that among the many assets seized, including a lot of money, there are portfolios totaling 213,519 bitcoins, or currently more than $2 billion![47] The legal proceedings are ongoing, but this sale would make it possible to solve several key budgetary problems, on the condition that it is spread out over time, otherwise such a quantity placed on the market at once would risk causing prices to fall. However, on 19 May, the prosecutor's office effectively confirms that there is an operation to dismantle this network, but denies that bitcoins have been seized.[48] Strange.

---

46. *2,000 Confiscated Bitcoins Create a Storage Puzzle in Finland*, Kati Pohjanpalo, Bloomberg, 20/02/2018.
47. *More than 200,000 bitcoins in value of 500 million USD seized by the Bulgarian authorities*, Selec, 05/29/2017.
48. *Bitcoin: Bulgarian banks terminate accounts of cryptocurrency exchanges*, The Sofia Globe, 12/08/2017.

International regulation?

As already mentioned, bitcoin is not regulated by any of the usual banking authorities. Inevitably, institutional and governmental voices, undoubtedly influenced by their commercial banks which see a source of profit escape them, as well as the control of what may be the financial system of the future (we will return to this in conclusion), are worried about the existence of cryptocurrencies and want to obtain their regulation.

This is, for example, the case of France, along with Germany, as they plan to take the issue of bitcoin to the next G20 summit, according to AFP[49]. The Minister of Finance, Bruno Le Maire, told AFP on 18 December: "The rise of bitcoin presents risks in regards to speculation and the possibility of illicit financing," hence the need for "a legal framework."

The notion of "risks versus speculation" is a false argument, however, because the very principle of speculation is risk! Would France like speculation without risk? If so, we must then close stock exchanges, ban futures markets, such as Forex, etc.

As for the "illicit financing," it should obviously be excluded, but for drug cartels, mafias, traffickers of all kinds, terrorist groups like Daesh, etc., is it cryptocurrencies that have allowed them to prosper for decades, or the current banking and financial system?

The French intention is confirmed during an interview of François Villeroy de Galhau, the Governor of the Banque de France (the central bank), on the BFM Business channel, who believes that "regulation only makes sense internationally." He adds, "I think it's time to ask the G20."

It will indeed be interesting to see what emerges from this initiative. Janet Yellen, President of the Federal Reserve, announces in February 2014 that her organization has no authority to regulate bitcoin, which she repeats in December 2017 (see Chapter 2).

This was also stated in September 2017 by Mario Draghi, President of the European Central Bank (ECB), before the Economic and

---

49. *La France portera la question du bitcoin au G20 (Bercy)*, AFP, in *Les Échos Investir*, 12/18/2017.

Monetary Committee of the European Parliament: "It would actually not be in our powers to prohibit and regulate" bitcoin and other digital currencies."[50] He added that the ECB needs to consider their potential impact on the economy, even if they are still too immature to be considered as a viable payment method, and that the ECB's primary concern is cybersecurity.

That France is concerned about regulation is undoubtedly positive, but do the authorities seem to understand that a revolution is underway and that it would be harmful to miss it?

Are bitcoin transactions anonymous?
In theory, this is the case: they are registered and public but linked to an e-mail address that does not display a direct link to their author, or even his purchases. This is one of the major arguments used by supporters of regulation to impose it: illicit transactions are possible because anonymity is absolute. However, many specialists have shown that although it is a working principle of bitcoin and other cryptocurrencies in general, anonymity is not total.

This is explained by an article in the *MIT Technology Review*[51] dated August 23, 2017: "Security experts call it pseudonymous privacy, like writing books under a nom de plume. You can preserve your privacy as long as the pseudonym is not linked to you. But as soon as somebody makes the link to one of your anonymous books, the ruse is revealed. Your entire writing history under your pseudonym becomes public. Similarly, as soon as your personal details are linked to your bitcoin address, your purchase history is revealed too."

So the question is how can the bitcoin address be recognized and identified in relation to its owner? The author of the article explains that the answer is provided by the work of Steven Goldfeder of Princeton University and several of his colleagues:

---

50. *Mario Draghi: European Central Bank Has 'No Power' to Regulate bitcoin*, Rachel Rose O'Leary, *Coindesk*, 09/26/2017.
51. *Bitcoin Transactions Aren't as Anonymous as Everyone Hoped*, Emerging Technology from the arXiv, *MIT Technology Review*, 08/23/2017.

"The main culprits are Web trackers and cookies—small pieces of code deliberately embedded into websites that send information to third parties about the way people use the site. Common Web trackers send information to Google, Facebook, and others to track page usage, purchase amounts, browsing habits, and so on. Some trackers even send personally identifiable information such as your name, address, and e-mail.

In this way, information about a transaction leaks onto the Web, where governments, law enforcement agencies, and malicious users can readily collect and analyze it."

What is worrying is that S. Goldfeder and his colleagues find that of the 130 largest merchant sites accepting bitcoin, including Microsoft, 40% "of merchants leak payment information to a total of at least 40 third parties, most frequently from shopping cart pages. Most of this information leakage is intentional for the purposes of advertising and analytics."

What is more worrying is that additional data is sent: "We find that many merchant websites have far more serious (and likely unintentional) information leaks that directly reveal the exact transaction on the blockchain to dozens of trackers."

This is not the only door through which anonymity is at times jeopardized, including for users of solutions such as CoinJoin[52]. Indeed, in addition to the vulnerabilities linked to commercial sites, startups have developed tools for tracking bitcoin transactions. One of the best known ones is Chainalysis[53], a software the IRS (Internal Revenue Service, the US tax service) has been using since 2015:

---

52. "CoinJoin is an anonymization method for bitcoin transactions proposed by Gregory Maxwell. It is based on the following idea: "When you want to make a payment, find someone else who also wants to make a payment and make a joint payment together."[1] When making a joint payment, there is no way to relate input and outputs in one bitcoin transaction and thus the exact direction of money movement remains unknown to third parties." Source: Wikipedia.

53. "Founded in 2014, Chainalysis is the leading provider of Anti-Money Laundering software for bitcoin. (...) Our customers have checked over $15 billion worth of transactions using our platform. Through formal partnerships with Europol and other international law enforcement, our investigative tools have been used globally to successfully track, apprehend, and convict money launderers and cyber criminals." Source: website of the company in *About*.

"This is necessary to identify and obtain evidence on individuals using bitcoin to either launder money or conceal income as part of tax fraud or other Federal crimes."[54]

The company Elliptic also provides similar services, as explained on its website[55]:

"Elliptic's technology traces entities' transaction activity through the blockchain instantly and automatically. It uncovers complex relationships between multiple entities with precision and complete transparency.

Elliptic's proprietary database delivers auditable proof of identity for millions of bitcoin addresses across thousands of real world entities. This gives law enforcement agencies and financial institutions the confidence they need to investigate and evaluate suspicious activity on the bitcoin blockchain."

Who would dare say that bitcoin transactions are completely anonymous?

WannaCry and cryptocurrencies

It seems, however, that the Chainalysis and Elliptic tracking tools do not always break anonymity, as the WannaCry case shows. It is a malware or malicious software, called "ransomware," which requires the payment of a ransom to be deactivated.

Considered the largest cyberattack with ransom in Internet history, WannaCry blocks, from May 12 to 17, 200,000 to over 300,000 computers using various versions of the Windows operating system, from XP to Windows 10. Spain and the United Kingdom are the first countries affected, but by the end more than 150 are affected, including the United States, Russia, India and so on.

Public services, universities, SMEs, multinationals such as FedEx, Vodafone, Honda, Hitachi, Nissan, Deutsche Bahn, Renault, PetroChina, Petrobrás, Telefónica, the National Health Service (United Kingdom), the Russian Ministry of the Interior, etc., are all affected.

---

54. *The IRS Has Been Using bitcoin Tracking Software Since 2015*, Stan Higgins, *CoinDesk*, 08/22/2017.
55. Https://www.elliptic.co.

General Overview of Cryptocurrencies

Here is one of the screens that appeared on infected computers:

Source of the image: Jacques Cheminat,
WannaCry et maintenant les variantes !
Silicon.fr, 05/15/2017.

The screenshot shows that the ransom is set at the equivalent of $300 in bitcoin, with the address for payment. The pirates have even included a tab explaining how to buy bitcoins.

According to Dune Lawrence of *Bloomberg Businessweek*[56], on the evening of May 17, the three portfolios received 277 payments totaling just over forty-five bitcoins, for a value of about $82,000.

On August 3, 2017, Selena Larson from CNN informed that:

"For months, the ransom money from the massive WannaCry cyberattack sat untouched in online accounts. Now, someone has moved it.

More than $140,000 worth of digital currency bitcoin has been drained from three accounts linked to the ransomware virus that hit hundreds of thousands of computers around the world in May.

It's unclear, though, who emptied the accounts and why. If the WannaCry hackers are finally trying to get their hands on the money, they'll have to outwit law enforcement agencies from around the globe.

---

56. *North Korea's bitcoin Play*, Dune Lawrence, *Bloomberg Businessweek*, 12/18/2017.

Chapter 1

It's a fresh twist in the mysterious attack that cybersecurity experts have linked to a hacking group associated with North Korea."[57]

Contacted by the website Gizmodo.com[58], Jonathan Levin, founder of Chainalysis, explained that these bitcoins began to be transformed into monero, a cryptocurrency "much more anonymous." According to research made by Chainalysis and Neutrino, a company specialized in cybersecurity, "the WannaCry hackers are using a service called ShapeShift to launder their bitcoins (...) which allows a user to provide an email address and anonymously convert one cryptocurrency into another." In this case, bitcoins become moneros, which are "totally anonymous so far," according to what CEO Neutrino Giancarlo Russo told *Forbes*. "It will not be possible to follow further movements."

Although the first analyses seem to indicate that the creators of WannaCry speak Chinese fluently, in the end North Korea is named the culprit by the governments of the United States, Canada, and Japan. It is said to have acted via the Lazarus Group, which is responsible for numerous hackings and attempts against financial institutions, including the theft of $81 million from the Central Bank of Bangladesh in 2016.

---

57. *Someone has emptied the ransom accounts from the WannaCry attack*, Selena Larson, CNN, 08/03/2017.
58. *The WannaCry Ransomware Attackers Are Cashing Out Their Bitcoin at a Dangerous Time*, Rhett Jones, Gizmodo.com, 08/03/2017.

How to Boost One's Stock Price?

It is currently quite simple: just announce an initiative in the cryptocurrencies and/or the blockchain, and it's done. Perhaps the most recent and emblematic case is that of Kodak, who announces the creation of KodakCoin as part of a project "to empower photographers and agencies to take greater control in image rights management."[59] Following the announcement, the Kodak share price jumps 120%.

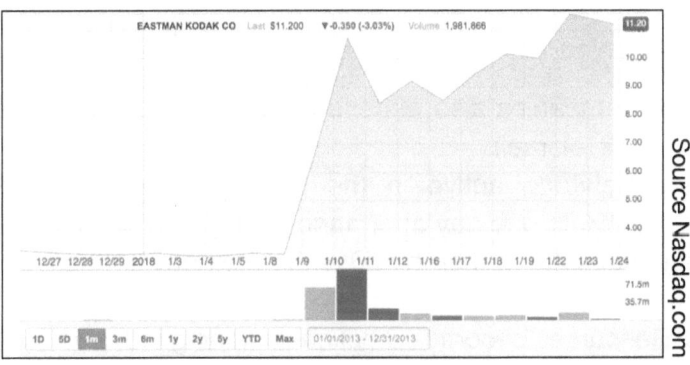

Guess when the creation of the KodakCoin was announced?

But there are even better and more vague examples: the tea beverage company Long Island Iced Tea Corp sees its share price quadruple on December 21, 2017 when it announces the transformation of its name into "Long Blockchain Corporation" and that "the parent company is shifting its primary corporate focus towards the exploration of and investment in opportunities that leverage the benefits of blockchain technology."[60]

---

59. *Kodak leads surge of companies exploiting bitcoin buzz*, Alex Hern, *The Guardian*, 01/11/2018.
60. *Long Island Iced Tea Corp. to Rebrand as "Long Blockchain Corp.,"* website of the company.

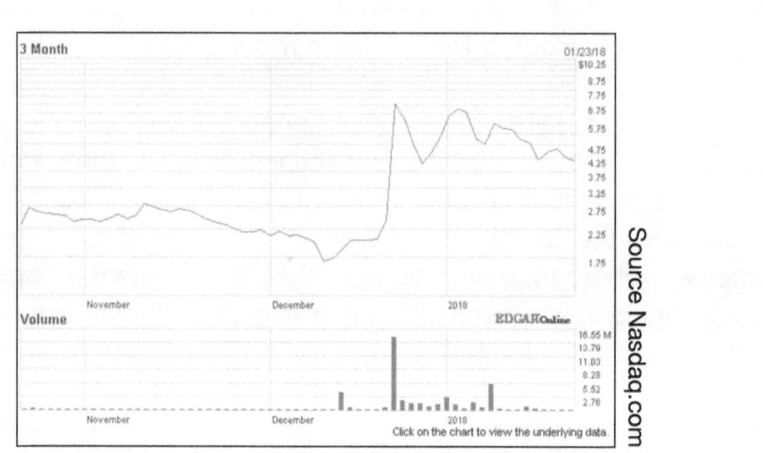

Two Israeli companies also experience the same striking results (see Chapter 2 – Israel):

- Fantasy Network, active in the gaming industry: its stock skyrockets 44% in one day after announcing the recruitment of a blockchain consultant, then by 80% the next day. In the end, the share has quadrupled;
- Natural Resources becomes Blockchain Mining Ltd. and its share price beats all records, with an increase of 5,144.76% between January 1 and December 31, 2017.

After this general overview, we will now present the position and strategy of many states regarding the issue of cryptocurrencies.

Chapter 2

Sovereign Cryptocurrencies

Introduction: The Bitcoin Market Potential Index (BMPI)
In August 2014, Garrick Hileman, a professor at the London School of Economics and the University of Cambridge, created a bitcoin index, which reads as follows:

"The Bitcoin Market Potential Index conceptualizes and ranks the potential utility of bitcoin across 178 countries to show which countries have the greatest potential to see bitcoin adoption. The index utilizes a data set with 40 variables related to bitcoin's current core functions: store of value, medium of exchange, and technology platform. The variables are grouped into the index's seven equally weighted sub-indices: technology penetration, international remittances, inflation, size of informal economy, financial repression, historical financial crises, and bitcoin penetration. Standardized and rescaled country level data both indicate that Argentina and Sub-Saharan Africa are the country and region, respectively, where bitcoin has the greatest potential for adoption. It is argued that while bitcoin regulation can play an important, and perhaps even decisive, role in bitcoin adoption it should be excluded as an index variable for now due to insufficient data and uncertainty over its ultimate impact."[61]

The study then explains the methodology adopted, including the description and analysis of the forty variables. From the 178 countries he analyzed with the BMPI, the researcher creates a table of the first ten countries likely to adopt bitcoin: the first column presents the standardized ranking while the second gives the re-scaled results (of course, the United States cannot appear in fifth place, this would be an attack on the image of the sacrosanct dollar and lose one's credibility):

---

[61]. *The Bitcoin Market Potential Index*, Garrick Hileman, London School of Economics.

Chapter 2

Ranking	Country (Standardized)	Country (Re-scaled)
1	Argentina	Argentina
2	Venezuela, RB	Venezuela, RB
3	Zimbabwe	Zimbabwe
4	Malawi	Iceland
5	United States	Malawi
6	Belarus	Guinea-Bissau
7	Nigeria	Congo, Dem. Rep.
8	Congo, Dem. Rep.	Belarus
9	Iceland	Nigeria
10	Iran, Islamic Rep.	Angola

Garrick Hileman concludes his work: "Finally, measuring actual bitcoin adoption against the BMPI forecast presents a number of challenges, including the lack of individual country data for many adoption metrics. Obtaining country level adoption data would help test the BMPI's accuracy."

Four years after the creation of this index, in spite of the quite understandable difficulties to elaborate it, in this chapter we will progressively explore how the adoption of private or sovereign cryptocurrencies has evolved in the world.

I. When bitcoin becomes the safe haven of a country

1) Cyprus, the first laboratory

The Cypriot financial crisis starts in 2012 and ends with a rescue plan the following year concocted by the Troika (IMF, ECB and European Commission), the same committee that intervened in the Greek crisis. Several measures are imposed on the government, one of the most symbolic states that deposits exceeding €100,000 will be taxed at a rate of 47.5% and converted into shares in the Bank of Cyprus, the island's main commercial bank. In short, this amounts to legally stripping owners of 47.5% of their account if over €100,000! (A similar scheme is then extended to the whole European Union as of 1 January 2016).

Two days after the presentation on March 25, 2013 of the second Troika rescue plan, here is what CNBC writes:

"The online alternative currency, previously little more than a curiosity in financial markets since its 2009 inception, has zoomed in trading value since the Cyprus banking crisis erupted two weeks ago.

With fears spreading that even insured deposits might not be safe in similar nations hit by banking crises, those looking for a haven to store their wealth have fled to the complicated world of digital cash. 'Incremental demand for bitcoin is coming from the geographic areas most affected by the Cypriot financial crisis—individuals in countries like Greece or Spain, worried that they will be next to feel the threat of deposit taxes,' Nicholas Colas, chief market strategist at ConvergEx, said in a report on the startling trend."[62]

Thus, the European Central Bank and its two Troika partners contributed to the first successes of bitcoin, by making it a safe haven to escape the drain on accounts in the event of bank restructuring.

---

62. *Bitcoin Bonanza: Cyprus Crisis Boosts Digital Dollars*, Jeff Cox, CNBC, 03/27/2017.

2) In Zimbabwe, bitcoin saves the day

According to CoinDesk's Bitcoin Price Index, bitcoin trades around US$7,000 on November 15, 2017. At the same time, in the capital of Zimbabwe, Harare, on the Golix platform, the only one in the country, it reaches the record sum of $13,499, almost double the price elsewhere. Why such a gap?

November 15 the Zimbabwe army places 93-year-old President Robert Mugabe under house arrest after almost forty years in power that has led his country to the abyss. The most serious failures concern agrarian reform and agricultural policy, coupled with poor harvests that caused famine in the 2000s. But the situation extends to the whole economy: "In the midst of chronic shortages of basic goods, the central bank ramped up its money-printing machines to finance imports. The result was rampant inflation. At the peak of the crisis, prices were doubling every 24 hours. Cato Institute economists estimate monthly inflation peaked at 7.9 billion percent in 2008. Unemployment soared, public services collapsed and the economy shrank by 18% in 2008."[63]

Zimbabwe even does something that is nearly unheard of, abandoning its currency in 2009 — the year bitcoin is created, although there is no link — replacing it with the US dollar and the South African rand, but also the euro, the British pound, the yen, the yuan, the Indian rupee and the Botswana pula.

The situation does not improve and in 2015 bank deposits in Zimbabwe dollars are exchanged for US dollars at the incredible rate of:

$$US\$1 = Z\$35,000,000,000,000,000$$

or Z$35 million billion for US$1!

Two years later, when the army takes power in Harare, it is therefore almost natural for Zimbabweans to turn to bitcoin as a safe haven, almost at any price. All you need is a smartphone to protect your

---

63. *How Robert Mugabe killed one of Africa's richest economies*, Alanna Petroff, CNN, 11/17/2017.

savings and retrieve them later, flexibility, speed and liquidity that few other values offer than cryptocurrencies. They can even be used to make direct payments, an advantage that is unique when confidence in the monetary and banking system disappears.

It does not seem to have returned yet because on the first day of 2018, the Golix platform shows bitcoin prices ranging from US$19,810 to US$21,000, an increase of 4.32%, i.e. a price about 50% higher than on the world's main exchanges (then around $13,300); even for Korean ones, which display a price around $17,600, i.e. up to 20% cheaper.

It should be noted that Zimbabweans are not the only Africans to use bitcoin, as it is easier and cheaper than Western Union or MoneyGram to send money. However, at current prices and given their volatility, it seems difficult to use it as a means of payment, including in stores. The Reserve Bank of Zimbabwe (RBZ) reminded people on 22 November 2017, one week after Robert Mugabe was placed under house arrest, that "in terms of the bitcoin, as far as we are concerned, it is not actually legal. In Southern Africa, what we have done as regulators, we have said that we will not allow this in our markets.

Research is currently being undertaken to ascertain the challenges and risks associated with these particular products and until we have actually established and come up with a legal and regulatory framework for them, it will not be allowed."[64]

Like most other central banks, the RBZ warned and advised citizens not to get involved in cryptocurrencies, because they risked losing their investments without having any possible recourse. The message seemed to fall on deaf ears as bitcoin continues to rise on the Golix platform: on January 15 it was quoted between $22,001 and $23,300, 10% higher than two weeks earlier.

Update: Bitcoin continues to remain disconnected from other exchanges, fluctuating between $13,050 and $15,800, compared to an average of $9,800 elsewhere on February 15, one month later.

---

64. *Bitcoin is not legal: RBZ*, Chronicle, 11/22/2017.

Chapter 2

3) The United Kingdom like Zimbabwe?

On 24 June 2016, the day after the UK voted in favor of Brexit, bitcoin increased by 9% while the pound sterling fell by 9% in two trading days. Did the English choose to take refuge in the cryptocurrencies to save their economies? Actually, no: "The price of the global cryptocurrency bitcoin spiked on Friday as the yuan dipped after Britain voted to leave the European Union.

Bitcoin moves are often counter-linked to the yuan because the majority of trade in the cryptocurrency comes from China. The yuan hit a five-and-a-half-year low on Friday, while the price of bitcoin jumped around 8.7 percent from the day's opening price, hitting highs of around $680.19, according to Coindesk which tracks the price of the cryptocurrency. (...) The correction from a day or two ago had more to do with a technical correction that it did with Brexit."[65]

The next day, bitcoin dropped to $673.87 but in any case, it was significantly higher on June 20, a few days before the vote, when it stood at $755.31:

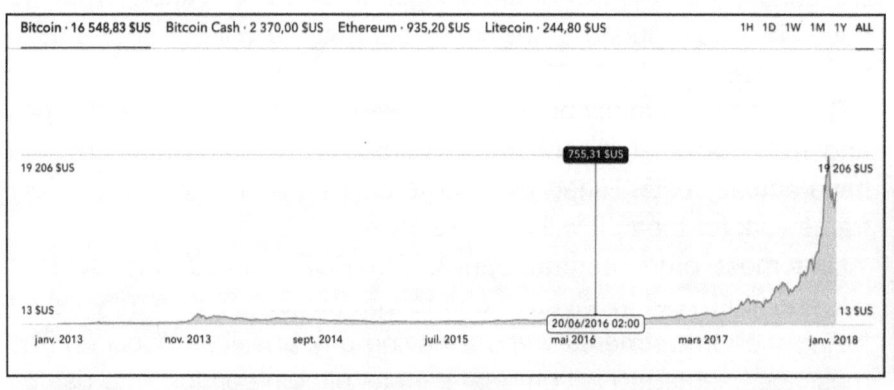

It is true, however, that many Britons speculated on currencies before the vote, however they opted for the euro or the dollar as there was much more chance that the Brexit would make the pound drop rather than raise the bitcoin.

---

65. *Bitcoin spikes as yuan hits five-and-a-half year low on Brexit*, Arjun Kharpal, CNBC, 06/24/2017.

4) Iran under sanctions and pressure

Brave New World Investments is a Swedish investment company specializing in operations in Iran. Here is what it communicates on its website:[66]

"The greatest opportunity in the Middle East region by far is post-sanction Iran. As sanctions are being dismantled, industries in dire need of investment will quickly be brought up to par with international standards. Information technology penetration is currently low in the country and is expected to boom in the coming years. (...)

A few US financial sanctions are still active that are effectively excluding large parts of the country's financial industry from the international financial industry. As these are gradually removed, the country's financial sector will begin to fully rejoin the international financial markets. As this is happening, and despite the challenges, Iran like the rest of the world is on the brink of a revolution in digital payments, taking full advantage of emerging technological advances.

While sanctions have been eased, it is still difficult to transfer money in and out of the country. Many western banks will not transfer money to or from Iran and indeed will not even open a bank account for companies explicitly stating business activities involving dealings with Iran. At the root of this reluctance is a fear of putting their activities in the US under any sort of legal or regulatory risk.

Brave New World Investments is building a remittance service, which solves these problems by utilizing blockchain technology. *We are currently preparing a pilot program (...)*."

The decision accelerated after the founders "initially took their idea of creating an investment vehicle for companies traded on the Tehran Stock Exchange to the six largest banks in Sweden, and each refused the idea."[67]

Consequently, they decide to use blockchain and bitcoin, including for the creation of their company. They get confirmation from their government that the use of the blockchain and the transfer of

---

66. Http://www.bnw.investments
67. *Sweden Incorporates Iran Investment Firm Using Only Bitcoin*, Michael del Castillo, CoinDesk, 04/12/2017.

bitcoins to Iran would not violate US sanctions, and that they can use bitcoins to build their initial share capital. What is all the more interesting is that the Swedish Accounting Standards Board has also agreed that Brave New World Investments can use a bitcoin account and be created without a traditional bank account. All is needed is a certificate from a certified public accountant.

Bitcoins, ethers, etc. are then sent to Iran where they are exchanged for rials, the country's currency, and then fund the company's local bank account to finance its investments. In this situation, the use of cryptocurrencies makes it possible to avoid the risks of sanctions, and even, if at least partially, of the banking system.

Indeed, Bloomberg points out in late 2012 that Iranians are turning to bitcoin to escape the fall of the rial and sanctions, the most important cryptocurrency already acting as a safe haven.[68] Moreover, many of them do not have access to international credit cards such as Visa and MasterCard, even after the signing of the nuclear agreement, so they can make purchases on foreign sites accepting bitcoin payments.

The authorities measure the situation, and the Deputy Minister of Information and Communication Technologies states in October 2017: "[We have] already conducted a number of research studies as part of efforts to prepare the infrastructure to use bitcoin inside the country. We as the main center in Iran dealing with the country's technology developments have taken the issue of preparing the infrastructure for the new currency very seriously."[69]

At the same time, a Member of Parliament declares in December 2017: "Deals and transactions made with bitcoin are in no way in accordance with Islamic and economic fundamentals, therefore related entities, especially the central bank, must exert the necessary supervision over these deals."[70]

---

68. *Dollar-Less Iranians Discover Virtual Currency*, Max Raskin, Bloomberg, 11/30/2012.
69. *Iran Preparing Cryptocurrency Infrastructure*, News BTC, 10/30/2017.
70. *Iranian Banker Calls for Cryptocurrency Acceptance*, Cindy Wang, Bitcoin.com, 01/09/2018.

Sovereign Cryptocurrencies

For the time being, although it has already issued warnings, the central bank has not yet given its stance on the adoption of bitcoin and other cryptocurrencies as legal means of payment, but it is expected to do so by September 2018.

The serious disturbances that shake Iranian cities in January 2018 with at least twenty deaths have an impact on the volumes traded, as Bitcoin.com points out : "Data published by Coin Dance indicates that peer-to-peer trade between the Iranian rial (IRR) and bitcoin witnessed record volumes during the build-up to Iran's protests over recent weeks. The record 70+ billion IRR worth of bitcoin traded during the week of 23 December comprised more than a 1000% increase in volume when compared to markets' preceding records of 6.3 billion IRR from early November."[71]

As can be seen in the price graph below:

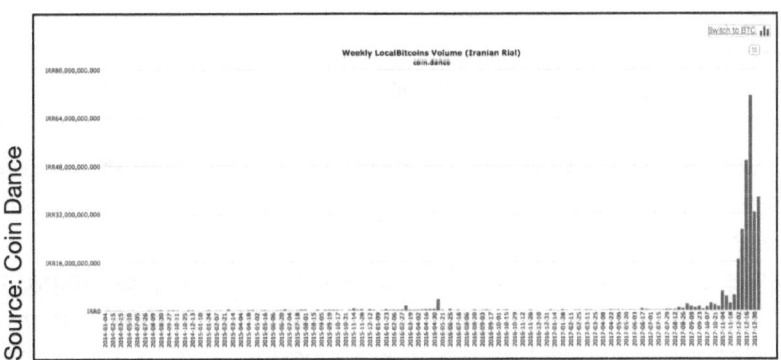

The same graph expressed not in value but in number of bitcoins exchanged gives another angle:

---

71. *Iranian Bitcoin Adoption Surges Amid Political Protests and Censorship*, Samuel Haig, bitcoin.com, 01/05/2018.

Chapter 2

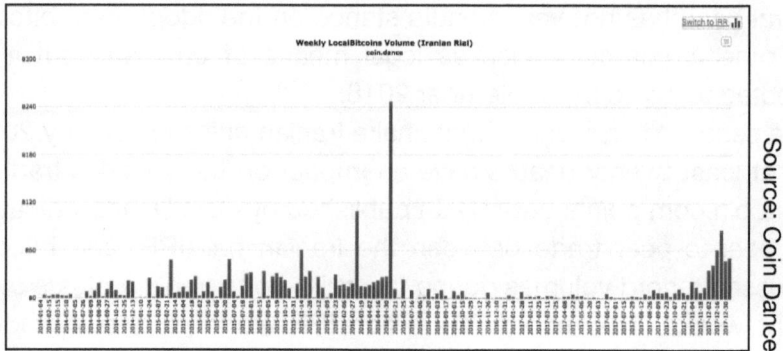

Indeed, it is in 2016 that the largest volume of bitcoins is traded. But, at the time, they are worth a few hundred dollars, which can give a distorted understanding of the situation. Nevertheless, the demonstrations in Iran clearly have an impact on the role of bitcoin as a safe haven.

Maintaining the sanctions imposed by the United States inevitably pushes the country towards an economy that will operate without the dollar and leaves a lot of room for cryptocurrencies, further accelerating the reduction of the influence of the greenback on the international scene—unless the central bank prohibits cryptocurrencies as a legal means of payment. But, by September 2018, the deadline it has set to take a position, who knows what can happen? Meanwhile, cryptocurrencies still seem to have a bright future in the event of a new political and/or economic crisis.

And in February 2018, Abolhassan Firouzabadi, Secretary of Cyberspace, reveals that discussions at the state level are underway for the creation of a digital currency based on the blockchain. The project is therefore in progress.

5) Afghanistan, hawala and bitcoin

This country would be among the richest if it had not experienced war for decades—unless it is at war because it is one of the richest? Indeed, in 2010, the United States announces that it has discovered, in addition to the already known reserves, the equivalent of $1 trillion in mineral resources, with gigantic deposits of iron, copper, cobalt, gold and strategic metals such as lithium. To this must be added oil, gas and uranium, present in the Helmand province, which also has poppy crops, whose planted areas have been constantly increasing since 2001—a year that also marks the beginning of the Western presence in the area—with a record 328,000 hectares cultivated in 2017. This means Afghanistan produces nearly 90% of the world's heroin, according to the UN.[72]

Although historically the first bitcoin transaction in Afghanistan appears to have taken place in 2013[73], the official government and its central bank (Da Afghanistan Bank) currently have other priorities than legislating or developing a cryptocurrency.

Roya Mahboob is an Afghan entrepreneur. She has created several structures, including Women's Annex, founded with an American investor and partner, to enable women to create blogs and earn money through advertising. Here is how *Forbes* relays the rest of the adventure: "That startup ran into problems paying the contributors, the majority of whom were women, since 99% of them did not have bank accounts. While legally women could have bank accounts, culturally, many families did not trust banks. The system they trusted, hawalah, was actually an ancient non-technological system that resembles blockchain technology, in which money is transferred from one person to the next, each of whom trusts the next link in the chain. It's basically an eighth-century version of bitcoin."[74] The origin

---

72. *Afghan opium production jumps to record level, up 87 per cent: Survey*, United Nations Office on Drugs and Crime, 11/15/2017.
73. *Afghanistan's first recorded bitcoin transaction?*, Robert Viglione, Coindesk, 07/02/2013.
74. *How Bitcoin Solved This Serial Entrepreneur's Problems*, Laura Shin, *Forbes*, 08/08/2017.

Chapter 2

of hawala is not known, but it was used as a means of payment for trade on the major trading routes of the Middle Ages, including the Silk Road, in the Middle East and the Indian subcontinent. To solve her payment problem, Roya Mahboob convinces the contributors to be paid in bitcoins, comparing it to hawala.

Since then, she has launched the Digital Citizen Fund, an NGO that has recruited 9,000 Afghan women in educational programs covering topics such as blockchain technology, bitcoin, ether, etc., and helped a hundred of them start their businesses.

This is further proof that cryptocurrencies are not only a safe haven and a means of payment in times of crisis, but also a gateway to the future.

Why Issue a Central Bank Digital Currency (CBDC)?

This is the exciting question posed by the IMF on page 43 of its study *Fintech and Financial Services: Initial Considerations*, published on June 19, 2017. Answers are organized around two types of arguments:

1) For efficiency reasons
- The blockchain would allow the central bank to ensure a more efficient payment system infrastructure. However, it must be ensured that the introduction of a CBDC will bring greater efficiency gains than the regulation of the payments industry. There are several examples, in Africa among others, that show that spectacular progress can be made without a national cryptocurrency, which is also demonstrated by Denmark, which is approaching a society without cash.

- Gradually replacing coins and bills with electronic money would generate savings for the state. "It may also significantly reduce transactions costs for individuals and small enterprises that have little or costly access to banking services in some countries or regions; and it may facilitate financial inclusion."
- A CBDC would counter certain external monopolies, including one or more private cryptocurrencies or payment system operators.

2) For monetary policy reasons
- The introduction and potential proliferation of private digital currencies could erode the demand for central bank money and the transmission of monetary policy mechanisms. A CBDC could prevent this phenomenon by relegating them to the background, even if the threat is not imminent.
- The challenge for central banks will be to carefully weigh the advantages and disadvantages of being, in addition to other functions, the operator of applications based on new technologies, for which the private sector is always ahead.

For readers wishing to explore the issue further, we recommend reading the entire study.[75]

---

75. *Fintech and Financial Services: Initial Considerations*, Dong He; Ross B Leckow; Vikram Haksar; Tommaso Mancini Griffoli; Nigel Jenkinson; Mikari Kashima; Tanai Khiaonarong; Celine Rochon; Hervé Tourpe, FMI, 06/19/2017.

II. Achievements and national projects

It is estimated that about more than ninety central banks around the world have begun to study cryptocurrencies and blockchain. We will look at some of them on each continent, because they are not all at the same level of progress and do not share the same visions and strategies.

The statements made on this subject in September 2017 by Christine Lagarde, Managing Director of the IMF, are interesting:

"For now, virtual currencies such as bitcoin pose little or no challenge to the existing order of *fiat* currencies and central banks. Why? Because they are too volatile, too risky, too energy intensive, and because the underlying technologies are not yet scalable. Many are too opaque for regulators; and some have been hacked.

But many of these are *technological* challenges that could be addressed over time. (...) So I think it may not be wise to dismiss virtual currencies. (...)

And yet, why might citizens hold virtual currencies rather than physical dollars, euros, or the sterling? Because it may one day be *easier* and *safer* than obtaining paper bills, especially in remote regions. And because virtual currencies could actually become *more stable*. (...) Issuance could be fully transparent, governed by a credible, pre-defined rule, an algorithm that can be monitored... or even a "smart rule" that might reflect changing macroeconomic circumstances.

So in many ways, virtual currencies might just give existing currencies and monetary policy a run for their money. The best response by central bankers is to continue running *effective* monetary policy, while being open to fresh ideas and new demands, as economies evolve."[76]

We will also present some situations where the central banks seem to have not yet made up their mind about cryptocurrencies but are nevertheless studying the benefits and uses of blockchain.

---

76. *Central Banking and Fintech—A Brave New World?*, Christine Lagarde, FMI, 11/29/2017.

1) Iceland

Everyone remembers the financial crisis that this country went through between 2008 and 2011, with the bankruptcy of its three main commercial banks, then the IMF loan blackmail in order that the population, although victim and not responsible for this situation, agrees to take on long-term debt in order to pay off the debt of commercial bank. Strict capital and exchange controls were put in place during this troubled period in order to limit the outflow of funds and currencies as much as possible.

It is in this context of crisis and capital control that the central bank confirms to the newspaper *Morgunbladid* in December 2013 that the law on exchanges does not authorize operations with bitcoin.[77]

Two months later, in February 2014, one or more Icelanders using the pseudonym Baldur Friggjar Odinsson launches a cryptocurrency called auroracoin, an alternative to bitcoin and the króna, the currency of the country. It is accompanied by a political manifesto: "The people of Iceland are being sacrificed at the altar of a flawed financial system, controlled by an elite that made astronomical bets supported by the government on behalf of the people and ultimately at the expense of the people. (....) Cryptocurrencies are a very important milestone in this fight for liberty. They bring the hope of a new era of free currencies, immune to the meddling of politicians and their cronies."

The terms of the launch specify that half of the 21 million auroracoins created will be distributed as of March 25 to nearly 330,000 citizens registered in the National Identity Register, namely 31.8 units per person. To do this, an airdrop is planned, which takes place in three phases over one year. During the first phase, just over 35,000 people ask for their auroracoins, followed by just over 5,000 and 2,600 during phases 2 and 3, for a total of about 13% of the population. Less than 50% of the planned distribution is reached, the balance being frozen:

---

77. *Höftin stöðva viðskipti með bitcoin*, Morgunbladid, 12/19/2013.

Chapter 2

	Auroracoins
Total issuance	21,000,000
Available for airdrop	10,500,000
Distributed	5,155,372
Made inaccessible	5,344,628
Donation to the Auraráð Foundation	1,000,001

The Auraráð Foundation is created on March 29, 2015 to promote the development and adoption of auroracoin. It receives for this purpose 1,000,001 units from the founders.

Here is the evolution of auroracoin prices since its inception:

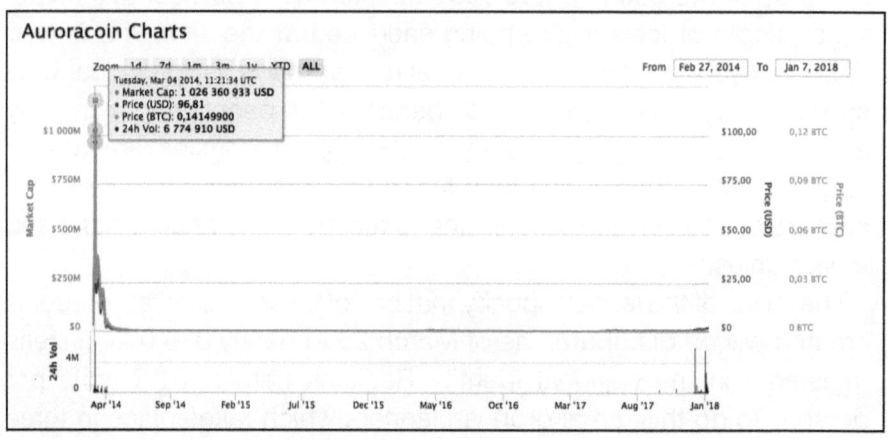

Source: Coin Market Cap

It appears on the graph that on March 4, 2014, some twenty days before the distribution, the auroracoin is already quoted at $96.81, which gives it a capitalization of $1.026 billion, making this new cryptocurrency the third largest, behind the bitcoin and the ripple, but in front of the litecoin.

As noted earlier, this data demonstrates that the criterion of the capitalization can be misleading by multiplying the price by the number of units issued, but in fact there were not 10.5 million auroracoins available—and still none at that time—and just over five million at the end of the airdrop.

The price quickly drops to around 0 and will not move for more than three and a half years. It should be noted, however, activity around auroracoin has resumed in recent weeks:

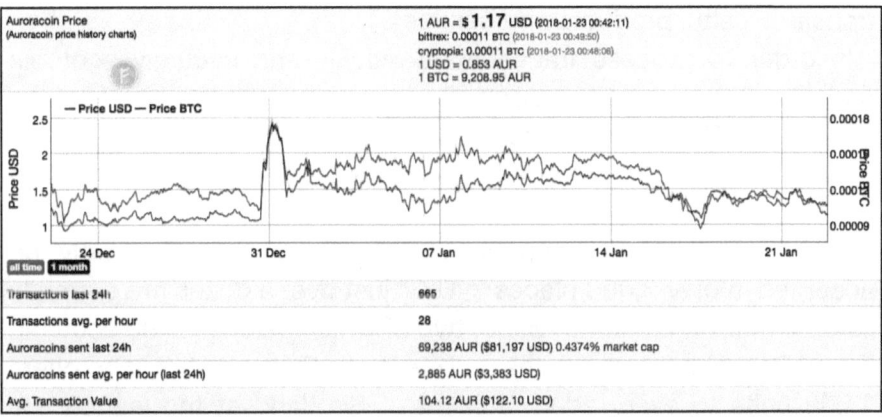

Source: Bitinfo Charts

Is this the announcement of a new dawn for the auroracoin? Pending verification in the medium term, it should be noted that the Icelandic Central Bank has not announced any plan to create a national cryptocurrency.

Chapter 2

2) Scotland

It is not (yet) a country and therefore does not issue its own currency — it uses the pound sterling, although Scottish banks may print their own banknotes. However, "its" cryptocurrency already exists: scotcoin. Here is what promoters say about it on the project's website:

"Scotcoin was established in 2013 and is one of the first and most successful country-related alternative digital currencies.

Scotcoin is proud of its Scottish roots but it is not limited to Scotland. It can be used by individuals and businesses worldwide to transfer wealth, products and services.

In order to process transactions quickly and securely scotcoin uses the Counterparty platform. Counterparty uses the power of the established Bitcoin Blockchain. (...)

Every scotcoin transaction piggybacks onto a bitcoin transaction where its details are recorded."[78]

Even if the website announces that "scotcoin will shortly be accepted in over 2,000 places in UK," just over a dozen are currently listed on the "Merchants" page, two of which belong to the scotcoin buyer, David Low. Indeed, the real creator is Derek Nisbet, who offers 1,000 units to every adult resident of Scotland at the launch. He explains his motivations as follows: "There is so much uncertainty with the current financial situation, that introducing a voluntary cryptocurrency, which may in the future act as a medium of exchange for the Scottish people, can only benefit them should there be major disruption."[79]

What looks like a communication coup is organized in August 2017: a friend of David Low buys his apartment, valued at £60,000, and pays him with ten million scotcoins, or a parity of £1 = S167.

Details of the transaction can be read on the online version of the *Daily Mail*, which presents the scotcoin: "(...) Like other digital currencies, such as the infamous bitcoin, payments are made directly between individuals or businesses, removing the need for banks. The

---

78. www.scotcoinproject.com.
79. *Bitcoin goes national with Scotcoin and Auroracoin*, Alex Hern, *The Guardian*, 03/25/2014.

Sovereign Cryptocurrencies

latest price of scotcoins, which can be bought online, is listed as £7 for 1,000. This is compared to £3,021 for a single bitcoin. There are one billion scotcoins in existence, meaning if demand for them rises, the value of each coin will also rise."[80]

The scotcoin deserves to appear in these pages, because even if it has not been created by a national institution, its site presents eight objectives for 2017, of which the last promises: "We will be offering Scotcoin IP and ecosystem to the Scottish government as part of a process to allow them to take control of monetary policy in Scotland."

A laudable ambition, but one that presupposes a prerequisite: Scotland's independence. If this event were to happen, at least sovereign cryptocurrency is ready, even if it is not (yet) worth much today.

Source: WorldCoin Index

---

80. *Two-bed flat worth £60,000 becomes the first in the country to be bought using digital currency as it sells for 10 million Scotcoins*, Keiran Southern, *MailOnLine*, 08/22/2017.

Chapter 2

There are other cryptocurrencies similar to auroracoin and scotcoin, that is to say carrying a national identity and born of private or even individual initiatives, such as GaelCoin (Ireland—it has almost disappeared since) or PesetaCoin, created in 2014, which, as its name indicates, originated from Spain. In the immediate future, such a project cannot be far-reaching, because the country's currency remains the euro, and the European Central Bank prohibits national cryptocurrencies, as we expose it below. The interested reader can nevertheless visit the official site: www.pesetacoin.info.

Source: WorldCoin Index

Sovereign Cryptocurrencies

3) Ecuador

Even if their founders give them a national identity, the first cryptocurrencies presented in this chapter have not been issued by countries. Let us now look at situations that are truly linked to states. The first case is Ecuador, which has the particularity of having abandoned its currency, the sucre, in 2000 in favor of the US dollar, as a result of monetary instability and repeated depreciation.

Fifteen years later, a CNBC headline: *Ecuador becomes the first country to roll out its own digital cash*.[81] It is the Dinero Electrónico, which, as presented in a study by the Bank for International Settlements, "is a mobile payment service in Ecuador where the central bank provides the underlying accounts to the public. Citizens can open an account by downloading an app, registering their national identity number and answering security questions. People deposit or withdraw money by going to designated transaction centers. As such, it is a (rare) example of a deposited currency account scheme. As Ecuador uses the US dollar as its official currency, accounts are denominated in that currency."[82]

On 30 August 2017, a new step is announced: "1. Ecuador's Central Bank will no longer maintain electronic money accounts as soon as banks and cooperatives put their systems into production. These platforms will respect international standards guaranteeing safety and quality."[83]

Though it is a real electronic money system, it does not correspond to the principle of a cryptocurrency, based on blockchain technology. Ecuador is even one of the first countries to ban the use of bitcoin, voted by the National Assembly on 24 July 2014 (Session No. 286). The central bank further recalls in an official communiqué on 8 January 2018 that "bitcoin is not an authorized means of payment in

---

81. *Ecuador becomes the first country to roll out its own digital cash*, Everett Rosenfeld, CNBC, 02/06/2015.
82. *Central bank cryptocurrencies*, Morten Linnemann Bech et Rodney Garratt, Banque des règlements internationaux, 09/17/2017.
83. *Dinero electrónico será manejado por la banca pública, privada y el sistema financiero popular y solidario*, Banco Central del Ecuador, communiqué du 08/30/2017.

the country (...) in accordance with Article 94 of the Organic Monetary and Financial Code," even if the purchase and sale of cryptocurrencies over the Internet are not prohibited.

4) Uruguay

Despite a year of analysis and already at the end of the year 2017, the central bank (BCU) still remains undecided about whether bitcoin can be considered as electronic money and therefore potentially subject to the supervision of monetary authorities. However, on 3 November, its president, Mario Bergara, announces the launch of a six-month "digital tickets" pilot project with ten thousand customers of the national mobile telephone company Antel.

They must download an application from www.epeso.com.uy that works on all types of phones, register and fund their account through the national payment system Red Pagos. Then they will be able to pay into the network of member merchants and send money between them, but it is not a cryptocurrency, based on the blockchain. In principle, this is similar to what Ecuador has put in place.

5) Canada

On 22 May 2017, the Enterprise Ethereum Alliance (EEA), which brings together many companies interested in the Blockchain Ethereum technology, announces by press release that it has been joined by eighty-six new members, including Toyota, Samsung SDS, Deloitte, Merck, Rabobank, and the National Bank of Canada. In fact, it was as early as 2016 that the latter began experimenting with blockchain technology, with the objective to analyze its benefits and risks. This experiment, called the "Jasper Project," is being developed in collaboration with commercial banks.

Although a digital currency is created for testing purposes, the CAD-coin, the Bank of Canada's June 2017 Jasper presentation paper, shows that the immediate focus is on testing the potential integration of blockchain technology into the overall payment system. This does not exclude the eventual use of a national cryptocurrency, especially since banks are already exchanging CAD-coins convertible into Canadian dollars as part of the experiment. However, it is still too early to know the Bank of Canada's direction on the issue of creating a sovereign cryptocurrency for the public, although it seems a likely option in the future.

6) The Netherlands

De Nederlandsche Bank (DNB), the central bank, informs in a report dated March 16, 2016 that it has conducted tests to develop a cryptocurrency based on the blockchain, "an innovation that could have far-reaching consequences, including for payments and securities transactions. While we acknowledge the new opportunities of digital currencies, we also see risks."[84]

The DNB cannot launch a national cryptocurrency because it is part of the euro zone. On the other hand, its experience is instructive, and here is a summary of its observations:

"Potential benefits of virtual currencies (...):

- Transactions can be effected directly between the originator and the recipient, without intermediaries and at low cost.

- The technology is fast and always available, allowing transactions to be processed almost in real-time and continuously. This means that a cross-border can be made within seconds.

- The data are reliable, because all transactions are verified [in a decentralized manner]. Furthermore, the system is resilient to cyberattacks, as information is stored in various locations across the network.

Potential drawbacks of virtual currencies (...):

- Governance issues: the network's decentralized nature obscures its members' responsibilities, meaning that none of them can be held accountable in the event of mishaps.

- The technology has not yet fully matured. Further standardization is needed to ensure interoperability of new systems.

- If the traditional financial institutions or transaction processors

---

84. www.dnb.nl => Virtual Currencies.

were to introduce the new technologies, operational risks would emerge in terms of robustness, security and interoperability."

In conclusion, here is what the DNB states:

"We acknowledge the possibilities offered by the new technology. Introducing it will also require adjustments on the part of central banks and supervisory authorities. One option would be for central banks to issue digital currencies themselves. Several foreign central banks are currently looking into this. We have built a test network based on blockchain technology for study purposes and to gain practical experience. We are also involved in a test in which a Dutch bank keeps its data in a blockchain network, which permits its supervisors to have current information at all times."

This experience has been shared with several other central banks, some of which have made progress in creating sovereign cryptocurrencies, as we will see with the following countries.

7) The United Kingdom

On its website, the Bank of England informs:

"We do not currently plan to issue a central bank-issued digital currency. However, we are undertaking research to better understand the implications of a central bank, like the Bank of England, issuing a digital currency. We first raised the possibility of a central bank-issued digital currency in our research agenda in February 2015."[85]

This project was developed in partnership with researchers from the University College London and the currency is called RSCoin.

On December 20, 2017, Governor Mark Carney tells parliamentarians that blockchain technology could improve the way transactions are conducted between financial institutions, "but there could be financial stability risks if such an approach were rolled out across the whole economy through a cryptocurrency intended for the general public."[86]

---

85. www.bankofengland.co.uk => Digital Currencies.
86. *BoE's Carney sees problems with central-bank issued cryptocurrencies*, Andy Bruce, Reuters, 12/20/2017.

He explained that as there would no longer be intermediaries with such a system, this could "create a situation where you can have an instantaneous (bank) run," where banks which may not have enough money to pay those who want to empty their accounts and open new ones, especially at the central bank. This could create serious turbulence in the economy, especially as banks would no longer have sufficient deposits to allocate loans, while the Bank of England would end up with huge cash reserves that it would not be able to distribute. This last point seems debatable to us, because the central bank could set up a distribution system, but this is another debate — we will return to it in conclusion.

In his intervention, he reiterated that bitcoin, despite its erratic movements, poses no threat to overall financial stability.

On 4 January 2018, the *Financial Times Adviser* publishes the information that the central bank has told them to give up launching a national cryptocurrency for the reasons given by Mark Carney above, but that it will continue research in this area. "It also expressed concern about its ability to maintain financial stability through interest rate policy in a world of digital currencies."[87]

There will therefore be no national cryptocurrency in the United Kingdom, at least in the coming months. In any case, the reasons given by the Bank of England, complementary to De Nederlandsche Bank's observations, can only inspire other central banks, particularly in the so-called "rich" countries, where the introduction of a national cryptocurrency could cause the collapse of the banking system.

It should be noted, however, that one or more private cryptocurrencies could gradually become sufficiently important to replace the pound sterling in certain areas of the economy. The Bank of England would still have a (major) asset to help it avoid a bank collapse: ban payments in any currency other than the currency it issues — with the negative consequences this could also have, which we will examine later.

---

[87]. *Bank halts crypto-currency plans over stability fears*, David Thorpe, *FT Adviser*, 01/04/2018.

8) Poland

In February 2018, the press reveals that the central bank—Narodowy Bank Polski—has spent about $27,000 in anti-cryptocurrency advertising campaigns on social networks, with Google, Facebook and a popular Polish YouTuber with more than 900,000 subscribers. One of the videos is entitled "I lost all my money!?" The problem is that the public is deceived because it is not specified that this is advertising, making them falsely believe that these are real messages. The practice is illegal, but it does not bother the central bank. In any case, it is an original method to fight against cryptocurrencies.

Meanwhile, Poland advances in the development of a sovereign cryptocurrency, as announced in January by the Polish daily *Puls Biznesu*. This currency, called the Digital PLN (dPLN), brings together the expertise of several partners, including the Polish Blockchain Technology Accelerator (PATB), the Ministry of Digitalization and Lazarski University in Warsaw. Prof. Krzysztof Piech, who is also the president of the Polish Blockchain Technology Accelerator, says to *Puls Biznesu*: "We have created a cryptographic currency, which we have deprived of speculative features. We want to give our economy unprofitable money that does not require expensive infrastructure, and by the way, its transfer is ultrafast."[88]

We believe that removing or at least limiting the possibilities of speculation on a cryptocurrency is a prerequisite for its long-term success. It seems to us, however, difficult to completely do away with them from the moment there exists the possibility of exchange with other currencies.

Although the project has not yet received government approval for its deployment, it is innovative and interesting, and can serve as a model for financial institutions in other countries. Professor Krzysztof Piech also explains how they explored the option of creating a blockchain-based decentralized bank, but abandoned the idea, because of the legal complexity, not for technical reasons.

---

88. *Poland is Developing National Cryptocurrency*, Arnab Shome, *FinanceMagnates*, 01/17/2018.

9) Russia

On 27 January 2014, the Central Bank of Russia issues a press release announcing that providing a virtual currency exchange service by commercial companies will be considered a violation of laws against money laundering and terrorist financing.

Two years later, on 28 February 2016, the Central Bank announces that it has "created a working group on the analysis of advanced technologies and innovations in the financial field. Among the priority issues are the study of distribution technologies (e.g. blockchain), as well as new developments in the fields of mobile telephony, payments and others."[89]

At the St. Petersburg International Economic Forum, on June 2, 2017, Olga Skorobogatova, Deputy Governor of the Central Bank of Russia, announces that "we are going to arrive at a national virtual currency, we have already started working on it."[90] Information circulates that it could be called "CryptoRouble."

In August, Deputy Prime Minister Igor Shuvalov confirms that Russia has plans to introduce its own virtual currency based on blockchain technology. It states that the FSB [the Russian Federal Security Service] "is actively working at the international level and wants to ensure that security issues are solved from the very beginning," since "blockchain technology has a far greater use than just cryptocurrencies," because "it also provides a mechanism for a professional, transparent and fast public service."[91]

The Cointelegraph publishes an article on 15 October based on Russian sources informing them that President Putin has confirmed that Russia will indeed create the "CryptoRuble," as then announced Nikolay Nikiforov, Minister of Communications. Issued, controlled and maintained by the authorities, it will not be mined and will be on a parity equal to that of the rouble.[92]

---

89. Банк России займется анализом и оценкой возможностей применения новых финансовых технологий, Central Bank of Russia, 02/28/2016.
90. ЦБ начал работу над созданием национальной криптовалюты, *Ria Novosti*, 06/02/2017.
91. *Kremlin considers crypto-ruble & use of blockchain in public service*, Russia Today, 08/24/2017.
92. *BREAKING: Russia Issuing 'CryptoRuble'*, John Buck, *The CoinTelegraph*, 10/15/2017.

Chapter 2

In December, Finance Minister Alexei Mosesev states that he is working with the Central Bank of Russia and the Parliament's Financial Markets Committee on a bill to regulate all activities related to bitcoin and other cryptocurrencies, including trading, mining, use as a means of payment, ICOs, etc. The bill is to be adopted by the Russian Parliament in December.

Mid-January, Arseni Scheltsin, Director of Russia's Cryptocurrency and Blockchain Association, announces that proposals for the creation and regulation of CryptoRouble will be presented in July 2018, for a launch that will not take place before 2019.[93]

At the end of January 2018, a bill is submitted to Parliament so that CryptoRouble is accepted as a (future) official means of payment, which implies amending the Civil Code. Another bill on the regulation of mining and the circulation of digital financial assets is also filed.

The world is now waiting for the next announcements, whether on this new legislation or the CryptoRouble, especially since the various officials who have spoken in the last six months do not intend for their cryptocurrency to only be used inside Russia. It is perhaps for this reason that the launch, although announced in October 2017 as planned "for the weeks to come," is postponed. In chapter 3 we'll come back to the international development of CryptoRouble.

10) Abkhazia

Located on the shores of the Black Sea, this small territory of 8,653 km^2 and less than 250,000 inhabitants declares its independence from Georgia in 1992. Georgia as well as the United Nations, refuses it, considering that it is still part of the country. As an independent state, it is only recognized by Russia, Venezuela, Nicaragua and Nauru.

Despite the ambiguous political situation, in early October 2017 Abkhazia announces "a plan to raise a billion dollars worth of cryptocurrency via an ICO. The breakaway state has long vied for international legitimacy and has struggled to attract investment to

---

93. *Russia Postpones "Crypto Ruble" Launch to Mid-2019*, Forklog, 01/16/2018.

fund its internal development projects—a situation it hopes to turn around by creating a state-sponsored cryptocurrency.

At a conference in Moscow [the week before], Abkhazian government officials Adgur Ardzinba and Evgeny Galiakhmetov state[s] that the fledgling country [will] soon begin selling Abkhazian Republic Coins (ARC). They [say] the cryptocurrency (limited to 8 billion coins) [will] be open to foreign investment and that ultimately it [will] become the country's sole legal currency. Abkhazians […] have a great incentive to adopt the ARC coins they [say], as for the first three years the government [will] waive a range of taxes for market participants who use the coins."[94]

This cryptocurrency will also allow possible international sanctions to be circumvented. No details have yet been provided on the implementation of this project, or even on its feasibility, given the political uncertainties. Indeed, the creation of a cryptocurrency could be considered as one more step towards independence and another towards war with Georgia.

11) Kyrgyzstan

This former republic of the USSR in the heart of Central Asia, of about 200,000 km^2 and six million inhabitants, probably began its official history with the cryptocurrencies on 18 July 2014, with a warning from its central bank:

"National Bank of the Kyrgyz Republic notes that recently the world has seen the emergence and spread of such new phenomenon of "virtual currency," in particular, bitcoins. They are also called "cryptocurrency," "digital currency," "decentralized virtual currency" (…). In Kyrgyzstan it could also be observed attempts to spread and use the "virtual currency," to popularize them among the population of our country.

At the same time we should not forget that under the legislation of the Kyrgyz Republic the sole legal tender on the territory of our

---

[94]. *Abkhazia announces ICO to fund first state-run cryptocurrency*, Luke Parker, Brave NewCoin, 10/19/2017.

Chapter 2

country is the national currency of Kyrgyzstan "som." And the use of "virtual currency," bitcoins, in particular, as a means of payment in the Kyrgyz Republic will be a violation of the law of our state."[95]

The beginning of this release is unambiguous, but here is how it ends: "Thus, persons or entities in any way using "virtual currency" subject to the abovementioned risks. And also, when involved in these activities, they assume all the possible negative consequences of the possible violation of the legislation of the Kyrgyz Republic." Why add "possible" to violation?

According to CoinDesk, data show that the official Bitcoin-Qt wallet has only been downloaded around 1,000 times at that time in Kyrgyzstan, which remains limited.[96]

Despite a warning from the central bank the previous year, the first bitcoin ATM is installed in a pizzeria in the capital, Bishkek, in September 2015—it would even be the first machine in Central Asia. "Many people attended the launch of the ATM. Especially bankers. There were also representatives from the National bank. Everyone was interested [to discover] what bitcoin is. Very few people had heard about bitcoin at that time," explained one of the two promoters of the project.[97]

Although bitcoin was still not legal, this installation could be done because even if "the law does apply to official institutions, for individuals it acts only as a recommendation," according to the article of Coinfox. Three to four customers come to the pizzeria each month to purchase bitcoin, which represents the equivalent of $1,500 on average. We do not know what has happened to this machine, but it does not appear on the map or in the ATM Radar listing (neighboring Kazakhstan has three in early 2018).

On June 14, 2017, the Prime Minister announces that Kyrgyzstan is planning to create a sovereign cryptocurrency backed by gold. With

---

95. *Warning of the National Bank of the Kyrgyz Republic on the spread and use of the "virtual currency", in particular, bitcoins (bitcoin)*, 07/18/2014.
96. *Kyrgyzstan: Bitcoin Payments Violate State Law*, Pete Rizzo, CoinDesk, 08/04/2014.
97. *Bitcoin enthusiasts advocate cryptocurrency in Kyrgyzstan*, Aliona Chapel, Coinfox, 10/01/2015.

Russia, it is the first project of its kind within the Eurasian Economic Union (EAEU: Armenia, Belarus, Russia, Kazakhstan and Kyrgyzstan), followed by that of Kazakhstan, which announces in October to work on the creation of its national cryptocurrency (see below).

One of the reasons for Kyrgyzstan is the fact that 32% of the national product of the country consists of money transfers from the Kyrgyz working abroad (it slightly exceeded $20 billion in 2016)[98]. Having a system as powerful and efficient as the blockchain would make it possible to receive tens of millions of dollars more, currently paid in transfer fees and therefore retained in part in the issuing countries (see box on page 106).

As for its cryptocurrency being backed by gold, this may seem surprising, but not if we look at how international agencies have rated Kyrgyzstan bonds: for 2017, Moody's rates them B2—definition: "Obligations rated B are considered speculative and are subject to high credit risk." This would mean that Kyrgyzstan aims to take its national cryptocurrency beyond its borders, because it would not need to be backed by gold if it were only used inside the country.

12) Kazakhstan

On June 13, 2017, the central bank issues a statement that it has completed the development of a blockchain-based mobile application.[99] Here is the summary:

"The proposed project will allow citizens to buy and sell the notes of the National Bank online from a mobile phone, bypassing intermediaries, namely brokers and dealers. No taxes and no commissions. Absolute liquidly and no restrictions on the periods of ownership."[100]

On June 16, Nursultan Nazarbayev, President of Kazakhstan, declares during a session at the 10th Astana Economic Forum:

---

98. *Bitcoin enthusiasts advocate cryptocurrency in Kyrgyzstan*, Aliona Chapel, Coinfox, 01/10/2015.
99. *Ұлттық Банкінің қысқа мерзімді ноттарын "блокчейн" технологиясын пайдалана отырып орналастыру жобасы туралы*, Central Bank of Kazakhstan, 06/13/2017.
100. *Kazakhstan Central Bank Develops Blockchain Mobile App for Securities*, Samburaj Das, CCN, 06/14/2017.

Chapter 2

"It's time to consider the introduction of the global payment unit. This will save the world from currency wars, speculation, avoid distortions in trade relations and reduce volatility in the markets. The currency should have a simple transparent mechanism of emission, subject to its consumers. A payment unit of account can be created in the form of a cryptocurrency taking into account digitalization and block-chain development (...). The introduction of a global currency is possible by creating a pool of central banks, for example, the Special Committee at the United Nations (UN)."[101]

While awaiting this global currency, CNBC announces on October 17 that the government is preparing to launch its own cryptocurrency, following statements by the director of the Astana International Finance Center, who signs an agreement to this effect with the company Exante, a provider in Malta.[102]

More information should soon be published on the progress of this sovereign cryptocurrency.

Costly Remittances

"A remittance is a transfer of money by a foreign worker to an individual in his or her home country. Money sent home by migrants competes with international aid as one of the largest financial inflows to developing countries. Workers' remittances are a significant part of international capital flows, especially with regard to labor-exporting countries."[103]

The World Bank estimated that they would amount to $585 billion by 2017, of which $442 billion will go to developing countries. They mainly transit through specialized services such as Western Union (WU), MoneyGram, Ria, etc.

---

101. *Kazakh President proposes international currency, climate solutions at AEF*, Zhanna Shayakhmetova, *The Astana Times*, 06/19/2017.
102. *Kazakhstan plans to launch its own cryptocurrency*, Ryan Browne, CNBC, 10/17/2017.
103. Wikipedia, https://en.wikipedia.org/wiki/Remittance.

The transfer fee amount is a crucial problem, which the World Bank, among others, has tackled with the creation of a specialized database entitled "Remittance Prices Worldwide" (RPW). The index has calculated an average cost of 7.09% of the amount sent (a figure that corresponds to the third quarter of 2017), with wide disparities between recipient countries, and at only 2.09% of the 5% target set by the G20. Moreover, as indicated on the RPW homepage, "cutting prices by at least 5 percentage points can save up to $16 billion a year."[104]

For example, in 2016, WU has sales of $5.4 billion and an operating profit of $1 billion, with 550,000 sites in over 200 countries and territories and 150 million customers.[105] If we take the average fee rate of 7.09%, this means approximately $75 billion circulated via the WU coffers. Let's have a look at the impact on the first nine recipient countries:

(in billions of $)	2016	2017 (estimations)	Fees 7%
India	62.7	65.4	4.578
China	61.0	62.9	4.403
Philippines	29.9	32.8	2.296
Mexico	28.5	30.5	2.135
Pakistan	19.8	22.3	1.561
Nigeria	19.0	19.8	1.386
Egypt	16.6	18.2	1.274
Bangladesh	13.7	13.8	0.966
Vietnam	13.4	12.9	0.903
Total	**264.6**	**278.6**	**19.502**

Source: Wikipedia (Remittance)

---

104. Https://remittanceprices.worldbank.org/en.
105. *CEO Letter*, Hikmet Ersek, President, Chief Executive Officer and Director, Western Union.

Chapter 2

As a result, transfer fees have deprived the top nine countries of nearly $20 billion—at least in all appearances, because some of the commissions collected are paid to local agents or offices. These amounts are significant, but they are even more crucial when they represent a major share of GNP, as for the following countries:

	% of remittances / GDP
East Timor	216.6%
Tajikistan	42.1%
Kyrgyzstan	31.5%
Nepal	28.8%
Moldova	24.9%
Lesotho	24.4%
Samoa	23.8%
Haiti	21.1%
Armenia	21.0%
The Gambia	19.8%
Liberia	18.5%
Lebanon	17.0%
Honduras	16.9%
El Salvador	16.4%
Kosovo	16.1%
Jamaica	15.0%
Bosnia and Herzegovina	13.4%

Source: Wikipedia (Remittance)

These countries, like the first nine, have a clear interest in developing or using cryptocurrencies to eliminate most of the transfer fees, not to mention other benefits such as the fact that recipients would receive the payments immediately and directly, regardless of the day and time of the transfer. This would help speed up the circulation of money, an important factor in wealth creation, even if it is not always taken into account at its fair value. Subsequently, blockchain-based networks are emerging, such as The Blockchain Network, describing itself on its website's homepage as "the blockchain enabling the cheapest money transfers for everyone," on average 86% less than average costs. The operating principle:

"The Blockchain Network partners simply exchange fiat money and cryptocurrencies between countries in a matter of minutes and at a small fee."

The G20 target of 5% of costs on the amounts transferred should soon be largely exceeded.

13) Singapore

The Monetary Authority of Singapore (MAS) replied on 2 October 2017, in a parliamentary question on the importance of cryptocurrencies, that only about 20 retailers accept payments in bitcoin; that is not much compared to other countries. Even speculative trading is relatively low, if only compared to Hong Kong.[106]

At the same time, MAS concludes phase 2 of its Project Ubin, of which there are five. What is it about? The creation of a digital central bank currency using the blockchain principle. Announced in 2016 and inspired by "the architecture, code and lessons learned from Project Jasper" developed by the central bank of Canada, Ubin tests are expected to be completed by the end of 2018. The MAS will then announce its launch or not, or partial launch. This cryptocurrency could, in fact, only be used in cross-border payments between banking institutions. Moreover, several major international banks are associated with Project Ubin, including Bank of America Merrill Lynch, Citigroup, Credit Suisse, HSBC, JP Morgan, Mitsubishi UFJ Financial Group.

At the same time, as MAS explains on its website, two complementary programs are being tested: "The first project, driven by the Singapore Exchange (SGX), focuses on making the fixed income securities trading and settlement cycle more efficient through DLT [Distributed Ledger Technology, or blockchain]. The second project focuses on new methods to conduct cross border payments using central bank digital currency."

14) China

Until 2017, it was one of the most important countries in terms of cryptocurrencies, and it continues to be, but for other reasons, in particular for the successive bans it imposes: banning exchanges in September 2017, banning ICOs, limiting mining while the world's largest companies are Chinese (they are, however, migrating to other

---

106. *Reply to Parliamentary Question on the prevalence use of cryptocurrency in Singapore and measures to regulate cryptocurrency and Initial Coin Offerings*, Monetary Authority of Singapore, 10/02/2017.

shores), impending blocking of access to offshore exchanges, etc. However, transactions between private individuals, at least for small amounts, have not (yet) been prohibited.

Financial institutions have also been targeted, since the central bank (People's Bank of China—PBoC) sent them an internal document January 2018, in which they stated:

"Every bank and branch must carry out self-inspection and rectification, starting from today," according to a document issued by the central bank on Wednesday. (...) Service for cryptocurrency trading is strictly prohibited. Effective measures should be adopted to prevent payment channels from being used for cryptocurrency settlement. (...) Banks should enhance their daily transaction monitoring, and the timely shut down of the payment channel once they discover any suspected trading of cryptocurrencies."[107]

While the prohibitions and limitations have not yet been deployed, as early as 2014 the PBoC assembles a team to develop its own cryptocurrency. It is one of the first central banks to announce this. In January 2016, it declares that the project is on track. Since then, little information has filtered through.

It is obvious that a national cryptocurrency would offer the central bank a perspective on the evolution of the economy in near real time, impossible today with the traditional banking system. This would enable it to steer monetary policy, which is particularly sensitive in China, and about which foreign media regularly forecast the next bursting of bubbles—in credit, real estate, etc.—and to take the necessary measures.

It would also make the payment system faster and cheaper, especially since the population is already widely familiar with mobile payment, via solutions like Alipay (Alibaba Group) or WeChat Pay (Tencent), which share 54% and 40% respectively of mobile payments, which were estimated at $5 trillion in 2016.[108]

---

107. *China orders banks to stop financing cryptocurrencies as noose tightens around disrupter*, Xie Yu, *South China Morning Post*, 01/19/2018.
108. *Cash is already pretty much dead in China as the country lives the future with mobile pay*, Evelyn Cheng, CNBC, 10/08/2017.

Chapter 2

Moreover, a cryptocurrency open to the world at large would be a decisive asset in the New Silk Road program (China's geostrategic project), given the number of countries affected (68 and 4.4 billion inhabitants, according to CNN) and the unprecedented trade volumes in world trade. When payments will finally be made in cryptocurrencies, the door will open to a world whose transformations and evolutions are still impossible to predict.

The New Silk Road[109]

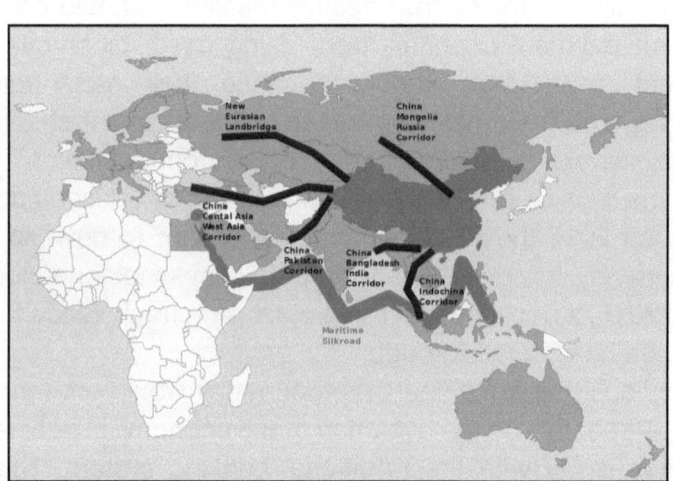

The six land corridors and the maritime route
(in gray, the member countries of the Asian Infrastructure Investment Bank — AIIB).
The corridors now extend to Western Europe,
and soon to West Africa, including Morocco.

---

109. Lommes, Wikimedia Commons.

15) Hong Kong

After China, it makes sense to look at one of the world's most dynamic financial centers, which has its own currency, the Hong Kong dollar. In March 2017, information is published by several media that "the Hong Kong Monetary Authority (HKMA) has teamed up with local banks and the R3 consortium to explore the creation of a central bank digital currency" based on the principle of the blockchain.[110]

"Local banks" are the three commercial banks that have the status of issuer of banknotes—the Bank of China, HSBC and Standard Chartered. The project is also developed with the Hong Kong Interbank Clearing Limited.[111]

The objective of this first phase is to study the feasibility of domestic interbank payments, intercompany payments and the delivery of debt securities in exchange for settlements. It is expected that the tests will be completed by the end of 2017 and that the HKMA will then position itself on the direction to take.

Pending the publication of the results, other projects related to the blockchain are being researched, including its use for securities trading. The studies are also being conducted with commercial banks, a collaboration scheme that is not the most widespread in terms of cryptocurrencies—it is however explained by Hong Kong's almost unique status and conditions.

16) India

As early as 2013, an Indian vintage themed pizzeria, in Bombay called the "Kolonial," accepts payments in bitcoin for the first time. Since then, the list continues to grow, even though, since 24 December 2013 and on several occasions, the Reserve Bank of India (RBI) has warned "users, holders and traders of Virtual currencies (VCs), including bitcoins, about the potential financial, operational, legal, customer protection and security related risks that they are exposing

---

110. *Hong Kong enters central bank digital currency fray*, Finextra, 04/11/2017.
111. *Legislative Council Panel On Financial Affairs*, Financial Services and the Treasury Bureau, 04/06/2017.

Chapter 2

themselves to."[112] Two days later, authorities carry out their first raid against the Buysellbitco.in exchange (which later became Zebpay), which leads other exchanges to suspend their activities. The first e-commerce site to accept payment only in bitcoin, HighKart.com, is launched in December 2013.

The latest RBI notice, dated December 5, 2017, includes the ICO risk and recalls the content of the previous press release, dated February 1, 2017, in which it states that it "has not given any license/authorization to any entity/company to operate such schemes or deal with bitcoin or any VC."[113]

A few days earlier, on December 1st, the Chinese leader in mining, Bitmain, announces on its Twitter account that it is suspending the sale of miners after Indian Customs informs the company that they will no longer accept these imports, while waiting for the decision of the DGFT (Directorate General of Foreign Trade, an emanation of the Ministry of Commerce and Industry).

Currently, India thus represents only about 2% of the global capitalization of cryptocurrencies.[114] Even if their status as a currency is not recognized by the authorities, they are not considered illegal: as long as they are not used to contravene the law, investors can buy and hold them.

This is when a unique action comes to our knowledge: a "public interest litigation," dated November 3, 2017, is filed in the Supreme Court of India by a lawyer, Dwaipayan Bhowmick, demanding the regulation, even the banning, of bitcoin and other cryptocurrencies, among other reasons because the transactions are untraceable, and that despite the warnings of the RBI, etc., 2,500 new users arrive on exchanges every day.

---

112. *RBI cautions users of Virtual Currencies against Risks*, The Reserve Bank of India, 12/24/2013.
113. *RBI cautions users of Virtual Currencies against Risks*, The Reserve Bank of India, 12/05/2017.
114. *Can the rise of cryptocurrency impact currency market in India?*, Kanishk Agarwal, Moneycontrol News, 01/05/2018.

The Court accepts the case on 13 November and asks authorities, including the RBI, the Securities and Exchange Board of India (SEBI), the Ministry of Finance, the Ministry of Justice to give their position. The first stages of the procedure are meant to take place in early 2018.

Before an attempt to establish a legal framework for bitcoin and its competitors was started, information began to circulate from mid-September 2017 in the Indian press that the RBI would work on a project focusing on a national cryptocurrency, named "Lakshmi," after the goddess of fortune, prosperity, wealth and abundance, wife of Vishnu. Since then, there has been no official announcement, but the project was meant to be developed in collaboration with other government departments. The launch of Lakshmi in a country like India would obviously be emblematic for the whole world.

17) Dubai (United Arab Emirates)

In September 2017, Dubai Economy signs a partnership with Emcredit, one of its subsidiaries, and the British company Object Tech Group, a start-up specializing in blockchains. The project, called "emCash," concerns the creation of a cryptocurrency that will be used both in the private sector and for public services.

It is presented as follows in the press release published on 26 September 2017 by Dubai Economy[115]:

"Founded on the latest blockchain technology, emCash will be the digital currency in emPay wallet, launched by Emcredit to support contactless payments. emPay allows UAE residents to make varied payments, from their daily coffee and children's school fee to utility charges and money transfers, through the near field communication (NFC) option in their phones. With emCash, emPay users will have the option of a secure digital currency."

Muna Al Qassab, CEO, Emcredit Limited, explains how "customers can choose between two payment options on the emPay platform—the existing dirham payment or emCash. While the dirham payment

---

115. *Dubai Economy launches partnership to expedite emCash*, Dubai Economy, 09/26/2017.

Chapter 2

goes through normal settlement procedures, intermediaries and costs, emCash payments are settled directly between the user and merchant. EmCash thus gives real time value movement and merchants can pass the cost benefit to the emCash holder." In addition, third parties such as banks and Visa / MasterCard will disappear.

The system "will harness blockchain technology to make financial transactions, cheaper, faster and more secure while demonstrating the huge advantages of embracing this technology for governments, business and customers alike," added Tom Morgan, Director and Co-Founder of Object Tech Group.

Muna Al Qassab sees other advantages for authorities. This system "also reduces fraud as well as inflation since currency is issued in real time based on actual demand."

In addition to implementation, however, other issues still must be addressed, including pricing and transaction fees, as well as possible authorizations to be sought from the other six Emirates constituting the United Arab Emirates so that all Emiratis may benefit from it.

The example of Dubai is interesting for many reasons, because the ambition consists in creating a new economic ecosystem from a cryptocurrency. Governments and institutions that wish to do the same will closely monitor the experience.

18) Saudi Arabia and the United Arab Emirates

During 2017, their central banks expressed skepticism about cryptocurrencies, with the United Arab Emirates one adding that they did not recognize bitcoin as an official currency.

Last December, Saudi Sheikh Assim Al-Hakeem decreed on Zad TV that bitcoin and other virtual currencies are prohibited by Islamic law because they are "ambiguous": "We know that bitcoin remains anonymous when you use it. This means that it is an open door for money laundering, drug money and "haram" money [i.e. contrary to Islamic principles]."[116]

---

116. *Le grand mufti d'Égypte émet une fatwa contre le bitcoin*, Russia Today, 01/04/2018.

Sovereign Cryptocurrencies

Reuters, meanwhile, announces on December 13 that the governor of the UAE's central bank, Mubarak Rashed al-Mansouri, has declared that his institution is working with the Central Bank of Saudi Arabia on a joint project to create a digital currency based on the blockchain, which would be accepted for the payment of transactions between two countries.[117]

Reuters adds, "Mansouri said the central banks wanted to understand blockchain technology better. He told reporters that the UAE-Saudi digital currency would be used among banks, not by individual consumers, and would make transactions more efficient."

It is the re-emergence of an old project, because "a decade ago, the UAE and Saudi Arabia discussed the possibility of creating a single currency among members of the six-nation Gulf Cooperation Council but the UAE pulled out of the project in 2009"[118] (the very year bitcoin was created).

Since then, the geopolitics of the region have changed, and it is not surprising that currencies are also affected, from the moment that "diplomatic and economic ties between the UAE and Saudi Arabia have been strengthening this year [2017], and last week [05/12] the UAE said it planned to establish a bilateral committee with Saudi Arabia on economic, political and military issues."

For the first time, both countries are jointly introducing VAT, which is one of the measures to improve their fiscal situation. Bahrain, Kuwait, Oman and Qatar have postponed this decision to 2019.

19) Israel

Since bitcoin is also successful in the Israeli society, two vending machines have been installed in Tel Aviv, with commission around 5%. The first was stopped because the processing time for transactions was too long but should re-open. As for the second, "less reliant on the cryptocurrency marketplace infrastructure, the service is still

---

117. *UAE, Saudi working on digital currency for cross-border deals*, Andrew Torchia, Reuters, 12/13/2017.
118. *Saudi Arabia, UAE poised to launch digital currency*, Richard Wachman, *Arab News*, 12/14/2017.

Chapter 2

operating, though it has been shutting down periodically to process pending purchases due to high demand. Operating hours were also cut back, and the ATM now closes at 6 p.m. every day."[119] Although various official departments warn against the dangers of this speculation, there are no immediate plans to legislate; in any case, not vis-à-vis buyers, because financial media report from December 2017 that the Israeli authorities plan to ban listed companies involved in cryptocurrencies from operating on the stock exchange. This is the plan that Shmuel Hauser, chairman of the Israel Securities Authority (ISA), says he wants to submit to his board: "If we have a company whose main business is digital currencies we would not allow it. If already listed, its trading will be suspended."[120] He added that the ISA must put in place appropriate regulations for such companies to prevent speculation on what he considers to be a bubble.

He does not cite the targeted companies, but at least two are concerned, as they officially describe cryptocurrencies or blockchain technology as essential to their activity: Fantasy Network and Blockchain Mining (we have already mentioned them in Chapter 1).

Fantasy Network, previously specialized in gaming, sees its share price increase by 44% in a single day after announcing the recruitment of a blockchain consultant. The next day the stock appreciates another 80%. In the end, the share quadruples, before losing 50% in two weeks (source: Reuters, Steven Scheer, article quoted).

The shares of Blockchain Mining Ltd. (founded in June 1981), "which on Sunday changed its name from Natural Resources, have soared some 5,000% in the past few months since it announced it would shift its focus from mining for gold and iron to mining cryptocurrencies."[121]

The day Shmuel Hauser makes the announcement, the share prices of both Fantasy Network and Natural Resources drop respectively by 28% and 54%, however their capitalization still remains

---

119. *Bitcoin ATM in Israel Shuts Down Due to Demand Overload*, Hagar Ravet, Calcalist, 12/11/2017.
120. *Israel regulator seeks to ban bitcoin firms from stock exchange*, Steven Scheer, Reuters, 12/25/2017.
121. *Israel regulator seeks to ban bitcoin firms from stock exchange*, Steven Scheer, Reuters, 12/25/2017.

significantly higher than it was before the release of their arrival in cryptocurrencies. But the next day, they go up again. In the end, that of Blockchain Mining Ltd increases by 5,144.76% between January 1st and December 31st, 2017.

The only mining activity where such stock market price "explosions" can be found in 2017 is the mining of cryptocurrencies, as evidenced by this table from Zonebourse.com:

Mining companies	Variation of the price in 2017 (in %)	Capitalization (M$)
Blockchain Mining Ltd	5,144.76	-
Bhp Billiton Ltd	18.00	116,459
Bhp Billiton Plc	16.53	116,459
Rio Tinto	24.81	94,229
Rio Tinto Limited	26.56	94,229
Anglo American	33.58	28,928
Freeport-Mcmoran	46.1	27,89
Grupo Mexico S.A. De C.V.	11.61	24,874
Teck Resources Ltd	19.14	15,274
South32 Ltd	26.91	14,118
Fresnillo	17.04	13,768
First Quantum Minerals Ltd	28.63	9,83
Turquoise Hill Resources Ltd	-0.92	6,87
Polymetal International	7.66	5,237
Kaz Minerals Plc	150.42	5,141
Lundin Mining Corporation	28.02	4,883
Eramet	74.53	3,122
Yamana Gold Inc.	2.89	2,965
Vedanta Resources	-8.53	2,927
Ivanhoe Mines Ltd	62.45	2,727
Independence Group Nl	10.19	2,181

Regulations have yet to be officially implemented by the authorities at the time of writing this book, but the question arises as to what the concerned companies will decide if they can no longer operate on the Tel Aviv stock exchange: will they go elsewhere to be listed?

It is one thing to want to regulate the market with companies' shares, another to create a cryptocurrency. Thus, "despite skepticism by the market regulator, Israeli media reported earlier this week that Israel's central bank and finance ministry were considering the creation of a state cryptocurrency—a digital shekel—for use in cellular transactions in the country, which would allow users to bypass banks in transferring cash between individuals and businesses."[122]

Based on what we currently know, the Israeli project seems to resemble Dubai's approach. Before it is completed, the first step will take place before Parliament, which will hold hearings starting from 21 December 2017, as announced by Calcalist on 14 December[123]:

"The Israeli parliament Finance Committee will hear from representatives from the Finance Ministry and Israel's central bank, [as well as] from regulators in charge of securities, capital markets and taxation. Experts on virtual currencies will also be invited to speak."

These hearings will take place following a motion by the leader of the Labor Party Isaac Herzog: "Israel cannot ignore what has become a worldwide trend that will clearly not disappear on its own in the foreseeable future."

The project even seemed to be accelerating at the end of the year 2017, according to *The Jerusalem Post*: "For several months now, regulators have been examining the possibility of a state-sponsored currency, and the government could review a tentative legal framework in January. The digital shekel would be identical in value to the physical shekel currently in use."[124]

---

122. *Israeli regulator becomes latest to crack down on bitcoin*, Ilan Ben Zion, Financial Times, 12/25/2017.
123. *Israeli Lawmakers to Hold First Policy Discussion on Virtual Currencies*, Shahar Ilan, Calcalist, 12/14/2017.
124. *Israel banking on 'digital shekel' cryptocurrency?*, Max Schindler, The Jerusalem Post, 12/24/2017.

One of the reasons for this forthcoming implementation according to an official who wished to speak anonymously would be the fact that the digital shekel will record each transaction carried out by mobile phone and will thus make the possibilities of tax evasion more difficult. It is indeed a scourge for public accounts because "sources close to the Financial Ministry [have] revealed that the country's black market accounts for at least 22% of Israel's GDP. Their hope is that a state-registered cryptocurrency would greatly decrease this number."[125]

At the same time, other measures are being considered, such as prohibiting the payment of wages in cash.

However, the implementation of a crypto-shekel raises many questions, such as whether the portfolio is located in an account at the Bank of Israel in the user's name or on the user's phone, with the risks that this implies in the event of theft. What will the consequences be if the central bank decides to practice *quantitative easing* with its digital currency, if only to save banks which will see large amounts of cash escape them? What kind of cybersecurity will need to be implemented? Etc.

Like Dubai, this national cryptocurrency project will be instructive for other states. It carries the seed of a (r)evolution, that we have not yet evoked, even if it is a question that is increasingly asked: will this mean the disappearance of cash as a means of payment? (we come back to this question in the conclusion.)

While waiting for the digital shekel, the Ramat Gan diamond exchange, one of the three largest in the world along with those of Antwerp and Bombay, announces in September 2017 that it will launch a cryptocurrency backed by diamonds. The terms are confirmed on February 7, 2018: there will be two versions, the Cut, launched just days after and reserved only for professional exchanges on the Ramat Gan stock exchange, and the Carat, which was meant to be available in May, intended for the public and investors, whose value will be backed 25% by diamonds, in order to make it attractive.

---

125. *Israel could soon be offering its own digital currency*, Jack Dean, Bitconnect.com, 12/28/2017.

Chapter 2

On February 19, the Israel Tax Authority confirms that it considers cryptocurrencies as financial assets and not currencies. It plans to tax the gains made at 25%. Traders and miners will be subject to a VAT rate of 17%.[126]

20) Lebanon

As early as December 2013, the Banque du Liban, Lebanon's central bank, officially warns against bitcoin and the use of unregulated electronic currencies.[127] On October 26, 2017, Riad Salameh, Governor of the Banque du Liban, announces that the project to launch a national digital currency is being studied.[128] However, he declares it is necessary to start "[developing] a protection system from cybercrime," in which two commissions are to be involved, including the Banking Supervision Commission.

At this stage, he does not provide any additional information; especially whether this future currency, supported by the state and controlled by the central bank, will be based on the principle of the blockchain. He takes the opportunity to repeat his opposition to bitcoin and other cryptocurrencies, because "bitcoin and similar currencies are a big threat to the consumer and payment systems." He warns that they "are not currencies but rather a commodity whose prices rise and fall without any justification. For this reason, BDL [bans] the use of this currency in the Lebanese market."

21) Tunisia

It is often presented as the first country having introduced a digital currency:

"Starting with eDinar, 'the first electronic payment platform in Tunisia both by its age and its volume,' according to Moez Chakchouk, CEO of La Poste Tunisienne (the Tunisian Post Office). Created in 2000 by

---

126. *Bitcoin Will Be Taxed as an Asset: Israel Tax Authority*, Samburaj Das, CCN, 02/20/2018.
127. Banque du Liban, *Risks related to electronic money*, 12/19/2013.
128. *Salameh: Central Bank to launch digital currency*, Brooke Anderson, *The Daily Star*, 10/27/2017.

this national organization and the Tunisian Ministry of Communication Technologies and Digital Economy after a law on e-commerce, eDinar is a virtual currency indexed on the dinar (one dinar is equivalent to one eDinar) and issued by the Tunisian central bank which allows Tunisians to pay by prepaid card, online, in tobacco shops or to withdraw paperless money from the ATM."[129]

Innovative at the time, this solution does not correspond to the principles of today's cryptocurrencies. However, according to the July 2015 edition of *African Manager*, "the Tunisian Ministry of Technology and Digital Economy is looking for a specialist who would help it introduce bitcoin and blockchain technology in the country."[130]

The results do not take long to arrive because in October 2015 La Poste, "in partnership with a Tunisian company and a Swiss company, creates Digicash, a new platform indexed on eDinar that operates with blockchain (...). It is not a currency because the central bank would not be happy, but a kind of eDinar that uses blockchain and an interface exclusively with the original eDinar."[131]

An excellent analysis about the central bank's point of view about bitcoin, as the Governor, Chedly Ayari, declares on 5 April 2016: "This currency is more complex than the traditional one because it can be used to finance terrorism."[132] Always the same leitmotif from bankers...

Tunisians can nevertheless obtain bitcoins and other cryptocurrencies from various exchanges, but by the end of 2017, their status as a means of payment is still not recognized. Similarly, Digicash from La Poste is still indexed on the eDinar, however, the central bank also prohibits it from being converted, which would have allowed it to be used outside the country, a plus given the number of Tunisians living abroad.

---

129. *En Afrique, les monnaies virtuelles se sécurisent*, Kevin Poireault, RFI, 06/02/2017.
130. *Tunis : Le bitcoin, monnaie numérique, met le cap sur la Tunisie*, African Manager, 07/31/2015.
131. *En Afrique, les monnaies virtuelles se sécurisent*, Kevin Poireault, RFI, 06/02/2017.
132. *La Banque centrale de Tunisie s'inquiète du recours au bitcoin, l'accusant de financer le terrorisme*, Antony Drugeon, *HuffPost Tunisie*, 04/07/2016.

Chapter 2

Finally, it is (only) in the context of a fight against cash, at a working meeting on 20 October 2017 on the theme *A Reflection on the Reduction of Cash (de-cashing) in the Economy: the Current State, Stakes and Roadmap*, that the Central Bank of Tunisia concludes in its press release: "Moreover, a reflection will soon be launched on the 'crypto-currency' [with the objective] to put in place a national strategy and make the necessary choices regarding this means of payment for the future."[133]

Tunisia, which was in advance in the area of electronic means of payment, thanks to the eDinar and Digicash, among others, however, for the moment has not even started "thinking" about a national cryptocurrency.

22) Senegal, WAEMU and WAMU

The West African Economic and Monetary Union (WAEMU) comprises eight countries: Benin, Burkina Faso, Côte d'Ivoire, Guinea-Bissau, Mali, Niger, Senegal and Togo. Created in 1994, its mission is to build a "harmonized and integrated economic space" in West Africa to ensure freedom of movement for people, capital, goods, services and factors of production, as well as the right of residence of citizens throughout the territory — over more than 3 million km^2 and 112 million inhabitants. The zone shares the CFA franc as its currency (see box on page 126).

WAMU is the West African Monetary Union, separate from WAEMU, but brings together the same eight countries to administer their monetary policies. The joint issuing institution is the Central Bank of West African States (BCEAO), based in Dakar, Senegal. It "has the following fundamental missions:

  - define and implement monetary policy within the WAMU;
  - ensure the stability of the WAMU banking and financial system;
  - promote smooth operations and ensure the supervision and security of payment systems in WAMU;

---

133. Banque Centrale de Tunisie, 10/20/2017.

- implement WAMU's exchange rate policy under the conditions decided by the Council of Ministers;
- manage the official foreign exchange reserves of WAMU member states."[134]

In November 2016, the media inform that Senegal will introduce a national cryptocurrency, based on the blockchain, named "eCFA," which will have legal tender, like the CFA franc (FCFA). It is the result of a partnership between the BRM (Banque Régionale de Marchés, a market, investment and asset management bank, as indicated on its website) and eCurrency Mint Limited, a provider specializing in issuing digital currencies, particularly for central banks. The eCFA will first be available in Senegal, then, in a second phase, extended to the other seven WAMU countries.

What is strange in this announcement is that the initiator is the BRM, not the BCEAO, although the issuing institution.

Indeed, a corrigendum initially published by *Enquête* is reissued on 19 January by OSIRIS (Observatoire sur les Systèmes d'Information, les Réseaux et les Inforoutes au Sénégal) on its website, following a note communicated by BRM's management:

"Contrary to what could have been understood or written, the BRM's electronic money issuance project could not involve the Central Bank of West African States."

The press release adds, "The BCEAO does not issue electronic money and, in order to avoid definitively any confusion between the FCFA issued by the BCEAO and the eCFA electronic money, the Banque Régionale de Marchés informs that it 'decided to withdraw the name eCFA from its project of issuing electronic money'."[135]

Since then, no information has been provided, either on the release date or the technical specifications. Senegal therefore does not yet have its cryptocurrency, nor the other states of WAMU.

---

134. Source: website of BCEAO.
135. *La BRM sur le projet d'émission de monnaie électronique : « Il ne saurait impliquer la BCEAO »*, Enquête, 01/19/2017.

The CFA Franc

Created in 1945, the CFA franc (FCFA) originally stood for "Franc des colonies françaises d'Afrique." Today, it corresponds to two currencies common to several African countries:
- The franc of Communauté Financière Africaine (African Financial Community), issued by the Central Bank of West African States (BCEAO) for the eight member states of the West African Monetary Union (WAMU): Benin, Burkina Faso, Côte d'Ivoire, Guinea-Bissau, Mali, Niger, Senegal and Togo;
- The franc of Coopération Financière en Afrique Centrale (Financial Cooperation in Central Africa), issued by the Bank of Central African States (BEAC) for the six member States of the Central African Economic and Monetary Community (CEMAC): Cameroon, Chad, the Central African Republic, Chad, Congo, Equatorial Guinea and Gabon.
"In Africa, the franc zones constitute monetary and economic spaces. (...) After independence, most of the new states remained in a homogeneous monetary unit, whose institutional framework was renewed and structured by a common exchange rate system. Both CFA francs have a fixed exchange rate to the euro, and their value is guaranteed by the French Treasury under the Maastricht Treaty."[136]
In return, countries in the FCFA zone must deposit 50% of their foreign exchange reserves with the French Treasury, i.e. around €14.3 billion in 2014.
Even if the FCFA system is sometimes criticized and called into question, it constitutes a model in the context of the reflection on inter-state cryptocurrencies, since it is the common currency in the eight member states of UMOA and the six of CEMAC, with a single central bank for each of the two zones, which manages

---
136. Source: Wikipedia.

Sovereign Cryptocurrencies

to deal with the interests and needs of each country for which it is responsible for monetary issuance. The creation of a common cryptocurrency for the WAMU and/or CEMAC countries may pose a problem: France's position.

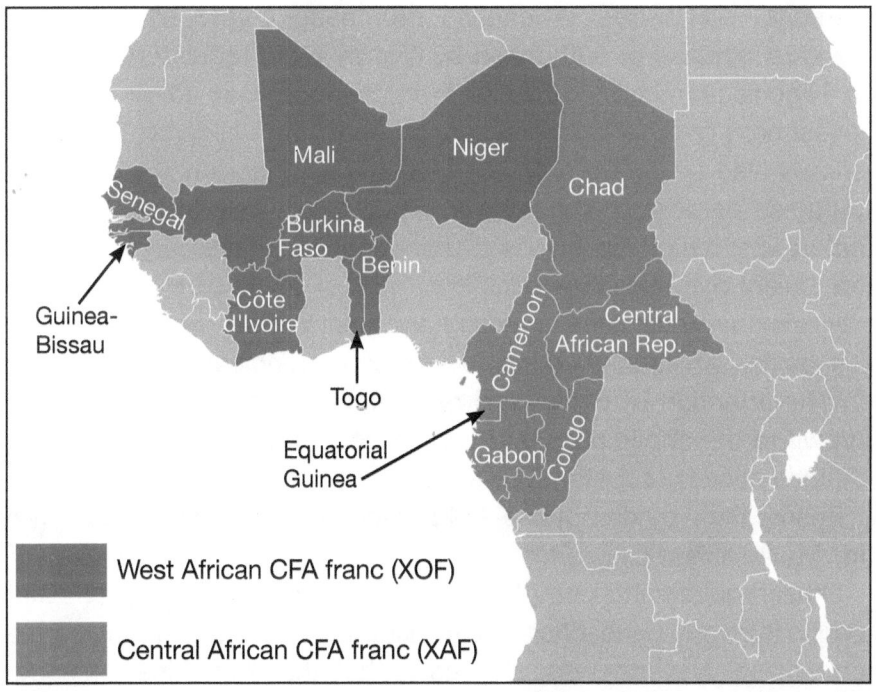

The CFA franc in Africa: WAMU and CEMAC[137]

---

137. Source: Jarry1250, Wikimedia Commons.

23) Nigeria

In the most populous country in Africa, with 190 million inhabitants, on January 12, 2017 the Securities and Exchange Commission issues an alert similar to that of the financial authorities and central banks of many other countries on the risk of these investments:

"The Commission wishes to alert the public that none of the persons, companies or entities promoting cryptocurrencies has been recognized or authorized by it or by other regulatory agencies in Nigeria to receive deposits from the public or to provide any investment or other financial services in or from Nigeria. The public should also be aware that any investment opportunities promoted by these persons, companies or entities are likely to be of a risky nature with a high risk of loss of money, whilst others may be outright fraudulent pyramid schemes."[138]

A few days later, on 17 January, the Central Bank of Nigeria (CBN) issues its own circular against the cryptocurrencies:

"The attention of banks and other financial institutions is hereby drawn to the above risks and you are required to take the following actions pending substantive regulation decision by the CBN.

Ensure that you do not use, hold, trade, and/ or transact in anyway in virtual currencies (…)."[139]

Other requirements complete the text, which amounts to prohibiting banks from any transactions of any kind with bitcoin and other virtual currencies. Nevertheless, it is estimated that Nigerians exchange about $4 million worth of cryptocurrencies each week on the country's thirteen platforms.[140]

Mid-September 2017, the press echoes the statement of the deputy director of payment systems of the CBN at a conference on cryptocurrencies in Lagos:

---

138. *Public Notice on Investments in Cryptocurrencies and other Virtual or Digital Currencies*, Securities and Exchange Commission (Nigeria), 01/12/2017.
139. *CBN bars banks from bitcoin, virtual currencies*, Mathias Okwe, *The Guardian*, 01/18/2017.
140. *Nigerians Trade $4 Million in Bitcoin Weekly, despite Warnings*, Lubomir Tassev, Bitcoin.com, 02/19/2018.

"[The Central Bank] cannot stop the tide of waves generated by the blockchain technology and its derivatives. Currently, we have taken measures to create four departments in the institution that are looking forward to [harmonizing] the white paper on Crypto currency."[141]

The reflection focuses on the creation of a national digital currency but also on the use of the blockchain in other areas, such as the management of securities on the stock exchange. At this stage, it is still impossible to specify the direction that the central bank will take, but it is moving forward.

24) South Africa

Trading by the local population is becoming increasingly important. Thus, the ICE3X platform estimates that between 200 and 300,000 South Africans are investing in cryptocurrencies, while the Luno platform indicates that the equivalent of 300 million rand (about $24.2 million) were exchanged in bitcoins on 1 December 2017 alone.[142]

Therefore, as is the case in many countries, the South African Revenue Service (SARS) is paying close attention to the issue in order to tax transactions, which was confirmed by Dr. Randall Carolissen, director of research at SARS:

"As you can imagine it is very difficult—the blockchain technology. Without revealing too much—we are talking to some of the top technology companies in the world that are doing similar work for Canada and the UK and we are hoping to get that technology."[143]

He added that, at present, capital gains on cryptocurrencies are taxed like those on capital, but that they have submitted the question to the OECD, along with other countries:

"We were part of the OECD working groups and that has certainly been incorporated into our policy environment. So we are on top of it. In fact, South Africa is cited as one of the leading implementers of this cryptocurrency environment."

---

141. *CBN mulls digital currency*, Ibukun Igbasan, *The Guardian*, 09/15/2017.
142. *South Africans riding the cryptocurrency wave*, eNCA, 12/08/2017.
143. *South Africa Wants to Track and Tax Bitcoin Trading*, Avi Mizrahi, Bitcoin.com, 12/17/2017.

Indeed, as early as February 2017, the central bank, the South African Reserve Bank (SARB), begins to study the possibility of issuing a virtual currency based on the blockchain principle, as its usage would strongly speed up transactions and lower fees. It is indeed what Tim Masela stated, head of the National Payments System at the SARB:

"If we go the route of issuing a digital currency, the objective would be to take advantage of emerging technologies so that we reap the benefits, (...) We foresee that these benefits could be realized, which would be good for the transacting public. But of course, the risks have to be borne in mind as well and that's what we want to balance."[144]

In July, it is announced that a provider of blockchain solutions has been selected for an initial test. The project is therefore in progress.

25) Venezuela

We end our world tour with this sovereign cryptocurrency, because it is emblematic and its stakes go far beyond Venezuela's borders.

Despite proven oil reserves that are among the richest in the world, not to mention other natural resources such as gas, gold, etc., this country, ravaged by serious civil unrest and sanctions imposed by the United States and the European Union, among others, has continued to see its situation deteriorate over the past year. According to the International Monetary Fund, Venezuela's economy was to fall by 12% in 2017 and its annual inflation rate is expected to exceed 2,300% in 2018.[145] As for the public debt, the year 2018 begins as badly as 2017 ends, with a new default of $35 million. The country, as well as its national oil company Petróleos de Venezuela (PDVSA), are declared in partial default by international rating agencies since December.

As a result of this disastrous situation in November, the bolivar (VEF)—the national currency—loses 57% of its value against the

---

144. *South African Reserve Bank Planning to Test Cryptocurrrency Regulations*, Ashour Iesho, Inside Bitcoins, 07/22/2017.
145. *Venezuela Announces the Creation of Oil-Backed National Cryptocurrency – the Petro*, Kevin Helms, Bitcoin.com, 12/04/2017.

Sovereign Cryptocurrencies

US dollar on the black market, falling from a parity of USD 1 = VEF 10,000 at the end of July to USD 1 = VEF +100,000 at the beginning of December; as poverty continues to spread across the country.

To escape this situation many Venezuelans begin trading bitcoin, with ever-increasing volumes, as this graph of LocalBitcoins picked up by Bloomberg shows:

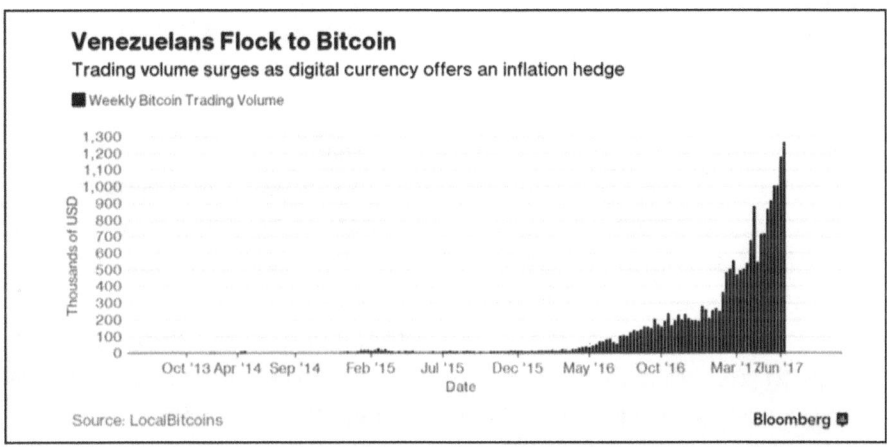

Trading literally explodes in just over a quarter, as the LocalBitcoins exchange, for example, sees its trading volumes quadruple between June and October 2017.[146]

Alongside the crisis, the mining of cryptocurrencies also begins, particularly adapted to Venezuela, because electricity is subsidized and costs almost nothing. Of course, bitcoin exceeds all the others in volume, but ether gains in popularity, because, as one miner explains, "mining ETH or bitcoin is pretty much the same principle: using free electricity to generate cash (...) but ETH mining is more affordable — all you need is free software and a PC with a video card. Any police officer is easily fooled into thinking your ETH miner is just a regular computer."[147] Indeed, the authorities are now raiding platforms or miners, in order to stop this activity considered as diverting the

---

146. *Localbitcoins in Venezuela Continues to set new Trading Volume Records*, JP Buntinx, NewsBTC, 10/19/2017.
147. *Venezuelan Bitcoin Mining Continues Despite Government Crackdown*, Samuel Haig, Bitcoin.com, 08/15/2017.

Chapter 2

principle of public subsidies on energy to enrich businesses and individuals—unless it is rather a question of their survival.

It is what made Daniel Osorio of Andean Capital Advisors told CNBC in September 2017 "that hyperinflation makes it impractical to use cash since dollars are in short supply in Venezuela. He elaborated, "we are beginning to see in Venezuela, potentially, the first bitcoinization of a sovereign state."[148]

From observation to decisions, the step is quickly taken, given the economic disaster, which continues to worsen. Consequently, on Sunday, December 3, 2017, President Maduro announces the creation of a national cryptocurrency called "petro," which will be backed by oil, gas, gold and diamond reserves. The goal is to help Venezuela "advance in issues of monetary sovereignty, to make financial transactions and overcome the financial blockade"[149] imposed by the United States.

This is the first time in the world that such a decision has been taken to resolve a (monetary) crisis situation. Usually, solutions are exclusively passed through the banking system, while this time, it is a national cryptocurrency without banks. The process then accelerates in the following days, with an announcement by President Maduro that he will sign the certificates to back petro with oil from the Orinoco Oil Belt. He commissions the Minister of Oil and the new president of the national oil and gas company PDVSA, Manuel Quevedo, to coordinate the team that will create the petro.

On 8 December, Decree No. 3.196 is published in the Venezuelan Official Gazette (*Gaceta Oficial* No. 41.296) authorizing the creation of the Superintendency of Cryptocurrency, whose role would consist in managing petro transactions. Article 3 states:

"The purpose of this decree is to establish, within the policies of integral development of the Nation and, in a legal manner, regulatory conditions set forth in the Venezuelan Civil Code, the purchase / sale of

---

148. *Venezuela Announces the Creation of Oil-Backed National Cryptocurrency – the Petro*, Kevin Helms, Bitcoin.com, 12/04/2017.
149. *Enter the 'petro': Venezuela to launch oil-backed cryptocurrency*, Alexandra Ulmer, Deisy Buitrago, Reuters, 12/03/2017.

financial assets, the application, use and development of blockchain technologies, mining, the development of new cryptocurrencies in the country, in order to bet on an economy capable of maintaining social cohesion and political stability."

On Tuesday, December 12, the Observatorio de la Blockchain de Venezuela is formally established. It will be in charge of governing the scheme of the new virtual currency and of "strengthening, evaluating and monitoring everything related to the use of cryptocurrency technology in Venezuela." It will also serve as the institutional basis for its launch, which will be distributed through "auctions or direct placement."

The Observatory also has the task of creating a Register of Cryptocurrency Miners, whose web page will be operational from 22 December (https://registro.blockchain.gob.ve/web/). All those who want to participate in mining have until January 21 to register. The Superintendent is also considering the establishment of large-scale mining farms in special economic technology development zones. Meetings are held with Corpoelec, the national electricity company, to ensure sufficient supply for this activity.[150]

On 27 December, President Maduro signs a decree guaranteeing five billion barrels of oil for the creation of petro, on the basis of 1 petro = 1 barrel. Some, particularly among opponents, point out the fact that, under these conditions, petro is not a cryptocurrency but an acknowledgement of debt backed by oil. It is, however, a

---

150. *Criptomoneda Petro: Venezuela abre Observatorio del Blockchain para registro de minería digital*, LaRed, 12/26/2017.

Chapter 2

cryptocurrency, but Venezuela's current financial situation does not allow it to launch a currency that would not offer any guarantee, especially since Venezuela intends to use petro for international payments, which would make it possible to circumvent the financial sanctions imposed by the United States, by freeing it from the dollar. At the time of writing this book, the price of a barrel of oil is currently trading between $60 and $70, so this would have secured a high value to petro.

On 9 January, Parliament declares it illegal because it contravenes the provisions of the Constitution. However, in a dramatic turn of events, it is announced on 23 January that the presidential elections scheduled for October 2018 will be held before 30 April. Like the Parliament's announcement, this decision does not interrupt the launch of petro, to take place in two phases:

- Phase 1: a pre-sale reserved for investors, with 38.4% of the total 100 million petros to be issued, or 38.4 million tokens at a face value of $60, sold at a discount;

- Phase 2: an ICO covering 44 million petros. It is meant to begin on March 20 and end when the total has been sold. The public will be able to buy some by paying in currencies or with other cryptocurrencies, based on the price of the Venezuelan barrel of oil.

The bolivar will not be accepted as a form of payment during these first two phases, but will be accepted on the secondary market. The government keeps the balance of petros, a little over seventeen million units.

The petro is pre-mined on the Ethereum blockchain using the ERC-20 standard.

End of January: 860,000 Venezuelans are now registered in the Register of Cryptocurrency Miners (the total population exceeds 31 million inhabitants).

On February 6, Foreign Trade Minister José Gregorio Vielma Mora announces that he has received a group of Brazilian investors willing to invest $300 million and that Poland, Denmark, Norway, Honduras and Vietnam, among others, have agreed to export food and medicines for the equivalent of $435 million paid in petros.[151]

Phase 1 begins on February 20 and from the first day, a total equivalent to $735 million is announced, which looks like a first success (logically, 735 = 435 + 300 announced by the Minister on 02/06). The Treasury Department of the United States does not fail to recall that buying it could be considered as an extension of credit in Venezuela, which would violate the sanctions regime and expose U.S. citizens to legal risks.[152]

Now, the first sovereign cryptocurrency in the world is born, and Nicolás Maduro declares on this launch day:

"Here is the petro and things must be done differently, in a new way. A new economic era is beginning for Venezuela."[153]

The stakes go far beyond the country's borders, as he has previously stressed:

"Venezuela has placed itself at the forefront of the world. It is the first country to create a cryptocurrency backed by its natural wealth."[154]

It is still too early to know whether petro will definitely succeed and save the country from economic catastrophe and bankruptcy, or in a word, chaos. If this is the case, it will have been achieved almost at the expense or even against the traditional banking system. This success will inevitably give rise to an intense debate elsewhere in the world: thanks to cryptocurrencies and blockchain technology, do we still need commercial banks? We will come back to this essential question in the conclusion.

26) Marshall Islands (RMI)

On 28 February 2018, the Parliament of this archipelago of about 1,100 islands in Oceania adopts a law giving birth to Sovereign (SOV), its future sovereign digital currency, which will operate alongside the US dollar, the current currency (until it can be replaced?).

---

151. *Brazil and Other Countries To Invest in Venezuela's Petros*, Telesur, 02/06/2018.
152. *Venezuela launches the 'petro,' its cryptocurrency*, Rachelle Krygier, *The Washington Post*, 02/20/2018.
153. *Estos son los servicios que se pagarán con El Petro*, Telesur, 02/21/2018.
154. *Decreto presidencial respalda al petro con reservas de la faja petrolífera*, *El Universal*, 12/27/2017.

The issue is planned for the end of the year via an ICO, with all residents benefiting from a free allocation (with a total population of a little over 70,000 inhabitants), before opening it to investors. The SOV will be based on a specific blockchain, which will require registration to combat anonymity and funds of questionable origin.

Here's what explains Dr. Hilda C. Heine, President of the Marshall Islands:

"The RMI will invest the revenues to support its climate change efforts, green energy, healthcare for those still affected by the US nuclear tests, and education."[155]

Isn't this a magnificent project being promoted thanks to this new cryptocurrency?

---

155. *Marshall Islands to be first to issue own sovereign cryptocurrency*, Samantha Herbert, *The Telegraph*, 03/01/2018.

Catalonia
From Independence to Cryptocurrency?

Elections to the regional parliament on 21 December 2017 give the majority of seats to the three separatist parties, although it is the centrist liberal party that takes the lead. It is therefore difficult to know what the future holds for Catalonia: independence or remain within Spain?

In the weeks leading up to these elections, Catalan leaders are warned that, in the event of independence, they will be excluded not only from the European Union but also from the Eurozone, which means that they will no longer have the right to use the euro, so they will find themselves without a currency.

This is obviously an unfortunate situation, but perhaps even more so for the euro, as the Catalan economy weighs around €220 billion, more than seven Eurozone countries, including Portugal. Its departure would inevitably have consequences for the parity of the euro with other currencies.

It is then announced in various media that an independent Catalonia would preferably turn towards the creation of a cryptocurrency based on the blockchain. It is also mentioned that Vitalik Buterin, the founder of Ethereum, is already involved as advisor for the possible future platform, the preparation of the etherCat and the ICO for the launching.

It should be noted that the region and the city of Barcelona have already acquired experience with cryptocurrencies, in particular to finance projects with a social dimension. It now remains to be seen how the political situation will evolve, because, in monetary terms, everything seems ready, or almost ready.

III. Other national situations

This part does not review the position of all countries on the subject of cryptocurrencies but presents several examples that illustrate different situations and visions, at different stages: where the process of creating a national digital currency has not yet begun to ones that have barely begun. We will start with three important countries in the world of cryptocurrencies.

1) The United States
At the legislative level, several initiatives have been taken by elected officials to encourage government agencies to monitor the use of cryptocurrencies by terrorists or for money laundering purposes. For example, on 16 May 2017 Democratic Representative Kathleen M. Rice files project H.R.2433 titled "Homeland Security Assessment of Terrorists Use of Virtual Currencies Act." It states:
"(Sec. 2) This bill directs the Department of Homeland Security's Office of Intelligence and Analysis: (1) in coordination with appropriate federal partners, to develop and disseminate a threat assessment regarding the threat posed by individuals using virtual currency to carry out activities in furtherance of an act of terrorism, including the provision of material support or resources to a foreign terrorist organization; and (2) to share such assessment with state, local, and tribal law enforcement officials."
The text is voted on in the House on 12 September 2017 and transmitted to the Senate the following day, where it was still under consideration at the time of writing this book.
Less than ten days after the House of Representatives, on 25 May 2017, a group of senators prepare the law S. 1241: Combating Money Laundering, Terrorist Financing, and Counterfeiting Act of 2017. Its goal is "to improve the prohibitions on money laundering, and for other purposes." In section 13, it adds cryptocurrencies, which will enter into the scope of the law once the Senate Committee of Justice has ruled (by the end of 2017 the law had not yet been passed).

On the other hand, the use of cryptocurrencies remains essentially in the private sphere, as the Federal Reserve (Fed) has not announced any project in this area. However, since 2014, there have already been voices calling for the Fed to create the Fedcoin, or at least use blockchain technology. It is clear, however, that the project is under consideration (see box on page 142).

The Federal Reserve has not lost interest in the phenomenon of cryptocurrencies. Thus, its president, Janet Yellen, reports in February 2014 that her organization has no authority to regulate bitcoin. She repeats this in December 2017, considering that bitcoin is not a stable source of value and constitutes a highly speculative asset. Although she adds that it plays a very limited role in the international payment system, she reiterates that "the Fed doesn't really play any regulatory role with respect to bitcoin, other than assuring that banking organizations that we do supervise are attentive, that they are appropriately managing any interactions they have with participants in that market, and [are] appropriately monitoring anti-money laundering, bank secrecy act responsibilities that they have.[156]"[157]

Indeed, several U.S. financial institutions have announced initiatives in the field of cryptocurrencies, starting with the Chicago Stock Exchange. Thus, the Chicago Board Options Exchange (CBOE) issues the first bitcoin futures on December 11, 2017.

"Launched at $15,000, these first futures, meant to mature in January 2018 took up 25.67% to $18,850 in their first session. At the close of European markets, they were being traded at $18,200, up 21.33%.

The exchanges had to be temporarily suspended twice in order to avoid excessive price fluctuations. And in the first twenty minutes of

---

156. The Bank Secrecy Act dates back to 1970 and requires financial institutions to work with the US government and its agencies in the fight against money laundering and fraud.
157. *Fed chief Yellen says bitcoin is a 'highly speculative asset'*, John Melloy, CNBC, 12/13/2017.

Chapter 2

the session, the traffic was so important that the CBOE website was temporarily rendered inaccessible."[158]

About 2,300 futures contracts are traded on this day, but that remains "a drop in the crypto ocean," as Bloomberg states in its chart summarizing the day, CBOE futures representing 3% of global bitcoin trading in the early hours:

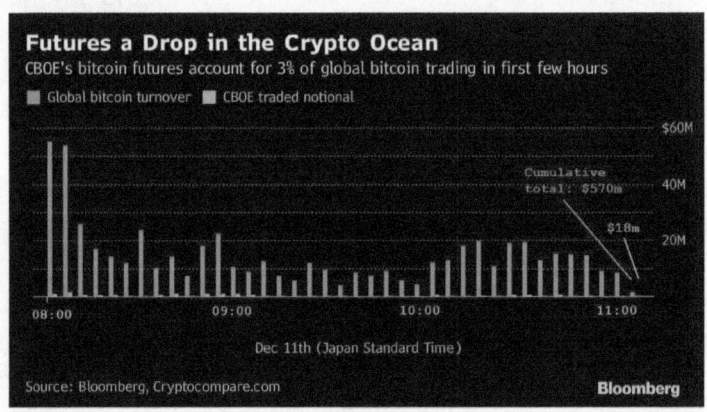

One week after the CBOE, on December 17, the Chicago Mercantile Exchange (CME), the other major U.S. futures market, launches its bitcoin contracts.

The fact that there is a listing on one of these major stock exchanges means that banking groups are not far away. Thus, Goldman Sachs announces in October 2017 its interest in cryptocurrencies and confirms in December that it wishes to open a specialized desk by June 2018. Other banks like Citigroup, JP Morgan, etc. already have more or less advanced projects in the field of cryptocurrencies. For the time being, it is more a question of offering services and products to their customers and speculating in this field than creating such currencies. But until when?

This should not be long in coming, as Citigroup Inc. president Michael Corbat said in a Bloomberg interview on November 8 that

---

158. *Le bitcoin fait des débuts prometteurs en Bourse*, Leila Marchand, *Les Échos*, 12/11/2017.

"our bank is experimenting internally with its own currency, dubbed Citicoin, which can reduce friction in international foreign-exchange transactions."[159].

On February 6, 2018, during a hearing before the Senate Banking Commission, Jay Clayton, Chairman of the Securities and Exchange Commission (SEC), and Christopher Giancarlo, Chairman of the Commodity Futures Trading Commission, are resolutely open and positive towards cryptocurrencies and the blockchain. Of course, it is necessary to ensure that consumers and users are protected, but it is more a question of accompanying and encouraging this innovation than restricting it by inappropriate regulation.

Remember, however, that the Federal Reserve belongs to the major U.S. banks and not to the federal government, so there is little chance that any decision that could go against their interests, including the creation of a sovereign cryptocurrency, could be implemented, regardless of the needs and situation of the population.

---

159. *Bitcoin, Beware: Citigroup's CEO Predicts State-Sponsored Digital Currencies*, Erik Schatzker et Dakin Campbell, Bloomberg, 11/08/2017.

Chapter 2

The Fedcoin

The Bank for International Settlements notes in a September 2017 study that there is still no cryptocurrency issued by a central bank for the public. However, it assumes the fedcoin hypothesis, because, according to it, it is one of the most debated:

"The concept, which was proposed by Koning (2014) and has not been endorsed by the Federal Reserve, is for the central bank to create its own cryptocurrency. The currency could be converted both ways at par with the US dollar and conversion would be managed by the Federal Reserve Banks. Instead of having a predetermined supply rule, as is the case with bitcoin, the supply of fedcoin would, much like cash, increase or decrease depending on the desire of consumers to hold it. Fedcoin would become a third component of the monetary base (…).

Fedcoins would only be created (destroyed) if an equivalent amount of cash or reserves [are] destroyed (created) at the same time. Like cash, fedcoin would be decentralized in transaction and centralized in supply."[160]

Most central banks are not yet ready to move towards the creation of national cryptocurrencies, as they would endanger the existence of commercial banks, which would lose their monopoly, even if it is more and more undermined by new solutions appearing all over the world, especially in so-called "emerging" countries.

---

160. *Central bank cryptocurrencies*, Morten Linnemann Bech et Rodney Garratt, Banque des règlements internationaux, 09/17/2017.

Sovereign Cryptocurrencies

Cryptocurrency Among the Sioux

The United States does not (yet) have its virtual currency, but one of the native nations, the Oglalas Sioux—one of the seven clans of the Lakota nation—has practically its own, the MazaCoin[161], since March 2014. As *Newsweek* explains, they are among the poorest tribes, with an average annual per capita income of $2,892, according to the United States Census Bureau (2013 data). Then, Payu Harris, descendant of Indians and resident of South Dakota, decides to create a cryptocurrency, the mazacoin, which "is designed to replace the more than $200 million in annual federal funding that supports the Oglala Sioux nation 'with funding we control. We can build our economy from scratch'."[162]

He wants to leave half of the funds in a tribal trust, which means safe from US taxes. Indeed, "bitcoin and its cousins are borderless currencies, not controlled by any centralized authority and cloaked in anonymity. By contrast, Harris wants mazacoin to be 'fully transparent' and controlled by the equivalent of a central bank for the Oglala Sioux and potentially other tribes, a tool for self-determination and nation building to help cure the virtual open-air economic prisons that many tribal reservations are."

A memorandum of understanding is signed in January 2013 with representatives of the Sioux Oglalas, to explore the potential of mazacoin and, depending on the results, adopt this currency within the Lakota nation. According to what was shred with *Newsweek* by W. Gregory Guedel, a tax lawyer, here is one potential scenario: "If the slowly growing number of national retailers now accepting bitcoin, which now include Overstock.com and Dell, ever move to

---

161. Le MazaCoin is named after the word lakota "mazaska," which means "money."
162. *Oglala Sioux Hope bitcoin Alternative, Mazacoin, Will Change Economic Woes*, Lynnley Browning, *Newsweek*, 08/14/2014.

Chapter 2

accept Mazacoin in exchange for goods, then a consumer in, say, Sweden, could use the tribal currency to buy books on Amazon, with a percentage of the transaction going to the tribal trust, Guedel says. Mazacoin, he asserts, "potentially opens up a global market to this tribe."

We are not there yet, but the idea is starting to progress, as shown by this graph released by CoinMarket on January 8, 2018:

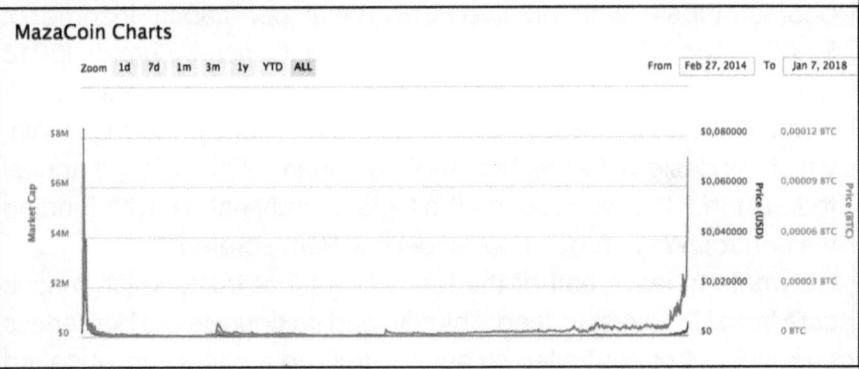

Data for the last month of transactions:

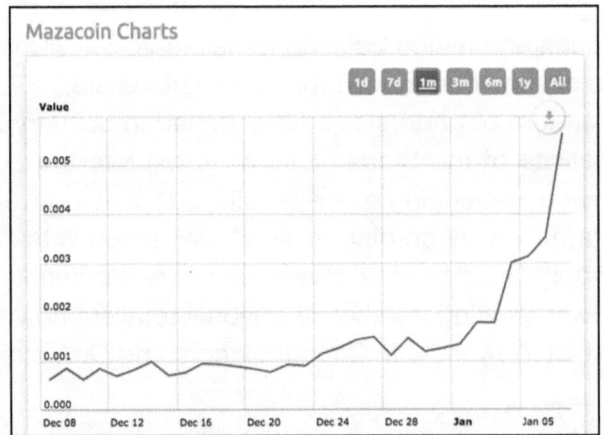

Source: WorldCoinIndex

It is from mid-November 2017 that the value of the mazacoin starts to increase, with an acceleration in December, which had not diminished. The total capitalization is still only $7.7 million, but nearly $130,000 had been traded over the last 24 hours. Will it be "the new buffalo? Once, it was everything for our survival. We used it for food, for clothes, for everything. It was our economy," declared P. Harris to *Forbes*.[163]

Will Oglala Sioux soon be an example of development to be considered by the world? All the more as "mining mazacoin is currently much more straightforward than mining bitcoin, requiring significantly less processing power. This makes it one of the world's more environmentally-friendly cryptocurrencies, as the mining calculations do not use as much power and can even be achieved using out-of-date machines which no longer have enough grunt to mine bitcoin."[164]

---

163. *The Battle of Little Bitcoin: Native American Tribe Launches Its Own Cryptocurrency*, Jasper Hamill, *Forbes*, 02/27/2014.
164. *The Battle of Little Bitcoin: Native American Tribe Launches Its Own Cryptocurrency*, Jasper Hamill, *Forbes*, 02/27/2014.

2) Japan

It has become the leading bitcoin trading market, ahead of the United States and South Korea. While China continues to attack everything that concerns private cryptocurrencies, Japan is following the opposite path, with measures almost unique to the planet. Tokyo is no longer the main financial center in Asia, but its decisions on virtual currencies could make it a leader in this highly strategic area in the future. However, it is in Japan in February 2014 that an exchange experiences the biggest bankruptcy, that of Mt. Gox, which causes enormous losses and, moreover, has still to reveal all its mysteries (see Chapter 1).

Here are the main measures taken by the authorities:

- March 4, 2016: a bill is introduced in the Diet (parliament) to regulate exchanges. A provision provides that cryptocurrencies may be considered as payment instruments.

- April 1, 2017: the law having been passed, the Payment Services Act is amended in order to recognize cryptocurrencies as a legal means of payment.

- July 1, 2017: the 8% consumption tax on bitcoin transactions is eliminated.

- On 29 September 2017, the Japanese Financial Services Agency officially registers eleven exchanges, which amounts to granting them a license to operate. At the same time, seventeen cryptocurrencies are approved for trading on these platforms, including bitcoin, ether, ripple, litecoin, etc.

Japan now ranks first in the world, with 30 to 50% of trade. It also has nearly 300,000 merchants who accept bitcoin at the end of 2017. The central bank has therefore not announced the creation of a national digital currency. On the other hand, private banks, including Japan's postal bank and its financial power, are currently studying the possibility of launching their own cryptocurrency, called "J-Coin." It would be linked to the yen and used via a mobile application. The project is still in its early stages, but the announced objective is for it to be operational for the Tokyo Olympic Games in 2020.

3) South Korea

It is considered to be the third largest cryptomarket in the world, after Japan and the United States, and is estimated to account for 20% of global bitcoin transactions. For a total population of more than 51 million, nearly one million Koreans are believed to possess cryptocurrencies. As we saw in Chapter 1, the demand for bitcoins is such that they trade at an average price 15-20% higher than in other countries.

Faced with increasing fraud and cheating, and the risk of what could prove to be a bubble bursting, with catastrophic consequences on a national scale, the Korean authorities are mobilizing to regulate this speculation of a new kind:

- September 29: all forms of ICOs and fundraising in cryptocurrencies are prohibited, under penalty of sanctions;

- Early December: the government sets up a task force on the subject of cryptocurrencies in order to take urgent measures;

- December 13: all financial institutions no longer have the right to use virtual currencies, or even to hold them; foreigners and minors are prohibited from trading. However, transactions remain authorized and are not subject to capital gains tax;

- December 28: it is announced that as of next month, anonymous accounts in cryptocurrencies are prohibited. Banks can no longer offer services for unidentified trade either, in order to combat money laundering; the authorities even threaten to close some exchanges, or even all of them. The announcement of these decisions makes decrease the value of bitcoin by almost 12% and ether by 8%;

- January 2: the government informs that the measures prohibiting anonymous accounts will take effect around 20 January. In addition, the accounts opened with the exchanges must correspond to real registered accounts, and only the account declared by an investor may be used for transactions.

If measures are carried out to the extreme, such as closing all Korean exchanges, this would have consequences that we cannot yet imagine, including in terms of civil peace. How would nearly a million Koreans who would consider themselves robbed by their government, because the price would inevitably fall, react? The impact would also spread to most Asian countries, and logically beyond.

Such a decision would not be without consequences, nor for the future of South Korea, since many groups have projects related to cryptocurrencies and blockchain technology:

"Despite the fluctuations, retail investors and several major Korean companies are getting in on the action. Samsung announced in May a project using blockchain—the platform for all cryptocurrencies—to track shipping orders in real time. Kakao, maker of the country's leading messaging app, acquired the fintech start-up Dunamu to launch its own cryptocurrency exchange in October, named Upbit. And video game giant Nexon is now the biggest shareholder in Korbit, Korea's third-largest cryptocurrency exchange."[165]

Moreover, deciding to close all exchanges would generate serious legal, economic and political problems, including before Parliament: the government could not survive the crisis it would have triggered. Is bitcoin now too big to fail in Korea?

Although the country has taken the lead in the fight to regulate cryptocurrencies, no public virtual currency seems to be in preparation or even envisioned. Maybe it should be thought about, in order to survive the crisis that could come from bitcoin.

All the more so as another crisis, which has worsened for more than a year, threatens South Korea—it is the risk of war with North Korea. Let's start by observing the evolution of bitcoin on the Korean exchange Bithumb.com over the year 2017:

---

[165]. *Why is South Korea suddenly terrified of bitcoin?*, **David Josef Volodzko**, *South China Morning Post*, **01/01/2017.**

Sovereign Cryptocurrencies

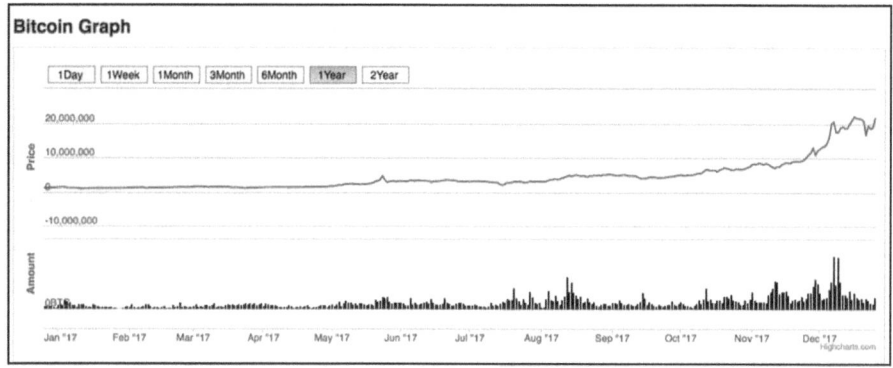

We note a fairly steady increase over the first ten months of the year, with the exception of 24 May when a strong peak appears:

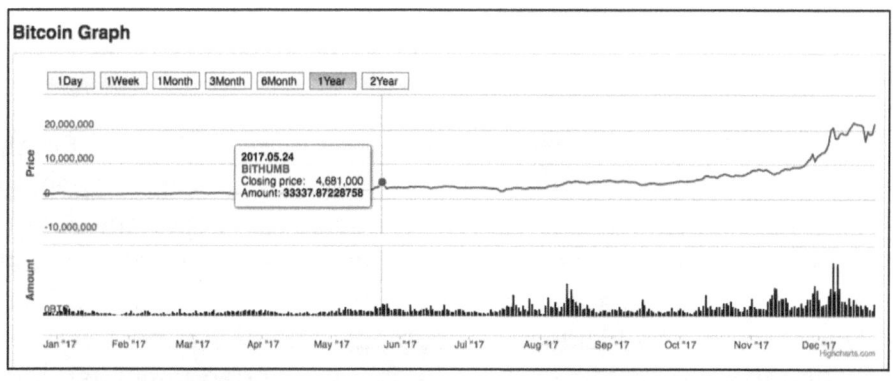

Source: Bithumb.com

That day, the closing price rises to $4,681, while the day before, it stood at $3,540 and fell the next day to $3,525, an increase of nearly 33% in one day. It even drops to $2,809 on May 26 before rising again the next day.

However, this 24 May, there is no major disturbance on the foreign exchange market, the parity between the won and the dollar is maintained at 0.00089:

Chapter 2

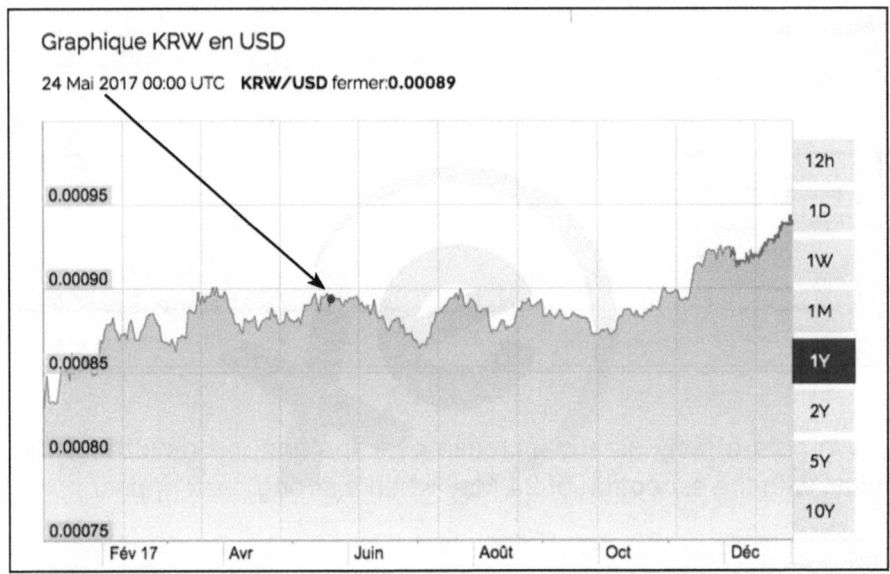

Source: www.xe.com

What is the reason for this sudden spike in bitcoin? Can a South Korean news event be the cause? We look at what was happening that day: economically, no news seems to justify the jump. However, the day before, the army fires more than ninety cannon shots against what appears to be an unidentified flying object from North Korea. The incident, undoubtedly one of the most serious during this period of high tension, is not reported until later, and it is only the next day, therefore the 24th, that the military finally declares that it was only balloons probably carrying propaganda. Nevertheless, the South Koreans may believe during a day that the war has begun. Like in Zimbabwe, does the prospect of war make people turn to bitcoin?

This could be an explanation, as well as for the sharp rise in prices from November onwards, which continues unabated till the end of the year despite threats of government regulation, and while rumors and preparations for war continue to grow, including in early January 2018 when the international press reveals that Chinese troops are gathering around the Yalu and Tyumen rivers and that villages on the border have been designated to receive North Korean refugees.

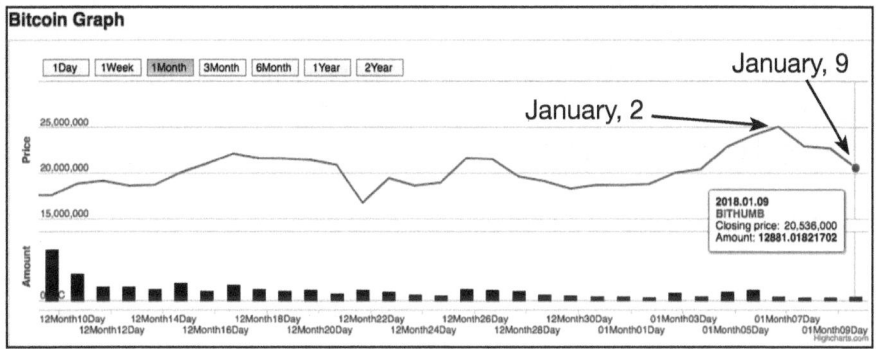

Source: Bithumb

The fact that bitcoin is at its lowest on one of the main South Korean exchanges, with a downward trend on January 9, could confirm the relationship between geopolitics and cryptocurrencies, as it is the day when the two Koreas meet for negotiations. That said, there are probably other parameters to take into account, and there is still insufficient hindsight to attempt any analysis. Especially since the latest news regarding the government ban is contradictory, but without doubt contributes to the decline in recent days. Indeed, Reuters reports on January 11, according to what the Minister of Justice says, that the government plans to ban the trading of cryptocurrencies, and that police raids have taken place against exchanges on the grounds of tax evasion. Faced with a dramatic drop in prices, the office of the Presidency takes corrective communication in the following hours and announces that the ban is only one of the measures envisioned, but that it has yet to be finalized. Prices remain above 30% of the world average.

It is obvious that a complete ban would cause prices to fall, not to mention the other consequences, but, as Reuters states, "once a bill is drafted, legislation for an outright ban of [the trading [of cryptocurrencies] will require a majority vote of the total 297 members

Chapter 2

of the National Assembly, a process that could take months or even years."[166]

Wisdom comes with time, Reuters reports on January 31 that Kim Dong-yeon, the Minister of Finance, says that the government does not plan to go as far as China and "there is no intention to ban or suppress cryptocurrency (market)," the immediate task remaining the regulation of exchanges.[167]

---

166. *South Korea plans to ban cryptocurrency trading, rattles market*, Cynthia Kim, Dahee Kim, Reuters, 01/11/2018.
167. *South Korea doesn't intend to shut down virtual coin trading: finance minister*, Reuters, 01/31/2018.

Bitcoin, Inflation, GDP and Debt

We have shown that bitcoin has already provided individuals and companies with a safe haven in the event of a political and/or economic crisis. What impact would it have on governments, public accounting, GDP, inflation, etc.?

In itself, bitcoin is not inflationary for a country because, even if it is a means of payment created from nothing, to acquire it, it must be exchanged for a currency or mined, an extremely slow process. As surprising as it may seem, bitcoin might even be better to withstand inflationary pressures than a national cryptocurrency, because its number is limited, which might not be the case of a public digital currency (history has shown how excessive central banks have been in printing money).

On the other hand, it could have inflationary consequences for a country in the event of a sharp rise in its price. Take the example of South Korea, where it is estimated that 20% of global transactions in bitcoin take place. Let us assume, for the sake of simplicity, that Koreans therefore own 20% of the total number of bitcoins emitted, or about 3.2 million units at the beginning of January 2017.

If the price is multiplied by ten in one year, from $1,000 to $10,000, they would also see their wealth multiplied by ten (all other things being equal), which would go from $3.2 billion to $32 billion. They could then decide to take advantage of the situation and, for example, sell 20% of it at the end of the year, i.e. the equivalent in won of $6.2 billion, thus doubling their initial wealth.

If they let the whole amount sleep in their bank accounts, the banks would welcome it. On the other hand, if this money goes directly into the economic circuit, through purchases of goods, services, real estate, etc., it is inevitable that such an amount of money— even if it represents "only" 0.4% of GDP ($6.4 billion out of $1,521 billion, the GDP expected by the IMF for South Korea in

2017) — would have an impact on prices, thus an inflationary effect. This is confirmed by Jim Edwards' article on *Business Insider* about Japan:

"The rise in the value of bitcoin could be adding 0.3% to Japanese GDP growth, according to Nomura analysts Yoshiyuki Suimon and Kazuki Miyamoto.

In a recent note to clients, they argued that the 'wealth effect' on Japanese bitcoin holders is likely to spur consumer spending that will have a measurable effect on GDP."[168]

They estimate it at $851 million, available for "extra-consumption." This analysis goes against what bankers and economists regularly say, who consider that bitcoin is too small to influence the economy, but we think exactly the opposite, at least for Japan and Korea. Indeed, even if "only three of the top 500 online retailers accept bitcoin as payment," according to the article, we consider that this is of little importance when speculation takes precedence over the payment function, because individual investors who have seen their bitcoin assets multiply by two up to ten, or even more, may wish to sell them at least partially, if only to protect themselves from a sudden fall in prices, from which they are not immune and which may occur at any time for multiple reasons. In this case, the national currency becomes a safe haven against the volatility of the cryptocurrency.

In any case, there is no doubt that the Korean authorities should take this economic dimension into account before legislating in an absolutist manner that could be detrimental to the whole country and beyond.

---

168. *Bitcoin could be adding 0.3% to Japanese GDP*, Jim Edwards, *Business Insider*, 01/01/2018.

4) North Korea

To our knowledge, it does not have a national cryptocurrency project. Moreover, what good could it do it given its geopolitical situation? Yet Kim Jong-Un's country occupies a special place in the media when it comes to this subject. Indeed, "for North Korea's rogue regime, the emergence of bitcoin provides new revenue possibilities to get around increasingly stringent sanctions."[169] Mainly in two directions:

A) Mining

According to available data, North Korea is a net exporter of energy. Obviously, the UN's economic sanctions following the development of the nuclear program and the firing of missiles have complicated the situation, both for the export of electricity and the import of petroleum products, now subject to quotas (Resolution 2397). Nevertheless, using the electricity produced to mine bitcoin is tantamount to exporting it free of sanctions, as long as the link between the bitcoin addresses and the origin of their holder has not been established.

Given current cryptocurrency prices, it may be even more attractive to mine bitcoin than to export electricity. Let us try to test this hypothesis, even if it is difficult to obtain reliable and precise data on the subject.

First of all, let us remember that the different technologies to generate electricity do not bear the same production costs. However, in order to be able to compare them, a mathematical tool has been created, the Levelized Cost of Electricity (LCOE), whose objective is to measure the production cost of 1 MWh according to its source. Since there are several LCOE calculation variants, we will use the one published by Lazard Bank in November 2015, generally considered an industry standard. However, it is problematic because it is based on costs in the United States, which are certainly higher than in North Korea. Nevertheless, it is a useful basis for comparison.

---

169. *North Korea's Bitcoin Play*, Dune Lawrence, *Bloomberg Businessweek*, 12/18/2017.

Chapter 2

According to the latest World Bank data, Kim's country produces its electricity mainly from coal, oil and hydroelectricity, but not nuclear. This information should be restated because, normally, since the extension of sanctions, Korea can no longer import as much oil as before; as for nuclear, satellite observations prove that the Yongbyon nuclear power plant has been re-opened, at least since early 2017.

Therefore, we will only retain, from Banque Lazard's table, the LCOEs for these two sources:

LCOE	(USD/MWh)		
Plant Type	Low	High	Average
Coal	65	150	108
Nuclear	97	136	117

As a result, to produce 1 MWh of electricity per coal-fired power plant costs between $65 and $150 in the United States.

We saw in the first chapter that to generate 500 bitcoin in mining revenue over a month, it takes about 4,000 MWh, which gives the following table, built from the previous one:

Mining of 500 BTC	(USD/4,000 MWh)		
Plant Type	Low	High	Average
Coal	260,000	600,000	430,000
Nuclear	388,000	544,000	466,000

Based on the average of the "Average" column for coal and nuclear, the cost to produce 500 bitcoins is around $450,000, which gives the following margin with the bitcoin at $10,000:

	(USD)
Energy Cost	450,000
500 BTCs at $10,000	5,000,000
Margin	4,550,000

To break-even the price of bitcoin would have to go down to $900 — knowing that the LCOE is based on the higher electricity production costs in the United States.

In the price grid for the kWh of electricity sold to South Korean consumers, the highest billing price is $0.62; multiplied by 1,000 to obtain the price of 1 MWh, it gives $620. By multiplying this amount by the 4,000 MWh in our example, we obtain a sale price of $2,480,000. Even if it is obvious that South Korea buys its electricity at a lower price, it is even more evident that North Korea no longer has any interest in selling it to its neighbor, but rather using it to mine bitcoin![170]

This example also applies to any country exporting electricity.

B) Hacking, robbery, ransom

The second reason why North Korea and cryptocurrencies are very present in western media is due to fraudulent transactions. Here is, for example, what Lee Dong-geun, director with South Korea's state-run Korea Internet and Security Agency[171] shared with CNN:

"It is a fact that North Korea has been attacking virtual currency exchanges. We don't know how much North Korea has stolen so

---

170. Note: For the calculation to be complete, the costs of mining should not only include electricity but also depreciation of the equipment, wages, premises, etc. However, these costs should be exorbitant to totally change the conclusion.
171. *North Korea may be making a fortune from bitcoin mania*, Sherisse Pham, CNN, 12/13/2017.

Chapter 2

far, but we do know that the police have confirmed the regime's hacking attempts."

North Korea has also been blamed for the global WannaCry cyber-attack, whose ransom had to be paid in bitcoin, which we presented in Chapter 1. Here is what *Bloomberg Business Week* wrote on December 18, 2017:

"Earlier this year, the cybersecurity company Recorded Future Inc. got a [data cache] from Internet usage in North Korea for the first half of the year. The data showed no bitcoin-related activity until May 17, until Priscilla Moriuchi, director of strategic threat development and previously a cyberthreat manager at the U.S. National Security Agency, when she realized it was mining. The data also showed the trails of users—presumably some of the few members of Pyongyang's political and military elite with permission to access the internet—making purchases using bitcoin."[172]

Bitcoin mining would have thus started a few days after one of the key dates of the WannaCry broadcast, especially active as of May 12. We find questionable to link the two events. It is interesting to learn, however, that North Korean dignitaries make purchases paid in bitcoin; it is a pity not to have any details on which sites in which country or countries. On North Korean websites?

5) Cambodia

In December 2017, the National Bank of Cambodia (NBC) reconfirms that it does not recognize bitcoin as a legal currency, and that it has also informed commercial banks of this fact.[173] On the other hand, it announces in April that it has signed a partnership to develop blockchain technology in order to offer the population a fast, secure and inexpensive money transfer system. This is all the more essential because Cambodia has limited financial and banking infrastructure (for example, there are only a few ATMs),

---

172. *North Korea's Bitcoin Play*, Dune Lawrence, *Bloomberg Businessweek*, 12/18/2017.
173. *Bitcoin Not Recognised by National Bank of Cambodia*, Mom Chandara Soleil, Agence Kampuchea Presse, 01/19/2018.

Sovereign Cryptocurrencies

while the penetration rate of telephones is much higher than that of banks. The immediate objective of using the blockchain technology is therefore to provide simple financial services, rather than offer a national cryptocurrency.[174]

6) Thailand

Thus far, the central bank does not seem to be leading in the use of blockchain technology and even less in the creation of a cryptocurrency, since it announces on 15 August 2017 that a meeting has been held with Vitalik Buterin, the founder of Ethereum. Achievements in this area are therefore not imminent. This is probably due to Thailand's progress with the launch, in January 2017, of PromptPay, a national interbank money transfer and electronic payment system. Here is, for example, what Finance Minister Apisak Tantivorawong had to say:

"For 10 years, we have been trying to change the method of payment from that of a cash society to a digital one. We have taken the first step to a cashless society at last."[175]

PromptPay is first used by the government in a pre-launch phase in December 2016, for the payment of social benefits to the poorest. About two million people have been registered as of January (the total population is around 68 million). The system has been rapidly achieving success, with 7.5 million transactions completed in four months and up to 100,000 per day.[176]

Thailand is also included in our presentation, as one of its major banking groups, Kasikornbank (or KBank), launches a blockchain-based letter of guarantee service in partnership with IBM in 2017. The goal is "through a blockchain-based system, to utilize Smart Contracts integrated onto a transparent ledger to avoid paperwork and process the operation of issuing a letter of guarantee in a transparent ecosystem."[177] Thus, KBank is set to process approximately $9 billion

---

174. *Cambodia taps Japanese blockchain tech for payment system*, Nikkei Asian Review, 04/21/2017.
175. *Thailand rolls out PromptPay money transfer service*, Yukako Ono, Nikkei Asian Review, 01/27/2017.
176. *PromptPay 'a big success'*, Jon Fernquest, Bangkok Post, 06/02/2017.
177. *Major Thai Bank and IBM Co-Launch Blockchain Platform to Settle Letters of*

worth of letters of guarantee this year and by 2018, the bank aims to process five percent of the letters of guarantee through the IBM Blockchain system. The percentage will increase according to the results of this first experiment.

7) Estonia, the European Union and the Eurozone

At the end of August 2017, Estonia announces that it wants to launch its Ethereum-based cryptocurrency, estcoin, as part of its e-Residency program. The problem is that this Baltic country is part of the euro zone, so Mario Draghi, the President of the ECB, reacts unequivocally in the following days:

"I will comment on the Estonian decision: no member state can introduce its own currency. The currency of the Eurozone is the euro."

As a result, the Estonian project is buried before it is born, because none of the nineteen states that have adopted the euro can create a cryptocurrency.

By the end of 2017, the situation has not changed since, according to Carl-Ludwig Thiele, member of the Executive Board of the Bundesbank, the central bank of Germany, the introduction of a sovereign cryptocurrency in the euro zone is still excluded, in any case, "for the moment," he states, before adding:

"There is, however, a vast debate on the advantages of digital currencies issued by central banks in a closed system, such as the prototype that we developed with the Deutsche Börse (German stock exchange). (...) The issue here is to explore the relevance of bitcoin technology for the settlement of payments and securities transactions."[178]

In his interview, he does not fail to point out that bitcoin is highly volatile and speculative. The European Banking Authority anyway has warned consumers about the dangers of virtual currencies as early as December 2013.[179]

Guarantee, Joseph Young, *The CoinTelegraph*, 08/10/2017.
178. *Bundesbank-Vorstand warnt vor Investitionen in Bitcoins*, Handelsblatt, 12/23/2017.
179. *Warning to consumers on virtual currencies*, European Banking Authority, 12/12/2013.

8) Sweden

Although part of the European Union, it has not adopted the euro and does not intend to do so in the near future. This is why it can authorize the creation of companies with a capital in bitcoin, as we have seen in the case of Brave New World Investments and its activities in Iran.

Sweden is considered one of the most advanced countries in the replacement of fiduciary money:

"At the end of 2016, more than 5 million Swedes (over 50% of the population) had installed the Swish mobile phone app, which allows people to transfer commercial bank money with immediate effect (day or night) using their handheld device (...).

The demand for cash is dropping rapidly in Sweden (...). Already, many stores no longer accept cash and some bank branches no longer disburse or collect cash. These developments are a cause for concern for the Riksbank [the central bank]."[180]

As a result, it is working on the project of an e-crown, which could appear within five years. Blockchain technology is part of the technical options, but no solution has been validated yet, as they are still under review. Depending on the choice, the e-crown would be more like a digital currency than a cryptocurrency, in the strict sense of the term.

Meanwhile, Sweden remains a host country for fintech-related activities. A platform has even been created, following the experience of the pioneer Brave New World Investments, in order "to guide individuals and companies who want to start and operate [a] Swedish company with cryptocurrency [and] without a Swedish bank account."[181]

The country could also become one of the most important in mining, especially after the decisions of China, whose farms will have to migrate. Sweden has already seen the first foreign operators relocate and set up, for which it has undeniable advantages: its political and

---

180. *Central bank cryptocurrencies*, Morten Linnemann Bech et Rodney Garratt, Bank for International Settlements, 09/17/2017.
181. http://bolag-utan-bank.se

economic stability, an ecosystem already largely oriented towards fintechs, a cold climate that naturally cools mining machines, and cheap electricity, thanks in particular to its hydroelectric power stations.

Mining, the New Eldorado

Sweden is not alone as a promising market, as Cui, founder and leader of a major mining pool in China, with more than 100,000 machines, told the *South China Morning Post* in November 2017: "Many of us have already paid a visit to Vietnam, Laos, Thailand, Russia and the US, negotiating electricity prices with local authorities and buying sites for future use. The business blueprint is bound to go overseas, even if there's only a 1 percent possibility that China's crackdown against bitcoin would extend to mining."[182] That was in November 2017; since then, 1% has become 100%, with China deciding in January 2018 to end mining activities on its territory.

This could, and indeed should, lead to lower bitcoin prices because until all facilities are relocated, there are risks that transactions will be validated in significantly longer periods of time due to the lack of processing capacity—it is estimated that China accounts for 60% of bitcoin operations. However, it should also be noted that the authorities did not act overnight, information circulated sufficiently in advance to give large organizations like Cui's the time to anticipate and move to other more welcoming destinations.

If there is an impact, it will occur almost exclusively to the bitcoin, because most other currencies do not require as much computing power and can be performed on "simple" computers, provided however that they have an adequate graphics card. In short, ether can be mined by a private individual, this is almost no longer the case for a bitcoin.

In addition to the countries that are positioning to replace China, the province of Quebec highlights its many assets, quite similar to

---

182. *China's bitcoin miners, wary of tighter government scrutiny, make plans to move overseas*, Sarah Dai, *South China Morning Post*, 11/18/2017.

Chapter 2

those of Sweden. David Vincent, Hydro Québec's development manager, explains that more than thirty-five potential customers have come to get information, and that he receives one solicitation a day, as demand has exploded. These customers' needs would represent nearly 70% of Hydro Québec's total generating capacity under development. Indeed, while the Montréal Canadiens hockey stadium requires 5 megawatts and a data center needs 30 to 60 megawatts, 200 to 300 megawatts must be supplied to each of the five largest mining farms in the world, currently in negotiations with Hydro Quebec.[183]

However, this situation poses a problem: industrial capacities need time to be amortized, and there is no guarantee that bitcoin mining will last long enough in such proportions. What then will happen to the power generation facilities?

The case of Iceland may also be sobering: HS Orka, a local producer of energy from geothermal energy, forecasts that electricity consumption in the country in 2018 to mine bitcoin will be 840 GWh, compared to only 700 GWh for all Icelandic households.

In any case, there is no doubt that China's decision will change the map of the mining world and perhaps rebalance the value of currencies among themselves, with other consequences in the world of cryptocurrencies that are still impossible to determine with certainty.

---

183. *Quebec Lures Cryptocurrency Miners as China Sours on Industry*, Aaron Stanley, CoinDesk, 01/10/2018.

Sovereign Cryptocurrencies

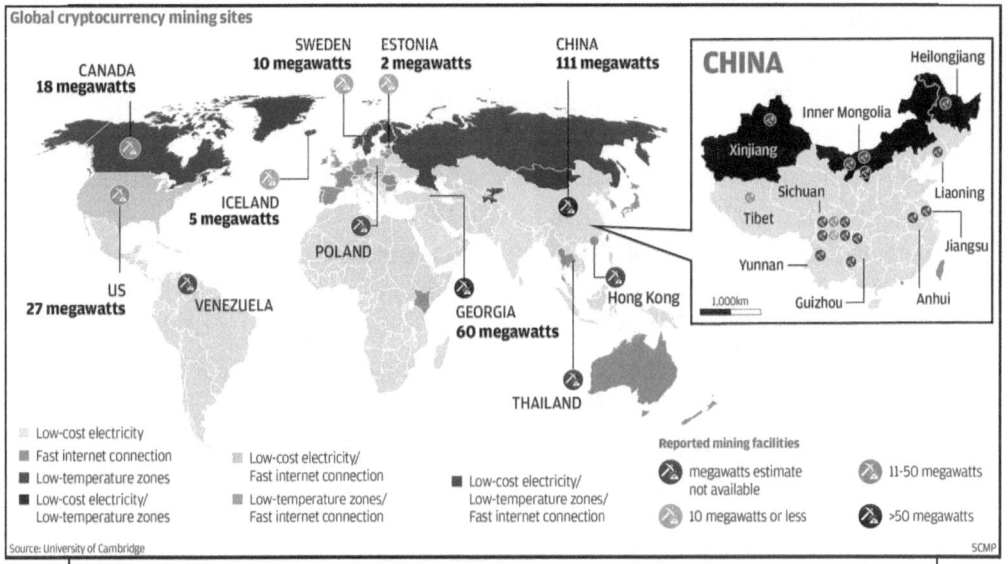

This map from the Cambridge University shows that countries with a competitive advantage in mining bitcoin are Canada, Iceland, Scandinavia and Russia (from west to east), as they benefit from cheap electricity, low temperatures and fast Internet connections.
(Note that indicated electricity consumptions are already out of date.)

It should also be noted that it is not common to witness industrial relocations from China to countries with higher labor costs. It is also because mining requires few staff, being mainly a capitalistic activity.
In fact, if the Chinese had really wanted to strike a fatal blow to bitcoin, they would have done otherwise, and could have gone even further, in banning, for example, the manufacture and export of miners.

9) Belarus

Resolution No. 279 of the National Bank of the Republic of Belarus of 11 July 2017 authorized banks to use blockchain technology for the transfer of bank guarantees.[184] They could already have a node of the blockchain network, especially since the technology has spread widely since 2008, as indicated by the central bank.

It also announced that the next step would be the implementation of the blockchain on the stock exchange, at the JSC Belarusian Currency and Stock Exchange, which "will create conditions for improvement of transparency and further development of the stock market in the Republic of Belarus."

At this point, the use of the blockchain technology does not include cryptocurrency transactions. The step is taken on 21 December 2017, when the office of President Alexander Lukashenko informs that a law on the digital economy has been signed, authorizing, among other things, transactions in cryptocurrencies on national territory.[185]

The ambition is great since it is announced that "Belarus will create an unprecedented regulatory environment for the circulation of cryptocurrencies and tokens."[186] The aim is to attract high-tech companies specialized in the field, by offering them a welcoming legal framework, including for ICOs. Important step, they will operate in part under British law, without comparison with Belarusian legislation, stemming from the former Soviet Union.

Even individuals are encouraged to get involved, as they "are entitled to possess tokens, perform mining, exchange tokens, buy and sell them for Belarusian rubles, foreign currency and e-money, as well as to present and bequeath tokens. The mining activity of individuals, tokens purchasing and sale shall not be considered entrepreneurial activity."

---

184. *The information network based on the blockchain technology was built up in the Republic of Belarus*, press release from the National Bank of the Republic of Belarus, 07/19/2017.
185. *Belarus adopts crypto-currency law to woo foreign investors*, Andrei Makhovsky, Reuters, 12/22/2017.
186. Media Kit of the decree, p. 5.

Cryptocurrencies thus even become exchangeable for currencies available on the local exchange markets, and all transactions will be tax exempt for the next five years, until January 2023.

These decisions are likely to attract new foreign IT investors[187], a field in which Belarus has been diversifying for several years. However, no project to create a national cryptocurrency has been announced yet.

This new law clearly has a geopolitical dimension, as the media kit presenting the measures includes a section called "14 Questions About The New Law On The Digital Economy," the last of which is formulated as follows: "Will Ukrainian and Russian IT companies relocate to Belarus?" Here is the answer in the document:

"It is important that Ukraine and Russia, our neighboring countries, [closely follow] the adoption of this Law. Each country has its own problems, which are reflected in the IT sector. In Russia, there are sanctions. (...) According to the latest crunchbase.com report, US investments in the Russian IT sector have fallen to zero. In Russia, a lot of high-level discussions on supporting IT and adopting legislation on blockchain were held. However, no legislation was introduced.

Ukraine has another problem—frequent searches of IT companies' offices. Worth mentioning—the recent case [being] ForkLog seizures[188].

With the adoption of the Law, conditions are being created in Belarus, which are unprecedented in the region. It may also be a good opportunity for IT companies in neighboring countries. It would be possible, for instance, to have a company's head office in Belarus, with the developers based in Russia or Ukraine. Given the simplification of the procedure for recruiting specialists from other countries, the relocation of entire teams to our country would not be a problem either."

This text presents no ambiguity.

---

187. IT for "Information Technology."
188. See on next page.

Chapter 2

The ForkLog Case in Ukraine

This company is the largest Russian-language online media covering the latest news and trends about cryptocurrencies and blockchain (www.forklog.net). On December 18, 2017, it publishes the following article:

"At 8 a.m., December 15, agents of Ukraine's Security Service (SSU) along with two civilian witnesses to the search entered Anatoly Kaplan's, founder and CEO of ForkLog online magazine, rented apartment in Odessa and conducted a search of the premises. (...) The alleged reason for the search was a criminal case involving a group of Ukrainian and US nationals who engaged in fraudulent activities with bankcards.

According to SSU, the suspects "have been exchanging bitcoin to hryvna (Ukrainian national currency) using online service 'ForkLog'. Representatives of the magazine were shocked and bewildered over these claims, since neither the main website, nor other associated resources have ever provided such services and do not even possess or run the required software.

Furthermore, none of the suspects were proven to have any connection with ForkLog or its founder. Neither does ForkLog offer any 'assistance' with such kind of activities.

While searching Mr. Kaplan's apartment, the SSU agents confiscated his laptop, several cold storage devices as well as other personal belongings.

Moreover, according to Mr. Kaplan, one of the agents tried to immediately transfer bitcoins to another address right in the middle of the search. The agent was stopped only after Mr. Kaplan's lawyer called the police, alarming them about what looked like an obvious robbery attempt.

However, already the next day a large amount in ETH was transferred from Mr. Kaplan's wallet to a newly created address. Additionally, Mr. Kaplan reported a failed attempt by an unknown party to withdraw 3,000 hryvnas (around $110) from his personal bank card."

The article continues with a statement from the ForkLog CEO:
"I believe that this strange situation perfectly illustrates one of the possible scenarios for the relationships between authorities and the crypto community. That is why we decided to make it public. It's not as much about protecting my personal interests as it is about protecting the interests of the entire community. This should send a warning to [anyone] who is in any way related to blockchain technologies."

At the same time ForkLog's Odessa office was also being searched, with the seizure of all available cash and expensive equipment (10 iMacs).

Artem Afian, Juscutum lawyer firm's managing partner and lawyer of ForkLog, "insists that this incident bears particular significance for the crypto community at large. (...) The latest wave of searches in IT companies' offices and personal homes of the industry's figureheads started as early as 2015, when more than 2,500 highly qualified professionals were forced to leave Ukraine. One of the most illustrative cases was the raid on the apartment belonging to Michael Chobanian, founder of Kuna Bitcoin Agency's and co-founder of Bitcoin Foundation Ukraine. The alleged reason for the raid was a criminal investigation pertaining to bitcoin trade information located on Kuna's website."

The country pays the consequences of this situation, as Artem Afian declares:

"According to various sources, [the] IT sector in Ukraine has lost approximately $40 million due to law enforcement pressure. Damages related to destruction and seizure of expensive equipment amounted to $9 million.

Recently, due to the exponential growth that crypto industry has been demonstrating in 2017, SSU also started targeting operators of mining farms, even though mining is not illegal in Ukraine."

At the end of December 2017, Pavel Lerner, General Manager of Exmo, an exchange, is kidnapped by strangers while exiting his office. His release is obtained after the payment of a $1 million ransom, according to various sources.

No doubt that with such actions, Belarus should quickly be considered by Ukrainians as a cryptocurrency paradise.

10) Ukraine

After reading the ForkLog case and the new Belarusian digital law, it is logical to want to look at the Ukrainian authorities' position on cryptocurrencies. In one month, three bills have been submitted to Rada, the Ukranian Parliament:

    a) On October 6, 2017, a group of deputies, in cooperation with the Ukrainian Blockchain Association, platforms and miners, proposes that cryptocurrencies should not be considered as means of payment but as goods that can be exchanged for other goods and services; that all transactions should be fully legalized; that mining should be legally recognized; and that owners should be free to dispose of their portfolios as they see fit. It is also proposed for the National Bank of Ukraine (NBU) to act as the regulator of the crypto market.[189]

The article adds that the NBU has not yet taken a position on the issue, with one of its representatives confirming that they observe what is happening abroad, with "countries treating them differently, some forbid, some regulate, some do not regulate."

    (b) The second text is submitted on 10 October and entitled *On the stimulation of the market of cryptocurrencies and their derivatives in Ukraine*, Bill No. 7183-1. The head of the Parliamentary Committee on Financial Policy and Banking proposes to recognize cryptocurrencies as a financial asset:

"It makes no sense to reinvent the wheel and invent new rules for it. The most effective model is the adaptation of cryptocurrencies to the already existing legislation. That is why we propose to recognize cryptocurrency as a financial asset."[190]

Exchanges will still need to obtain a license for their activities. A second part of this bill aims to stimulate mining.

---

189. *Ukraine Proposes Law to Completely Legalize Cryptocurrency Transactions*, Kevin Helms, Bitcoin.com, 10/10/2017.
190. *Ukraine's New Bill Treats Bitcoin as Financial Asset and Encourages Mining*, Kevin Helms, Bitcoin.com, 10/19/2017.

(c) On October 30, Project No. 7246, submitted by the Committee on Tax and Customs Policy, requests to amend the tax code to exempt profits from the purchase and sale of cryptocurrencies and from mining. The following note accompanies the text:

"In order to create an effective mechanism for stimulating the market of cryptocurrency in Ukraine, the logical step is the exemption from taxation of profits of enterprises... Income from cryptocurrency operations should not be included in the calculation of the total monthly (annually) taxable income, and transactions with cryptocurrency and mining crypto goods are classified as transactions that are not subject to taxation."[191]

Overall, it appears that Ukrainian authorities are rather favorable to the development of cryptocurrencies, as confirmed by the Minister of Finance on October 16:

"There are many open issues and in Ukraine the status of cryptocurrency is not defined by law, but this does not mean that cryptocurrency is prohibited. Ukraine should monitor world trends and not miss a chance to use new technologies and innovations in the financial sector."[192]

On November 28, at a session of the Kiev City Council, deputies decided "to petition the country's President, Parliament, and the National Bank of Ukraine regarding support for fintech startups and crowdfunding," so that they do not have to go abroad and Ukraine starts developing a sovereign cryptocurrency. Thus, "Igor Ovadychy—a deputy of the Kiev City Council—said that creating a cryptocurrency will signal to the world community that the country is an open and innovative state."[193]

On January 11, 2018, the National Bank of Ukraine reported in a Facebook post, that it is studying "new and innovative technologies,

---

191. *Ukraine Drafts Law to Exempt Crypto Income and Profits from Taxation*, Kevin Helms, Bitcoin.com, 11/03/2017.
192. *Ukraine's New Bill Treats Bitcoin as Financial Asset and Encourages Mining*, Kevin Helms, Bitcoin.com, 10/19/2017.
193. *Ukraine to Develop National Cryptocurrency? Kiev City Council Deputies Hope*, Miguel Gomez, Cryptovest, 11/28/2017.

as part of the country's so-called Cashless Economy project, of which the potential e-hryvnia is a part." But the NBU drew a distinction between a digital currency and a state-issued cryptocurrency:

"However, the National Bank would like to specify that what is meant here is the possible introduction of an electronic hryvnia, not our own cryptocurrency."[194]

Indeed, the solution of the blockchain is not retained, "at least for now," although the reflection continues. At the same time, in response to the legislation proposed in October, it is announced that a working group will be created to study the consideration of cryptocurrencies in Ukrainian law.

11) Switzerland
How can we not end our tour of Europe with the country of banks and foundations? In fact, our visit will be short: there is no national cryptocurrency in preparation, no specific legislation, no specific prohibition as long as the laws are respected, notably on money laundering and terrorist financing. However, "the Swiss National Bank (SNB) itself closely monitors and analyses the development of encrypted currencies and maintains a dialogue with market participants, regulators and other central banks on this subject."[195]

Similarly, the FINMA (the Swiss Financial Market Supervisory Authority) is scrutinizing the growing number of ICOs and has already stopped projects that it considers to be potentially fraudulent. Like almost everywhere, authorities and bankers have already warned the public against the dangers of bitcoin and cryptocurrencies.

Nevertheless, Switzerland aims to position itself as a world center for blockchain and cryptocurrency technology. The Canton of Zug is known for its attractive tax policy and now as the "Crypto Valley," an ecosystem that wishes to attract fintechs from all over the world. Several major players have already established themselves there, including Bitmain, the Chinese mining leader, Bitcoin Suisse AG and the Ethereum Foundation.

---

194. *Ukraine Wants A National Digital Currency, Not Its Own Cryptocurrency*, William Suberg, The CoinTelegraph, 01/12/2018.
195. *Le bitcoin commence à envahir la Suisse*, Philippe Rodrik, *Tribune de Genève*, 08/25/2017.

Many other foundations are joining Switzerland, as notes Swissinfo:

"These legal structures were largely set up in Zug to house crowdfunding campaign products, which raised seed capital for global fintech companies. In the first half of the year [2017], about a quarter of the $1.2 billion raised worldwide by ICOs—a new way for start-ups to raise money in exchange for tokens entitling them to their products—ended up in these Swiss foundations."[196]

Before leaving Switzerland, we should mention a rare experiment that was launched by SBB, the Swiss Federal Railways, on 11 November 2016, which allowed the possibility to buy bitcoins on more than a thousand ticket machines accessible in stations 24 hours a day and even to pay for "purchases without a credit card or a bank account in more than 10,000 points of sale throughout the world."[197] For those who wish to know more about how this solution works, read the article *Blockchain : Nous avons testé le distributeur de bitcoins des CFF*, by Charles Kangnivi Azanlekor, in the link in footnote.[198]

12) Brazil

On 8 July 2015, Bill PL 2303/2015 is introduced by the deputy Áureo, whose summary reads as follows:

"Provides for the inclusion of virtual currencies and air mileage programs in the definition of 'means of payment' under the supervision of the Central Bank."[199]

After a process through various committees, the Presidency of the House makes the decision on May 23, 2017 to create a Special Commission "to give an opinion on the Draft Law No. 2303." The deputy Expedito Netto is appointed rapporteur.

On November 16, 2017, Banco Central do Brasil issues an "alert on risks arising from custody and trading operations of so-called virtual

---

196. *La Suisse se rêve en centre mondial des cryptomonnaies*, Matthew Allen, Swissinfo, 08/31/2017.
197. Source: www.sbb.ch.
198. https://fr.linkedin.com/pulse/blockchain-nous-avons-test%C3%A9-le-distributeur-de-des-azanlekor-pmp
199. Câmara dos Deputados, PL 2303/2015.

Chapter 2

currencies."[200] Nevertheless, the statement ends as follows:

"Finally, the Central Bank of Brazil affirms its commitment to support financial innovations, including those based on new technologies that make the financial system safer and more efficient."

Eventually, the principle of the blockchain is not excluded.

On December 12, Jonatas Ramalho, its executive director for digital business, declares during a hearing before MPs in the framework of the bill PL 2303/2015:

"A possible regulation of the market of virtual currencies, like bitcoin, could allow for an environment more conducive to the use of these products, reduce risks, favor consumers and enable the participation of financial institutions."

An interesting and open position, not always shared among central banks.

On 20 December, the statements of the deputy Expedito Netto, rapporteur of the Special Commission on cryptocurrencies, are presented on the website of the Chamber of Deputies:

"I defend the ban on the issue of cryptocurrencies on the national territory, as well as their marketing, intermediation and as a means of payment. They may continue to circulate by mutual agreement, but, according to the text, companies that buy and sell bitcoin, for example, can be charged for a crime."[201]

This text is added to the Criminal Code. At most, it allows "the possibility of issuing a cryptocurrency for use in a restricted environment, under the responsibility of the issuer, and only for the acquisition of goods and services offered by the issuer or by third parties." The future looks bleak for cryptocurrencies in Brazil.

But it does not take long for responses to come, first from the deputy Áureo, the author of the bill, who states that "this is not what we want for Brazil." Then, the President of the Commission, the deputy Alexandre Valle, announces that the rapporteur was hasty and that he himself would not present a bill that has not been further

---

200. Comunicado n° 31.379, Banco Central do Brasil, 11/16/2017.
201. *Relator quer proibir emissão de moedas virtuais*, **Câmara dos Deputados**, 12/20/2017.

developed on such a "very important" subject. The House website adds that "in addition, unlike the report, MP Thiago Peixoto (PSD-GO) presented a separate vote and argued that, contrary to the ban, it is necessary to create conditions for Brazil to benefit from the use of virtual currencies."

On 12 January 2018, "the Comissão de Valores Mobiliários (CVM), which regulates financial markets in Brazil, decides to ban the direct purchase of virtual currencies such as bitcoin by regulated investment funds registered in the country."[202] The CVM considers that "cryptocurrencies can not be considered as financial assets," hence this prohibition.

It seems that, despite the sometimes contradictory positions expressed during this legislative process, Brazil will end up adopting regulations favoring the development of cryptocurrencies. It is currently considered as the fourth largest market for transactions worldwide. As for the creation of a sovereign virtual currency, it is not yet relevant.

13) Mexico

It presents a particular legislative situation, with the Law to regulate financial technology institutions, known as the "Fintech Law." Prepared with all stakeholders in the sector, it includes three areas: electronic payments, collective financing and virtual assets, which deal with cryptocurrencies. On this third part, Mexico's originality comes from Article 30: it stipulates that they may be used as means of payment provided that they have been previously entered on a list drawn up by the Central Bank of Mexico. It will have 25 months to prepare it after the implementation of the law.

December 5, 2017, the Fintech Law is passed unanimously by the Senate and then must be approved by the Chamber of Deputies. Many professionals want it to be definitively ratified before the end of December, but the vote cannot take place before the next legislature to start in February 2018.

---

202. *CVM proíbe fundos de investir em Bitcoin e outras criptomoedas*, Darlan Alvarenga, *Globo*, 01/12/2018.

The stakes of this law are high, at least on three levels:

- according to the Comisión Nacional Bancaria y de Valores, only 39% of the population has access to traditional banking services;

- according to the Inter-American Development Bank, the Mexican fintech sector is the second largest in Latin America, after Brazil, with between 200 and 300 companies;

- Mexico is the fourth country in the world to receive the most remittances (see box p. 106), with an estimated $30 billion for 2017. If the transfers were made via blockchain systems, this would represent several hundred million dollars more received by beneficiaries and injected into the economy.

It now remains to be seen how the deputies will vote in favor of this law, and what criteria the National Bank will use to draw up the list of cryptocurrencies that can be used as means of payment. Will it be extended to a large number of values or limited to a few? In any case, there are no immediate plans to create a national cryptocurrency.

14) Argentina

Let's recall that it is ranked first in the Bitcoin Market Potential Index (BMPI), a tool presented in the introduction of this chapter.

Indeed, given the evolution of its economy and currency, restrictions on foreign exchange and an annual inflation rate of over 25%, the population is rapidly adopting bitcoin as a means of payment, including in daily life.

According to the *Panam Post*, in July 2014 the first bitcoin ATM is installed in a restaurant in Buenos Aires.[203] During the same month, the Unidad de Información Financiera (UIF) publishes in the Official Bulletin its Resolución 300 on money laundering and the financing of terrorism, which requires financial and banking institutions to report monthly transactions carried out in cryptocurrencies as of 1 August—businesses are not concerned.[204] The declarations must

---

203. *Instalaron el primer cajero automático de bitcoin en Argentina*, Belén Marty, *PanamPost*, 09/08/2014.
204. *Prevención del lavado de activos y de la financiación del terrorismo*, Resolución 300/2014, Unidad de Información Financiera, 07/04/2014.

be entered online before the 15th of each month on the UIF website (www.uif.gob.ar). For the purposes of this resolution, "virtual money" means the digital representation of a security which may be the object of digital commerce and whose functions are to constitute a means of exchange, and/or a unit of account, and/or a store of value, but which is not legal tender, is not issued and guaranteed by any country or jurisdiction. At the same time, BCRA (Banco Central de la República Argentina) issues a statement confirming that cryptocurrencies "are not legal tender" in the country.

Nevertheless, it is in Argentina that the launch of the Crypto Assets Fund, Latin America's first private investment fund in bitcoins, ethers, litecoins, ripple, dash, etc. is announced in July 2017.

Even if it does not directly concern the cryptocurrencies, let us note an original initiative of the BCRA, which informs on May 4, 2017:

"(...) To have authorized from that day forward the installation of ATMs by non-bank entities. In this way, the current network of nearly 20,000 ATMs owned by financial entities can be extended with devices installed by supermarkets, gas stations or any other commercial entity, which can even be recharged with the banknotes they have collected.

Today, Argentina has a lower penetration rate of ATMs than neighboring countries. In fact, 20% of communities in the country do not have an ATM, which forces their inhabitants to travel to obtain money."[205]

Four months later, it is announced that two thousand ATMs compatible with cryptocurrencies are to gradually be installed in the country.[206]

However, it did not seem since this authorization that the central bank announced the creation of a national cryptocurrency.

---

205. *El BCRA impulsa la instalación de cajeros no bancarios*, Banco Central de la República Argentina, 05/04/2017.
206. *Instalarán en el país 2000 cajeros automáticos compatibles con criptomonedas*, Andrés Krom, *La Nación*, 09/14/2017.

15) Colombia

On 29 August 2017, R3, the company that developed the Corda platform, announces in a press release that it has signed an agreement with the Central Bank of Colombia (Banco de la República Colombia—BRC) to enable it to discover and experiment with the latest advances in blockchain technology. The Director of Technology at the BRC confirms that "it is in our interest to test the benefits of this technology for the safe and efficient management of securities exchange in the Colombian financial system"[207]

The central bank then confirms that "this participation has nothing to do with the creation or the transaction of cryptocurrencies."[208] Apparently, Colombia is not yet on this path, but a first stone has been laid.

16) Peru, Chile, Paraguay and others

The other Latin American countries are more or less at the same level, with warnings published by the authorities as those already presented in the previous pages, central banks that follow the evolution of the situation, possibly begin to study the principle of the blockchain, but, in the immediate future, there is no officially declared project to create a national cryptocurrency.

17) Namibia

In this part of Chapter 2, we have not yet passed through Africa. Let us start in Windhoek, the capital of Namibia, because it has a particularity: the Bank of Namibia Act (1997) recognizes the Namibian dollar as legal tender, but also the South African rand. Both currencies are therefore legal tender in the country, but the reverse is not true in South Africa, which is Namibia's largest economic partner. This is facilitated by the fact that both countries belong to the Multilateral Monetary Area, which also includes Lesotho and Swaziland.

---

207. Banco de la República Colombia se vincula con R3 para fomentar innovación financiera, R3, 08/29/2017.
208. *"Sabemos que Banrep se ha acercado a empresas de bitcoin y Blockchain": Fundación Bitcoin*, Dinero, 12/19/2017.

For the record, Namibia is a former German colony conquered by South Africa in 1915, which received the mandate of administration by the League of Nations in 1920. Integrated as a fifth province, it begins the fight for its independence in the 1960s (creation of the SWAPO—South West African People's Organization), and obtains it in 1990, after a long armed conflict that also involves Cuban troops and the People's Armed Forces of Liberation of Angola. On March 21, 1990, the day of the proclamation of independence, President Samuel Nujoma declares:

"Africa's last colony is, from this hour, liberated. (…) The destiny of this country is now fully in our own hands. We should, therefore, look forward to the future with confidence and hope."

In September 2017, the Bank of Namibia, its central bank, publishes a paper entitled *Position on Distributed Ledger Technologies and Virtual Currencies in Namibia*.[209] We find in it the usual opinions that monetary institutions usually hold on cryptocurrencies that we have already presented. Let us note, however, the end of Article 3.8.2:

"The bank however understands that virtual currencies, when exchanged for legal tender / fiat currency can be used to facilitate payment transactions, remittances and many other financial services. However, due to the lack of a legal premise, the bank is unable to endorse such activities in Namibia at the moment."

But Article 3.10.3 states:

"(…) Although the potential risks and implications are not entirely clear and fully understood, this technology is seen to have the potential [to transform] financial sector infrastructure and consequently, the operations.

The Bank intends to conduct further research on the plausible uses distributed ledger technologies and establish a position accordingly."

So, wait and see.

---

209. *Position on Distributed Ledger Technologies and Virtual Currencies in Namibia*, Bank of Namibia, 09/2017.

18) Swaziland

A former British colony, this absolute monarchy of 17,363 km² and about 1.4 million inhabitants proclaims its independence on September 6, 1968. Its currency is the lilangeni, but like in Namibia, the South African rand is legal tender. South Africa is also its largest economic partner. Life expectancy is barely fifty years, among other reasons because Swaziland has the highest AIDS rate in the world, with more than a quarter of the adult population affected (source: CIA World Factbook 2012).

According to the *Swazi Observer* of October 31, 2017, although the Central Bank of Swaziland (CBS) remains cautious about the use of cryptocurrencies, its governor, Majozi Sithole, says that they are evaluating the possibility of using them in the future:

"It may not be wise to dismiss virtual currencies and as the CBS we are learning and we want to accept and support innovation. If this is innovation, we do not want to stifle it. We want to learn more about it. Even with Mobile Money it took time for us to know what it [was] and we liaised with countries that [had] succeeded at it."[210]

Indeed, such a small country, almost without fintech, can hardly develop a cryptocurrency project alone, despite all the benefits it could derive from it. We will return to this in the next chapter.

19) The East African Community (EAC)

Founded in 1967, dissolved in 1977, and re-created in 2000, it forms a set of six countries with a total population of approximately 170 million people spread across Burundi, Kenya, Rwanda, South Sudan, Tanzania (where the EAC headquarters are located) and Uganda. It is a common market, a customs union, but cooperation also covers other plans, including, eventually, the constitution of a political federation.

In November 2013, the five member states—South Sudan joins in 2016—sign a memorandum of understanding for the constitution within a decade of a monetary union, with a central bank and a

---

210. *CBS Cautious, but Assessing Possibility of Embracing Cryptocurrencies*, Majaha Nkonyane, *Swazi Observer*, 10/31/2017.

common currency. The goal is to increase economic exchanges and attract international investors to create prosperity for all.

On January 2, 2018, the *Daily News*, Tanzania's leading newspaper, interviews the country's central bank (BoT) "on the threat of [the] growing use of digital currencies to the region's intention to have a single currency to be used across its six member [states]."[211] Bernard Dadi, Tanzania's Central Bank Director of National Payment System, explains that the process for the adoption of a common currency is still ongoing, despite new challenges that have appeared, such as the development of cryptocurrencies. He recalls that African central banks, as well as others, have warned people against the dangers of bitcoin. He also tells the reporter that the Bank of Tanzania will soon issue a directive on its use in the country and that British experts in cryptocurrencies have organized workshops on these issues for the management team.

It is therefore still too early to know what will be the future currency of the East African Community, or even if it will be based on the blockchain, but given current developments in the world, it could constitute one of the first common cryptocurrencies for a group of countries that have renounced their national currency. This justifies the fact that this is at least a medium-term project.

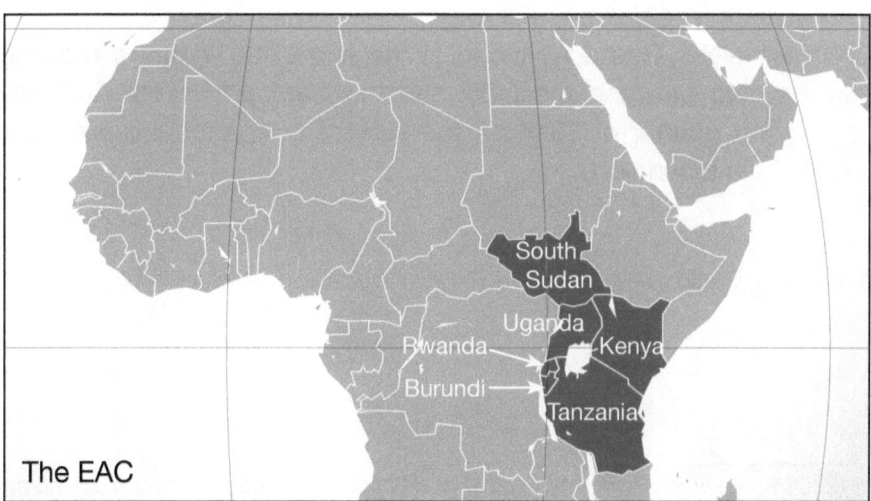

---

211. *EAC wary of surrogate coins*, Sauli Giliard, *Daily News*, 01/02/2018.

20) Kenya

The EAC common currency project, which Kenya is a part of, does not prevent its central bank from developing national initiatives, as it is believed that the experience gained could also be used by the entire community. In an interview with *Standard*, the country's leading daily, Patrick Njoroge, governor of the Central Bank of Kenya (CBK), begins by warning once again, as they did in 2015, about the dangers of bitcoin and other cryptocurrencies, which could be pyramid schemes. Kenya is also considered one of the four most important African countries for bitcoin, along with South Africa, Nigeria and Ghana. The governor also mentions the risk of a bubble, money laundering, financing of terrorism, etc. He acknowledges, however, that "these cryptocurrencies are using a technology known as blockchain. There may be a future for blockchain. We are working with our peers around the world on things that could lead to using this technology in particular ways."[212]

He does not give more details, but the launch of a national cryptocurrency is logically not a priority for the CBK because, on the one hand, it participates in the creation of the common currency of the EAC and, on the other hand, Kenya is one of the countries in the world where mobile payments have been the most developed for many years (see box on next page).

Nevertheless, it is announced at the end of 2017 that a meeting will be held between the CBK and the Capital Markets Authority in the first quarter of 2018 on the subject of cryptocurrencies and blockchain technology.

---

212. *CBK Governor Patrick Njoroge warns Bitcoin rush could be pyramid scheme*, Otiato Guguyu, *The Standard*, 11/25/2017.

The Fabulous Success of Kenyan Mobile Payments

In March 2017, Kenyan telecom operator Safaricom celebrates ten years of its mobile payment platform M-Pesa. The success is unprecedented:

"In a country with few banks but where 54% of the population has a mobile phone, the initial results far exceed expectations. In eight months, M-Pesa has gained 1 million customers and that number triples by June 2008. Today, the application claims to have 30 million regular users worldwide, including 18 million in Kenya, representing 70% of the country's adult population."[213]

The system consists of loading money to the telephone through a network of over 100,000 agents, also present in rural areas where there is no bank, which may be, for example, the supermarket or the telephone shop. Originally designed to facilitate access to microcredit, the service now makes it possible to:
- deposit and withdraw money
- transfer money to other users
- pay bills
- purchase airtime
- transfer money between the service and, in some markets like Kenya, a bank account.[214]

Other services are gradually being added, such as M-Shwari, which allows to create a savings account and earn interest, and to use microcredit.

"In ten years, M-Pesa has fundamentally transformed Kenya's increasingly digital economy, with faster, more secure and, above all, traceable transactions. A study by the Massachusetts Institute of Technology estimates that 2% of Kenyans have been lifted out

---

213. *Mobile banking : une success-story nommée M-Pesa*, Laure Broulard et Mark Anderson, *Jeune Afrique*, 04/03/2017.
214. Source: Wikipedia.

> of poverty through mobile microcredits. According to Safaricom, the platform has generated some 860,000 jobs and about $1 billion in economic activity."[1]
>
> The General Manager of M-Pesa says his company contributes 6.5% of Kenya's GDP.
>
> Since its inception, the service has been extended to Tanzania, South Africa, Mozambique, Lesotho, Egypt, Afghanistan, India and Romania.
>
> ---
>
> 1. *Mobile banking : une success-story nommée M-Pesa*, Laure Broulard et Mark Anderson, *Jeune Afrique*, 04/03/2017.

21) Mauritius

In a speech on November 3, 2017, Ramesh Basant Kings, Governor of the Central Bank, warns against cryptocurrencies and declares that "there is now an acceptance slowly emerging that if digital currencies are to be issued, central banks should necessarily be the issuer. But it is also recognized that the risks associated with digital currencies are far from minimal."[215]

Nothing suggests in his statement that the island could have a cryptocurrency soon, or use the blockchain. That being said, the central bank is one of the oldest in sub-Saharan Africa to have adopted electronic payment and real-time transactions, starting in 2000. Other initiatives are also under development, such as the National Payment Switch, which offers benefits for card payments, including reduced fees and speed.

In fact, SBM (State Bank of Mauritius), a private bank, announces in October 2017 that it has signed a partnership with Secured Automated Lending Technology (SALT) to enable its customers to provide their bitcoins and ethers as security for their loans. It is an original and interesting approach.

---

215. *Governor of the Bank of Mauritius warned people for cryptocurrency*, Ujjainee Chakraborty, UITV, 11/04/2017.

22) Australia

On December 13, 2017, Philip Lowe, Governor of the Reserve Bank of Australia (RBA), speaks at the Australian Payment Summit:

"(...) Today I want to share with you some of our thinking about this future and to address a question that I am being asked increasingly frequently: does the RBA intend to issue a digital form of the Australian dollar? Let's call it an eAUD.

The short answer to this question is that we have no immediate plans to issue an electronic form of Australian dollar banknotes, but we [continue] to look at the pros and cons. At the same time, we are also looking at how settlement arrangements with central bank money might evolve as new technologies emerge.

As we have worked through the issues, we have developed a series of working hypotheses."[216]

The last one deals with the use of the blockchain, which raises a number of questions, including the consequences it would have on the financial system; indeed, the role of the banks would be reduced to the point of putting them in danger. Here is how the Governor concludes:

"We do not see a case for the RBA offering every Australian a bank account for the purposes of making payments. Doing so would fundamentally change our banking system in a way that would not promote the public interest.

A convincing case for issuing Australian dollars on the blockchain for use with limited private systems has not yet been made. It is certainly possible that this type of system could lead to more efficient, lower-cost business processes and payments. My working hypothesis here is that such a case could develop, although we need to work through a range of complex operational and policy questions.

As we work though these various issues, we look forward to an ongoing dialogue with the payments industry and other interested parties."

An Australian cryptocurrency is thus far from being planned, nor even acquired in principle.

---

216. *Address to the 2017 Australian Payment Summit*, Philip Lowe, Reserve Bank of Australia, 12/13/2017.

23) New Zealand

In a speech on cybersecurity in July 2014, Toby Fiennes, Head of Prudential Supervision at the Reserve Bank of New Zealand (the central bank), states that "we're working with other agencies, such as the FMA and Ministry of Business, Innovation and Employment, to ensure that New Zealand presents an environment where digital financial innovation can flourish, provided it is done safely."[217]

In November 2017, it publishes on its website an analytical study, which in the conclusion states:

"Cryptocurrencies and blockchain technology could well become an important part of global payment systems, but wide-scale adoption will depend on competition from alternative transaction technologies, and on regulation to provide users with security. Crypto-currencies will also need to address technical, scalability issues if they wish to [be the intermediary of] the volume of transactions undertaken globally."[218]

This is obviously a problem that cryptocurrencies will face, namely the number of transactions to process permanently. When the authors of the study talk about "alternative transaction technologies," they think, among other things, of the Snapper solution, introduced in Wellington in 2008. It is a contactless electronic card using the NFC (Near Field Communication), rechargeable by telephone, which makes it possible to pay for bus tickets and other services of daily life, such as food, bars, taxis, etc. Snapper has already been existing for ten years and its mode of operation is interesting (www.snapper.co.nz).

At the beginning of December, Grant Spencer, Governor of the Central Bank (RBNZ), declares in an interview on a New Zealand television channel that the bitcoin constitutes a bubble, etc. On the other hand, he goes on to say:

---

217. *Reserve Bank outlines stance on cyber issues*, Reserve Bank of New Zealand, 07/19/2017.
218. *Crypto-currencies – An introduction to not-so-funny moneys*, Aaron Kumar, Christie Smith, Reserve Bank of New Zealand, Analytical Notes, 11/2017.

"I think digital currencies, cryptocurrencies, are a real and serious proposition for the future. I think they are part of the future, but not the sort that we see in bitcoin," he said. "I think a cryptocurrency that has a more stable value will be the sort of cryptocurrency that's more useful for the future."[219]

The article also tells us that the RBNZ is doing research about the New Zealand dollar and the possibility of replacing it with a digital alternative.

24) Vanuatu

Like Swaziland, it is not common for this country of about eighty islands in the southern Pacific Ocean to be featured in books and media dealing with international finance, even though it has been an offshore financial center since 1972—but that's what *Newsweek* did in October 2017:

"The Pacific island nation of Vanuatu has become the world's first country to accept the virtual currency bitcoin for its citizenship program.

The Vanuatu Information Centre (VIC) announced that its Development Support Program (DSP) [would] allow foreigners to qualify for Vanuatuan citizenship through a one-time payment of $200,000—or its cryptocurrency equivalent."[220]

At the time of the article, this represented just over forty-three bitcoins. Because Vanuatu belongs to the British Commonwealth, this citizenship has many advantages: the ability to travel visa-free in one hundred and twenty-five countries, including the European Union, Russia, as well as tax benefits, not to mention the beauty of these islands.

Newsweek quotes Geoffrey Bond, president of the VIC, as saying:

"In this case, the government of Vanuatu has explicitly expressed a desire to be at the forefront of adopting new technologies, officially encouraging the VIC to receive payments in bitcoin."

---

219. *Bitcoin 'Looks Remarkably Like A Bubble,' New Zealand's Central Banker Warns*, Matthew Brockett, Bloomberg, 12/09/2017.
220. *Bitcoin Now Buys You Citizenship in Pacific Nation of Vanuatu*, Anthony Cuthbertson, *Newsweek*, 10/09/2017.

All bitcoin transactions for Vanuatuan citizenship will be run through an Australian cryptocurrency exchange, which complies with requirements imposed by the Australian financial regulations."

Also reproduced in the article are the statements from a press release, where Christian Nesheim, an investment migration specialist and advisor to the VIC [states]:

"Many early investors in bitcoin would like to realize some of their earnings without incurring large capital gains taxes. Ideally, then, they would convert their cryptocurrency into tangible assets in a low-tax jurisdiction (...) As Vanuatu will now be the only country to offer citizenship for bitcoins, I think the program will see a surge in interest more or less immediately."

This information is repeated in other media, but a few days later, Samuel Garae, Acting Secretary General of the Vanuatu Citizenship Office, declares them false, and that the citizenship program would only accept the dollar as a payment currency.[221] Was the Vanuatu government pressured into retracting their offer? In any case, the explanations that followed were not clear on what appeared to be a complete reversal of the situation.[222]

---

221. *Vanuatu Citizenship Office: Bitcoins? What are those? Dollars please*, Vila Times, 10/17/2017.
222. *Vanuatu Government fails to explain the "bitcoin screw-up"*, Vila Times, 10/19/2017.

Evaluation and Taxation of Cryptocurrencies

This is the question that concerns most legislators around the world: are bitcoin and its digital cousins currencies or financial assets? The answer has major consequences, particularly on the tax rates to be applied, but not only.

We are obviously not going to deal with this in depth in these pages, but since the OECD is seized of the matter, we recommend that the portfolios of cryptocurrencies that companies have built up be valued in their balance sheets at their acquisition cost or at the value of the day of receipt (for payments), and not at their price on the last day of the fiscal year, because this could totally distort the results and generate a tax to pay too high if the prices have risen significantly in the meantime and they were to later fall.

Our remark amounts to considering that the real value of a (private) cryptocurrency can only be determined when it is sold or used as a means of payment.

We therefore think it desirable not to impose tax and accounting rules that could penalize companies in their strategy and management of these values at volatile prices, for example by pushing companies to sell them at an inappropriate time, because the tax that they are subject to would not be fair in its calculation and valuation methods.

It should also be noted that a company may end up with a portfolio of bitcoins or ethers, or even future sovereign cryptocurrencies, without the intention to speculate but simply because some of its customers abroad or locally have opted for this payment method.

Chapter 2

IV. Countries where bitcoin is illegal

Following the bankruptcy of Mt. In Gox in February 2014, many countries issue warnings about the dangers of bitcoin and cryptocurrency speculation, without however normalizing transactions or totally prohibiting them. Let us now turn to those who have gone the furthest in the prohibitions.

1) Egypt and the Muslim world

Before January 1, 2018, the country of the Pharaohs would have appeared in the previous category. Since then, Egypt has changed dramatically. Let's summarize the events:

- June 2017: information is widespread that the Central Bank may allow cryptocurrencies to circulate and be traded, which it denies quickly after.

- August 2017: two entrepreneurs announce that they will launch the exchange Bitcoin Egypt by the end of the month, the first in the country. According to one of the founders, bitcoins have so far been sold over the counter, on the black market, and there are barely a few hundred people active on a daily basis, from online forums[223] (Localbitcoins.com lists, in fact, less than ten sellers/buyers for Egypt). He adds that those registered on Bitcoin Egypt will have to provide their contact information:

"We will only be doing it to deter potential money launderers from abusing anonymity on our exchange, and to of course be roughly prepared for any future regulations set by the Egyptian government."

- August 23: "The Central Bank of Egypt (CBE) said that it has no intention of passing a law or issuing legislation to allow the trade of cryptocurrencies in Egypt. An official at the CBE said in a statement that the bitcoin—a famous kind of cryptocurrency—is not officially recognized in financial and banking transactions and that the sale of bitcoins in exchange for Euros or US dollars would be considered a crime."[224] At the same time, one of the founders of Bitcoin Egypt

---

223. *First Bitcoin Exchange Launching in Egypt*, Kevin Helms, Bitcoin.com, 08/11/2017.
224. *CBE has no intention of allowing cryptocurrency in Egypt: official*, Reem Hosam El-din, *Daily News*, 08/23/2017.

explains to the journalist that they expect the government to put the appropriate legislation in place, as they cannot operate for the time being. He states that "cryptocurrencies will be a reality soon, whether the Egyptian government agrees to be part of it or not."

- January 1, 2018: Egypt's Grand Mufti, Shawki Allam, [confirms] that "it is not permissible to trade, purchase or sell 'bitcoin' currency as it poses many risks to people; the currency may lead to fraud or falsifying its value. (…)

He [stresses] that he [has] met with economic experts to reach a final decision regarding the bitcoin by analyzing its effect on the economy. (…) Consequently, Allam [says] that based on what was mentioned the terms required for any money circulation are not available in bitcoin as it does not have a physical form and it leads to fraud in its banks and value, resembling it as counterfeit money. In this regard, bitcoin is forbidden in Islamic Sharia as it leads to more corruption, because it is a decentralized and anonymous system and difficult to trace who gave how much to whom."[225]

From the moment when the Grand Mufti speaks out against it, it seems almost impossible that civil authorities of the country do not follow, which they have already expressed at least since the summer of 2017.

Now that bitcoin is prohibited under Islamic Sharia, the repercussions of this *fatwa* go far beyond Egypt's borders and could extend to the entire Muslim world and its 1.5 billion believers, including in Asia. It should be noted, however, that this statement had no impact on the prices of the main cryptocurrencies, which are much more sensitive to what happens in Japan or Korea. In any case, given that blockchain and cryptocurrency technology is revolutionizing the global payment system, there is a strong chance that these declarations will become inaudible in the near future.

However, Muslim countries, including Morocco, Algeria and Bangladesh, ban bitcoin to varying degrees without having based their decisions on religious principles.

---

225. *Bitcoin leads to fraud in its banks, value: Grand Mufti*, Egypt Today, 01/01/2018.

2) Morocco

In November 2017, the web host and Internet company MTDS declares that it accepts bitcoin as a means of payment, a first in the Kingdom. The Foreign Exchange Office and the Central Bank replies by press release that all transactions carried out in cryptocurrencies are prohibited and will be punished by fines. Therefore, no business can accept bitcoin or any other virtual currencies as payment for goods and services.

It is nevertheless estimated that the equivalent of $200,000 is exchanged every day in Morocco.[226] The Localbitcoins.com site shows that there are offers to buy and sell in most major cities, mainly in Casablanca, the economic capital. Indeed, using bitcoin or ether as a means of payment is prohibited, but not speculation, provided that the extremely strict exchange regulations in Morocco are respected. Given current bitcoin prices, buying it in foreign currency requires circumventing the law, but the size of the Moroccan diaspora is undeniably a solution, against whom the authorities will find it difficult to fight.

Given Morocco's particularities, it seems to us that they should seriously examine the situation and consider the creation of a national cryptocurrency, notably for geopolitical reasons. We will come back to this in Chapter 3.

3) Algeria

The position of the authorities is definitely clear, as an article[227] of the 2018 Finance Bill states that "the purchase, sale, use and holding of the so-called virtual currency, are prohibited. The virtual currency is the one used by Internet users through the web. It is characterized by the absence of physical support such as coins, tickets, payments by check or bank card. Any breach of this provision is punishable in accordance with the laws and regulations in force."[228]

---

226. *Bye-Bye Bitcoin: Morocco Bans Cryptocurrencies*, Morocco World News, 11/21/2017.
227. Initialy Article 113, which became No. 117, after amendments.
228. *Crypto-monnaies : Le gouvernement algérien dit non !*, Lyes Bensid, Cap Algérie, 11/23/2017.

This Finance Bill is voted on November 26, 2017 and signed by the President of the Republic on December 27. It is the subject of several amendments, but not on the text banning virtual currency, which is therefore adopted. Indeed, even mining is now impossible, since it is paid in cryptocurrencies and their possession is officially prohibited.

A first consequence is the departure of the startup KodePay, which has to cancel the launch of its virtual bank and its cryptocurrency:

"I wanted to launch my business at home in Algeria, but the law has become so tough that we had to look elsewhere. In Kenya, they opened their arms to us," explains one of the two founders.[229]

Indeed, this country of the Maghreb does not look like the paradise of the fintechs. However, during the CARE conference (Circle of Action and Reflection on the Society) which is held on November 20 in Algiers on the theme *The contribution of blockchain and cryptocurrency to the digital economy in Algeria*, it is stated:

"Cryptocurrencies exist in Algeria and their use is important: there are more than 300,000 transactions that are made every day, which represents about 60,000 users. So do not ban cryptocurrencies. On the contrary, it is necessary to create a national one to enable Algeria to move from a cash-based economy to a digital economy."[230]

The current power does not seem to have heard the message. For things to change, we will probably have to wait until 2019 and the result of the next presidential election.

4) Bangladesh

With 170 million inhabitants for 143,998 km^2 of land, of which 105,000 are occupied by the Ganges delta, this country with a Muslim population of 90% is one of the most densely populated in the world. Despite difficult weather conditions and one of the lowest per capita incomes, Bangladesh has annual growth prospects above 5%. Did it take into consideration that it might be able to take advantage of the

---

[229]. *Start-up de la semaine : déboutée de l'Algérie, la cryptomonnaie de KodePay met le cap sur le Kenya*, Nelly Fualdes, *Jeune Afrique*, 01/04/2018.
[230]. *300.000 transactions se font en crypto-monnaie chaque jour en Algérie* (CARE), Amar Ingrachen, *Maghreb Émergent*, 11/20/2017.

cryptocurrency phenomenon to accelerate its development? Here is the answer, according to a statement from AFP[231] on September 15, 2015:

"Bangladesh's central bank has warned against dealing in bitcoin, saying anybody caught using the virtual currency could be jailed under the country's strict anti-money laundering laws.

The Bangladesh Bank (BB), which regulates the impoverished country's banking industry, said it issued the order after the local media reported on bitcoin transactions carried out through various online exchange platforms. (...)

Bank officials told AFP separately that anyone found guilty in Bangladesh of using bitcoin could be sentenced up to 12 years in jail."

Indeed, supposedly enough to deter offenders. Yet this is not enough, and two years later, at the end of December 2017, it has to issue the same warning because "transactions in cryptocurrencies like bitcoin, ethereum, ripple and litecoin are being made on exchanges in Bangladesh."[232] Contacted by the media, the spoke-person of the BB confirms that "the bank issued the notice so that no one makes transactions in cryptocurrencies under any circumstances." That is definitely clear. It remains to see if this will be enough to do away with the transactions now banned.

A few weeks earlier, the Vice-Governor of the Central Bank declares at the Digital World Summit 2017 in Dhaka, the capital of Bangladesh, that "the matter of the issuance of cryptocurrency by the central bank in the country still needs lots of research as it has both good and bad sides. We are seriously thinking about it. (...) An inter-operative platform [made up] of the central bank as well as other public private bodies will be formed by June next year [2018] with a view to expediting the penetration of digital currency in Bangladesh."[233]

Then, all what people have to do is wait.

---

231. Source: AFP, in *Why Bangladesh will jail bitcoin traders*, The Telegraph, 09/15/2014.
232. *Bangladesh Bank warns against transaction in 'illegal' bitcoin, other cryptocurrencies*, Abdur Rahim Harmachi, bdnews24.com, 12/27/2017.
233. *Bangladesh to expedite introduction of digital currency*, Shariful Islam, *Dhaka Tribune*, 9/12/2017.

5) Vietnam

It is a different situation from the countries presented so far, in particular by what could be akin to internal dissent. Let us see the sequence of facts and positions.

On February 14, 2014, the central bank issues a statement announcing that it does not recognize bitcoin as a legitimate means of payment.

Following the bankruptcy of Mt. Gox (see Chapter 1), a few days later it publishes a new notice prohibiting financial institutions from offering services in cryptocurrencies:

"The statement also refers to warnings issued by other countries: namely Thailand, Russia, France, China, Malaysia, Indonesia, and Norway as evidence the bitcoin menace is international. It doesn't mention, however, that at least two of those countries (France, Malaysia and possibly Indonesia) have chosen to avoid any restrictions on bitcoin for now."[234]

On August 25, 2017, the Vietnamese News Agency (VNA), a public service and official communication channel of the State, announces that:

"Prime Minister Nguyen Xuan Phuc this week approved a plan to scrutinize and streamline the legal framework for the management of cryptocurrencies such as bitcoin in Vietnam.

With this go-ahead, it is expected that such currencies will be recognized legally in the country soon.

The PM has asked the Ministry of Justice to preside and co-ordinate with other relevant ministries and institutions, including the State Bank of Vietnam, Ministry of Information and Communications, Ministry of Public Security, Ministry of Industry and Trade and Ministry of Finance, to scrutinize the current legal framework, provide a comprehensive assessment and propose suitable solutions and revisions in the [governmental] framework.

---

[234]. *Vietnam Warns Against Bitcoin, Invokes the Ghost of Gox*, Jon Southurst, CoinDesk, 02/28/2014.

The assessment must be completed before August 2018, and all legal normative documents on the currencies must be ready by the end of next year, the PM's decision stated."[235]

The article concludes with the following:

"It is expected that once the legal framework for the currencies is finalized, bitcoin and several other cryptocurrencies will be officially recognized in Vietnam, opening up possibilities in financial technology and online payments."

The sun looks bright for this new world. But, on October 30, the central bank issues a notice prohibiting the use of cryptocurrencies as a means of payment from 1 January 2018. "Fines of around US$9,000 apply to those who accept or offer payments in virtual currencies."[236] It is, indeed, a deterrent. On the other hand, exchanges and mining are not forbidden.

On January 6, 2018, the Vietnamese media report that the Deputy Prime Minister however asks the Minister of Justice and the State Bank of Vietnam to accelerate and complete the legal framework governing cryptocurrencies in the country:

"The report on the progress must be submitted to the Government for consideration before the end of January."[237]

At the end of December, the media report that customs has noted the importation of 7,005 miners from January 1 to December 21, 2017:

"Previously, the department announced that it received 98 import declarations for 1,478 mining rigs from January 1 to October 31, valued over $2,182 million (...).

Then, from the beginning of November to December 21, 2017, the number of mining rigs imported into Vietnam jumped by another 5,527, making the total number of rigs imported 7,005 in total. The 5,527 machines were mostly brought in from China through 8 organizations and individuals, the news outlet noted."[238]

---

235. *Government considers recognising bitcoin in Vietnam*, VNA, 08/25/2017.
236. *Vietnam bans bitcoin as payment for anything*, Simon Sharwood, *The Register*, 10/30/2017.
237. *VN needs cryptocurrency laws*, Viet Nam News, 01/06/2018.
238. *Cryptocurrency Mining Soars in Vietnam – Over 7000 Rigs Imported*, Kevin Helms, Bitcoin.com, 01/03/2018.

This means that there are mining farms developed in Vietnam, because 5,527 divided by 8 gives an average close to 700 devices, which is too big an investment for an individual. The journalist added that Customs even questioned officially the State Bank of Vietnam, the Ministry of Information and Communication and the Ministry of Industry and Commerce to know if they should ban the import of this material. "The central bank confirmed that mining rigs for bitcoin and other cryptocurrencies are not related to the use of virtual currency as a means of payment. As such, they are not part of the management functions and tasks of the State Bank."

For now, the mining can continue, while waiting the legislative framework. As for the creation of a sovereign cryptocurrency, no public announcement has been made yet. But until when? (Let us point out, however, that less than 30% of the population owns a smartphone).

6) Nepal

On June 30, 2017, Kedar Prasad Acharya, Deputy Director of Nepal Rastra Bank (NRB), the central bank, says that bitcoin is illegal in this country of just under thirty million people.

A few weeks later, on August 13, the NRB issues a warning prohibiting the use of bitcoin, which is not recognized as a legal currency. As a result, transactions are considered illegal. One of the concerns is that the purchase of cryptocurrencies could lead to the exit of the country's foreign currency reserves.

On October 6, "a police team deployed from the Central Investigation Bureau (CIB) of Nepal Police for the first time arrested seven persons for allegedly running bitcoin exchange business from various parts of the country," wrote *The Kathmandu Post*.[239] A spoke-person from the CIB explains that "if convicted, the accused can face a fine three times the amount in question and a jail term up to three years."

On the same day, the two founders of www.bitsewa.com, Nepal's main cryptocurrencies exchange, suspend their activity (see their

---

239. *7 nabbed for running bitcoin exchange business*, The Kathmandu Post, 10/06/2017.

Chapter 2

October 6 message on their Twitter account); nevertheless they are apprehended, on October 26:

"The Central Investigation Bureau of Nepal Police has arrested two persons for allegedly operating a bitcoin racket in Kathmandu and Pokhara under the cloak of an online technology business."[240]

There is still no new information published on these arrests. Nepal's policy against cryptocurrencies is, in any case, one of the most restrictive.

As for mining, there is no mention of it being prohibited, all the more as various reports show that it has been practiced there for several years. However, mining bitcoin should become more difficult or even impossible, at least for those wishing to start, as this activity requires specific import equipment, which will inevitably attract the attention of the authorities and should at least lead to the confiscation of the equipment. Moreover, what should be done with bitcoins, moneros, etc. received in payment for mining?

There is no mention either of the creation of a sovereign cryptocurrency. Yet, Nepal should study the issue, because it receives a lot of remittances, about $3.5 billion for the fiscal year 2012/2013, equivalent to between 15 and 20% of its GDP, about $21 billion (2016 figure). The gain, in addition to an increased speed of transactions, could be fifty times what the central bank saves by having its banknotes printed in China, as we learnt from Xinhua:

"The quality is as good as the ones that were printed earlier in another country but the cost is less than half of the amount we had earlier paid. (…) Getting 200 million notes printed in China saved the Nepalese central bank 3.76 million U.S. dollars."[241]

---

240. *Two arrested for operating bitcoin racket*, The Himalayan Times, 10/30/2017.
241. *Nepal saves millions by printing banknotes in China*, Tian Shaohui, Xinhua, 02/14/2017.

7) Bolivia

The country of Evo Morales is one of the first to totally ban cryptocurrencies. Thus, the Central Bank of Bolivia (BCB) formalizes the situation with the Resolution of the Directorate No. 044/2014 dated May 6, 2014, Article 1 of which states:

"As of today it is prohibited to use currencies not issued or regulated by states, countries or economic zones, as well as electronic money orders and currency denominations not authorized by the BCB as part of the national payment system."[242]

In April 2017, it issues a statement reminding the population of its resolution of May 2014. It is on this basis that sixty people are arrested one month later, "who, presumably, [are caught] giving training on how to invest money in virtual currencies. [The Autoridad de Supervisión del Sistema Financiero—ASFI] reminds the population that these activities are prohibited throughout the national territory, because they are linked to pyramid schemes whose sole purpose is to seek to appropriate the money and savings of Bolivians."[243]

So even training activities are hunted down. The statement also tells us that leaflets are seized during another operation, and that ASFI, "to date, is preparing a bill that will add pyramid scams to the Penal Code, to thwart and generate the necessary legal instrument for the purpose of combating and punishing anyone who adapts their conduct to such activities."

In the immediate future, there is no reason for the Bolivian sun to shine brighter on the cryptocurrency universe, especially since the repression even extends to the information published on social networks. However, Bolivia and other countries in this section should think about a sovereign cryptocurrency and the use of the blockchain, if only because they receive a lot of remittances but also because they are not among the highest bank account penetration rates in the world.

---

242. Website of the Central Bank of Bolivia.
243. Press release n° 20/17 of the Autoridad de Supervisión del Sistema Financiero (ASFI).

Chapter 3

Geopolitics of Future Cryptocurrencies

In an interview to Bloomberg[244] on November 8, 2017, Michael Corbat, CEO of Citigroup Inc., explains that bitcoin is a sufficiently serious threat to the financial system that the authorities would have no choice but to issue their own versions of cryptocurrency:

"I don't think governments are going to take lightly to other people coming in and potentially disrupting their abilities to manage data, collect taxes, combat money laundering, (...) It's likely that we're going to see governments introduce, not cryptocurrencies—I think cryptocurrency is a bad moniker for that—but a digital money."

We have also thought so for some time now, but not only for the reasons given by Michael Corbat. Indeed, in a world where sanctions can fall on a country sometimes in defiance of international rules, it is inevitable that states may want to protect themselves, i.e. no longer depend on the dollar and Western-dominated financial institutions, such as the World Bank, the IMF, Swift, Visa, MasterCard, etc. It is no coincidence that Venezuela and Russia are among the first countries to move towards the creation of a sovereign cryptocurrency.

Such currencies could be great accelerators of exchanges, and therefore sources of wealth, if the following criteria are respected:
- reliability, which is the basic principle of any currency;
- stability, therefore no or little speculation;
- security, so that hackers cannot gain access to accounts;
- anonymity vis-à-vis the public, but not for the public issuers.

---

244. Article previously quoted.

Chapter 3

A cryptocurrency seems to have little meaning if a single country issues it, although we will come back to this fundamental point in the conclusion. On the other hand, it can become much more important when it is managed by two or more states, because it offers the following advantages:

- no foreign exchange risks between the currencies of the participating countries;
- money will circulate a lot faster compared to the use of still indispensable current intermediaries like banks or money transfer companies. Transactions will be immediate, therefore no more lag time during which banks and central banks hold the funds to the detriment of the payer and the payee, but also no more "weekends," "bank holidays," "cut-off times" or "closing time," "transit time," "local correspondent," "computer bugs," etc.;
- no more expensive international transfer costs, at least transaction fees of a small amount.

In addition, if one of the countries is under international sanctions, a cryptocurrency can help maintain or even save its economy while preserving the anonymity of companies from third countries that trade with it, which keeps external economic exchanges from drying up.

On the other hand, creating and managing a currency between two or more states can quickly become a conundrum, perhaps more complicated than presiding over the creation of the euro, where many countries were involved, which diluted (a little) the power of each, even if Germany carried more weight. Indeed, such a situation inevitably create problems of governance, which, moreover, must be able to evolve and adapt according to the political, social, and economic circumstances of each of the issuing countries. African currency unions are already proving that it is possible with fiduciary money.

In order to illustrate different situations and models, we will present fifteen scenarios for the creation of cryptocurrencies between states. We will limit ourselves to the basic principles, because the detailed study of their implementation would go beyond the scope of this book.

1) BRICS

The BRICS nations (Brazil, Russia, India, China and South Africa) have many reasons why they should be the first group of states to look into establishing a common cryptocurrency, including their economic weight and trade. The idea, however, is making progress because, at the 9th BRICS Summit held in Xiamen (China) September 3-5, 2017, they agreed "to promote the development of BRICS Local Currency Bond Markets and jointly establish a BRICS Local Currency Bond Fund, as a means of contribution to the capital sustainability of financing in BRICS countries, boosting the development of BRICS domestic and regional bond markets."[245]

The project to create a common cryptocurrency is discussed with journalists by Kyrill Dmitriev, head of the Russian Direct Investment Fund: "While there is a focus on settlements in national currencies, cryptocurrencies are also being discussed as one of the possible settlement mechanisms." He adds "that within BRICS cryptocurrencies could replace the US dollar and other currencies used in settlements among the member states."[246]

On December 28, Olga Skorobogatova, First Deputy Governor of the Central Bank of Russia, said at a Russian finance ministry meeting that "the issue of a common cryptocurrency for a number of countries is very promising, more than that for a single nation.

The participants of different economic events [in which] I usually take part... [have] all come to the conclusion [that] the issue of a virtual currency is not [very useful if one country has it on its own]. It therefore makes sense to discuss a cryptocurrency [for] several countries such as the BRICS and EEU."[247] (Eurasian Economic Union: Armenia, Belarus, Russia, Kazakhstan and Kyrgyzstan).

No concrete decision has yet been made, but discussions are scheduled for 2018, and they inevitably will depend on the results of

---

245. 9th BRICS Summit – BRICS Leaders Xiamen Declaration – Xiamen, China, September 4, 2017.
246. *BRICS countries considering own cryptocurrency as settlement mechanism*, Russia Today, 09/04/2017.
247. *Russia suggests creating single virtual currency for BRICS and EEU*, Russia Today, December 28, 2017.

Chapter 3

the Russian presidential elections, which will be held in March 2018 and Brazil's, to take place in October 2018. In addition to Russia, the EEU will also be concerned by the presidential election in Armenia (February 2018). New members should also join—the next one should be Iran. India, already a member of BRICS, as well as Turkey and Pakistan, are also candidates. If these countries manage to create a common virtual currency, it would carry a weight gradually approaching that of the dollar, or in the least the euro.

However, given the economic, development and infrastructures disparities between them, the creation of a cryptocurrency of this scale is necessarily a medium to long-term project. It seems logical that it should be implemented in several stages, so as not to risk upsetting the vigor of the various economies, perhaps on a bilateral (China-Russia) or trilateral basis with Brazil and / or South Africa, as a first step, or within the EEU.

The first step could be to study a cryptocurrency similar to the SDR (Special Drawing Rights), an international monetary instrument created by the IMF in 1969 and consisting of a basket of currencies revalued every five years. It would promote state-to-state payments, possibly involving large companies and those carrying out import-export transactions, before later being extended to the whole populations.

2) The Russian-speaking area
In Chapter 2, we indicated that the project to create the CryptoRouble had the ambition to go beyond Russian borders, as confirmed by Olga Skorobogatova and cited above. Beyond the Russian-speaking EEU countries, an area seems even more suitable for sharing CryptoRouble: Novorossiya, the People's Republics of Donetsk and Luhansk. The bulk of their foreign trade is now with Russia, so having a common means of payment would probably increase exchanges. Moreover, since war began in Donbass, about 1.2 million people have fled to Russia. For those who will stay there after the war, the power of the blockchain technology would allow them to send money to

their relatives without going through the banking system, with all that this implies in terms of speed and economy.

For obvious geopolitical reasons, it is impossible for CryptoRouble's expansion to Novorossiya to be more than a whisper until it is formally declared that the Minsk Protocol is to be torn apart and that both republics will definitely remain independent.

Even if it is not being talked about does not mean it is not being prepared, as well as its deployment when the day comes, especially since bitcoin and its digital cousins have demonstrated that it is easy to implement cryptocurrencies without worrying about borders, even in the most extreme conditions, such as in Zimbabwe.

CryptoRouble could also be developed beyond Russian-speaking countries, for example in Syria, or even in Yemen and Libya, which would have enormous advantages over the traditional banking system: the "only" thing to do would be to rebuild telecommunication lines, where they had previously been destroyed, so that a means of payment could be made available. Nonetheless it is not as simple as that because the implementation process will have firsts to be defined, including the conditions of access, parity with the local currency, etc. Moreover, all members of the community must have smartphones.

CryptoRouble could also prove to be a formidable weapon in the economic conquest of Africa—where the Chinese have taken a significant lead—including among Russia's long-standing allies, such as Algeria. Indeed, it would encourage exchanges, always for the same reasons already mentioned. One of the vectors of dissemination would be African students pursuing studies in Russian institutions and universities, which can accommodate up to 200,000 per year. CryptoRouble would be the ideal way to send money across oceans. As for the 15,000 foreign scholarship holders hosted by the Russian State in 2017 (Study In Russia figure), to receive payments in the new cryptocurrency should not give rise to any debate.

3) Africa

In the previous chapter, we presented the situation and position of several African countries in regards to cryptocurrencies; in fact, the entire continent should be a fertile land for them, for several reasons:

- Remittances: according to the African Development Bank, more than $65 billion were sent to the continent in 2016 by its diaspora. However, as we have shown above, blockchain and cryptocurrency technology has major advantages for money transfers compared to conventional banking tools and even those of specialists such as Western Union, MoneyGram, etc. The amount of fees paid is also a strain on remittances, because fees for certain destinations can exceed 10% of the amount sent, a cost higher than for any other continent.

- Low bank account penetration rate: it is estimated that one in five households holds a bank account. "The account penetration rate varies greatly, ranging from 1.5% in Niger, 5% in the Central African Republic, DR Congo and Guinea, to more than 25% in Côte d'Ivoire and up to 80% in Mauritius (UNCTAD, 2016). Several kinds of barriers to financial integration exist. The physical distance of banks explains why a majority of the rural population does not have access to their services."[248] Pierre Jacquemot, the author of this article, reports that telecom networks are spread throughout villages while banking agencies are absent, preferably present in large cities.

- The growth of the smartphone penetration rate is high: according to various estimates, more than 350 million devices will be in service by the end of 2018, for a total population of 1.2 billion inhabitants.

- E-banking and mobile banking are experiencing faster growth than any other continent: "In this area, sub-Saharan Africa is showing good health. Financial digitization is spreading and the innovations we encounter are sometimes spectacular. According to the World Bank, 10% of adults possess an account that allows them to carry out financial transactions from their mobile phone, versus only 1 to 2% on average on other continents. This wave of mobile finance is

---

248. *L'Afrique, épicentre de la bancarisation numérique*, Pierre Jacquemot, Iris, 12/20/2016.

part of a revolution already joined by startups labeled "fintech." They mobilize a third of the investments allocated to African companies in new technologies."[249]

- The impact that the launch of cryptocurrencies, and inherently the economy, will have on commercial banks will be far less than their impact in northern countries, where they could definitely falter if they no longer have the virtual monopoly they currently have over collecting funds.

Even if the continent has many assets to make cryptocurrency prosper, it does not seem like a Pan-African bitcoin can be created in the near future. The conditions for its creation can, however, be progressively prepared, starting, for example, with a standardized, common regulatory framework, at least by zones, before extending it to the whole continent. Then it is up to the countries to work together to develop their common cryptocurrency. The WAMU (West African Monetary Union) and CEMAC (Economic and Monetary Community of Central Africa), which share the CFA franc between their respective member states, seem to be the first to be able to create a collective cryptocurrency. They even constitute a model for monetary governance, which has been rather immune to political uncertainties.

On the other hand, even though the ECOWAS (Economic Community of West African States) announces at its February 2018 summit in Accra, Ghana, that it wants to develop a new roadmap for the creation of the ECO, the single currency of the zone by 2020, this declaration raises a few questions: indeed, ECOWAS comprises sixteen member countries (+ Mauritania, which has an association agreement), and create a common currency, whether digital or not, for so many countries with such drastic economic disparities is complicated—if the final result is a sort of euro on the African continent, it would be better to think twice about it. However, Ghana's declaration of wanting to use the ECO from 2020 is promising[250],

---

249. *L'Afrique, épicentre de la bancarisation numérique*, Pierre Jacquemot, Iris, 12/20/2016.
250. *Ghana : Création de la monnaie unique de CEDEAO, les critères*, Mensah, Koaci, 02/21/2018.

and in the meantime perhaps the project could be studied first with Gambia, Sierra Leone and the Liberia of George Weah, three of the poorest countries in Africa. When the ECO has increased exchanges and proved successful, then it could be expanded to other states of the region.

We will not present all the opportunities of the continent, but let us start with two regional groups, then follow with suggestions bringing peace and development before going to other countries.

4) The East African Community (EAC)

In Chapter 2, we presented this group of six states, with a total population of about 170 million people, including Burundi, Kenya, Uganda, Rwanda, South Sudan and Tanzania.

In November 2013, the EAC members create a monetary union, but the process for adopting a common currency is still ongoing. Rather than go through the fiduciary phase, why not directly create a shared cryptocurrency, which would, overall, create fewer problems for its implementation, including logistics? In the beginning, it could circulate as a complementary national currency.

In addition, deployment would be facilitated by the fact that most EAC citizens are already accustomed to mobile payments. Another major advantage would be to reduce the costs of remittances, which are important for each of the member countries.

5) The Multilateral Monetary Area and Southern Africa

Formerly called the "Common Monetary Area," it becomes the Multilateral Monetary Area (MMA) in 1992 when Namibia joins South Africa, Lesotho and Swaziland. This area has a feature that is unique to the planet: the South African rand is legal tender in the other three countries, alongside national currencies—the Lesotho loti, the Swaziland lilangeni and the Namibian dollar.

The creation of a cryptocurrency could happen faster in the MMA than in the EAC. It remains to be seen what the position of South Africa's central bank (the South African Reserve Bank) would be and the part of power it would agree to share with its counterparts, the three other countries in this joint project—unless a "RandCoin," a purely South African cryptocurrency, is created and adopted by all.

The disadvantage of this solution would result in it being more difficult to export, for example to countries like Botswana, which is part of the Southern African Customs Union (SACU) along with the four other countries of the MMA, which it decided not to join. It could also be gradually extended to one or more countries of the Southern African Development Community (SADC), which has fifteen members, including five from SACU, plus Angola, the Democratic Republic of Congo, Madagascar, Malawi, Mauritius, Mozambique, Seychelles, Tanzania, Zambia and Zimbabwe. Let us note that as Tanzania is part of the EAC, it would open a door to this geopolitical set that has planned for a common currency.

SACU and SADC[251]

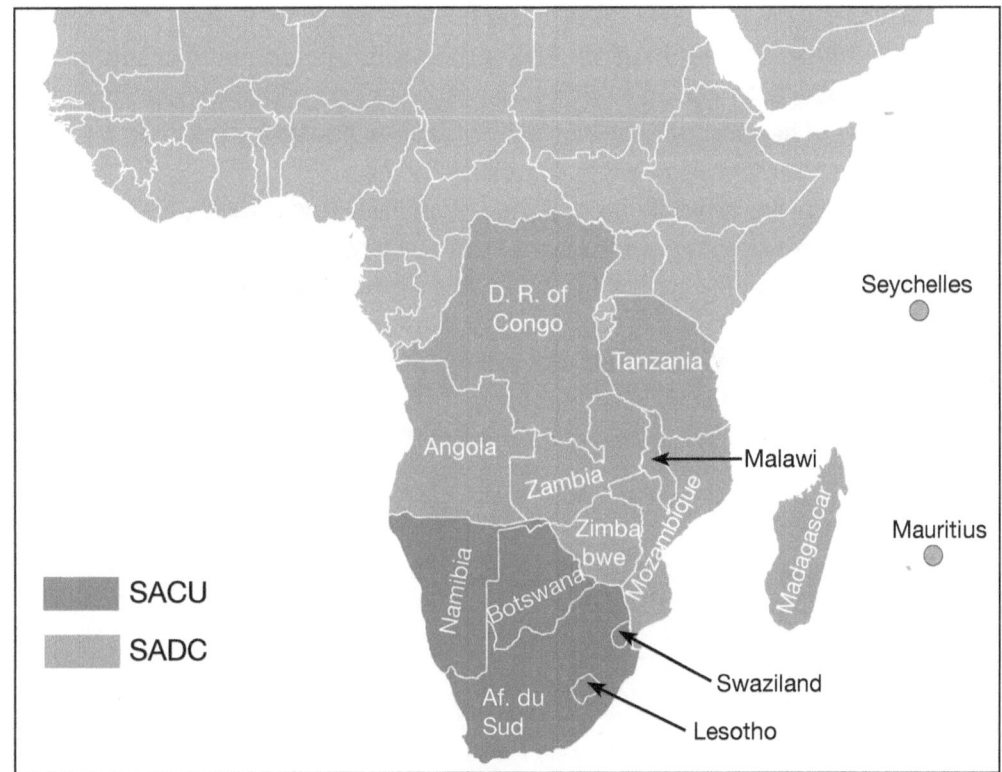

251. Source: Wikimedia Commons, Treehill.

6) Western Sahara and the Arab Maghreb Union (AMU)

Created in 1989, the AMU includes Algeria, Libya, Morocco, Mauritania and Tunisia. In reality, this Union has had virtually no influence for more than ten years, due to disputes, mainly between Morocco and Algeria over Western Sahara. It is an area of 266,000 km^2, including 1,200 km of Atlantic coast between Morocco and Mauritania, and bordering Algeria to the east. A long time Spanish colony, the Madrid Accords signed on November 14, 1975 formalized the retrocession of the Western Sahara: two-thirds to Morocco and one third to Mauritania.

In response, the Polisario Front, movement born in 1973 as the armed struggle against Spanish colonization, proclaims on February 27, 1976 the creation of the Sahrawi Arab Democratic Republic (SADR) throughout the territory. Supported by Algeria, it triggers attacks against Morocco and Mauritania to bring about its demand for independence.

A peace treaty is signed on August 10, 1979 with Mauritania, which cedes its part to the Polisario Front. Four days later, Morocco announces the annexation. The armed struggle continues, and, for its defense, Morocco erects what is called "the Wall of Sands," a barrier of separation between the two zones constituting the de facto border, the Polisario Front controlling the east.

A cease-fire is proclaimed at the end of 1991 and is followed in 1992 by a referendum organized under the auspices of the United Nations to decide definitively the status of this former Spanish colony. Since then, it is regularly postponed. In the meantime, Western Sahara is considered as a "Non-Self-Governing Territory" by the UN.

Western Sahara[252]

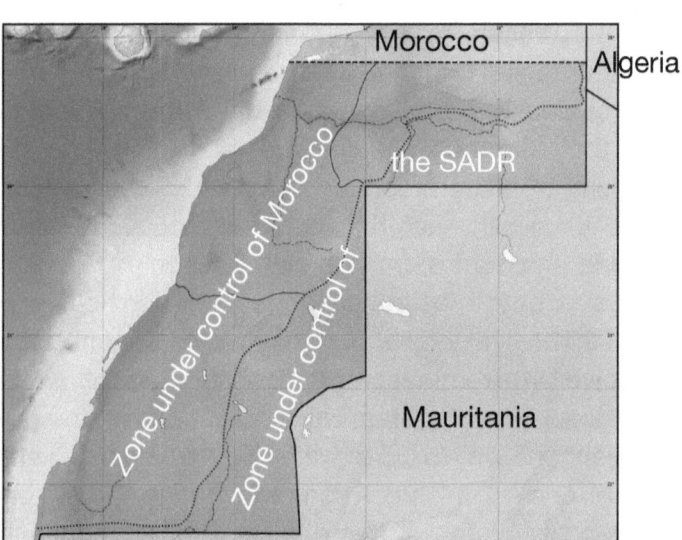

This situation has serious humanitarian consequences, as tens of thousands of refugees still live in camps on the Algerian side. Their number is estimated at 165,000 by Algeria, 155,000 by the European Union, and 90,000 by the UN agencies, but Morocco disputes all these figures. Moreover, this dispute between Morocco and Algeria hinders economic and cultural exchanges between both countries, and beyond, since it blocks the entire functioning of the AMU, while its five members and their populations could have benefitted from a calmer situation—however, Libya certainly has other priorities at the moment.

In monetary terms, the Moroccan dirham is mainly used, for the most part, in the western area. As for the east and in the refugee camps are circulating:

- the Saharawi peseta, issued by the SADR and originally based on

---

252. Source: Eric Gaba – Wikimedia Commons user: Sting, and Wikimedia Commons user: NordNordWest.

the old Spanish peseta. Adopted in 1997, it is materialized in the form of coins, but there is no banknote,

- and the currencies of neighboring countries: the Algerian dinar and the Mauritanian ouguiya, which replaced the CFA franc in 1973.

We will obviously not take a position in the political debate, but we think that Morocco should take the initiative to propose the development of a common cryptocurrency with Mauritania and Algeria. It is unlikely that the latter will accept given the current context and the future presidential election of 2019. Mauritania could however be interested, although it will also hold its presidential election in 2019. This digital currency would benefit both countries, which receive large remittances, especially Morocco, with $6.4 billion in 2015. It would also facilitate NGO operations on the ground.

Since telephone waves cross walls, it could even be used gradually in the SADR, or even in refugee camps in Algeria, the two communities also receiving remittances from at least a dozen thousand migrants, mainly settled in Spain. The number of smartphones in use could however be a problem, but this is a situation that can be managed.

If this shared cryptocurrency is mined, on the same principle as bitcoin, the annual sunshine should be taken advantage of by setting up vast solar farms in the Western Sahara, which will contribute to its wealth, a decisive asset to strengthen the population's support.

The energy produced will be in surplus and would reduce energy imports—they currently represent 94% of Morocco's total needs[253]. It could even be used to mine bitcoin and other digital currencies.

In the event that neither Mauritania nor Algeria—or even Tunisia— would want to get involved in this project, Morocco should still study it. To finance it, it could launch an international ICO, in addition to more traditional financing solutions. Moreover, wanting to be the end of one of the corridors of the Belt and Road Initiative (BRI), the Kingdom could appeal to China, whose companies are at the forefront in solar energy and mining.

---

253. *Le Maroc importe 94 % de ses besoins énergétiques*, Thierry Barbaut, Énergies Renouvelables Afrique, 06/01/2016.

Furthermore, such an initiative would strengthen its economic policy towards sub-Saharan Africa, as it is only a matter of time before their digital currencies are created. In the long run, when disputes are settled, this cryptocurrency could also be used throughout the AMU.

We can only focus on general principles in this book and not go into the details, but we think that Morocco, especially since joining the African Union in January 2016, would benefit from thinking about the development of a cryptocurrency, either sovereign or shared with its neighbors wishing to go down the same road.[254] There is no doubt that the geopolitical advantages it could derive from such a monetary advance will be significant.

7) Ethiopia, Egypt and Sudan: a cryptocurrency or war?

The Nile, the world's longest river with 6,700 km, runs through ten countries and is regularly the subject of political tension. As a result, many treaties including the share of this precious water have been reached for more than a century, the oldest dating back to 1891, between England and Italy, at the time colonial powers. The last agreement dates from 1959 and involves Egypt and Sudan. It was re-updated in 2015, after Ethiopia announced the construction of the colossal Grand Ethiopian Renaissance Dam, on the Blue Nile, which will be the largest in Africa. Although Egypt opposes the project, construction began in 2013 and is expected to end in 2018, unless there is a change with the future new Prime Minister.

The main problem stems from the fact that during the three or even five years required to fill the dam, it is estimated that Egypt would be deprived of at least 40% of the vital water flow of the Nile. The consequences on agricultural production, on which the population depends, and on hydroelectric production, the second in Africa, would be dramatic.

---

254. Let us note that the Western Sahara continues to oppose Morocco and Algeria at all levels, including the African Union, where paragraphs of the report of the Commissioner for Peace and Security, the Algerian Smaïl Chergui, presented on January 28, 2018 to the heads of state, were firmly rejected by the Moroccans.

Chapter 3

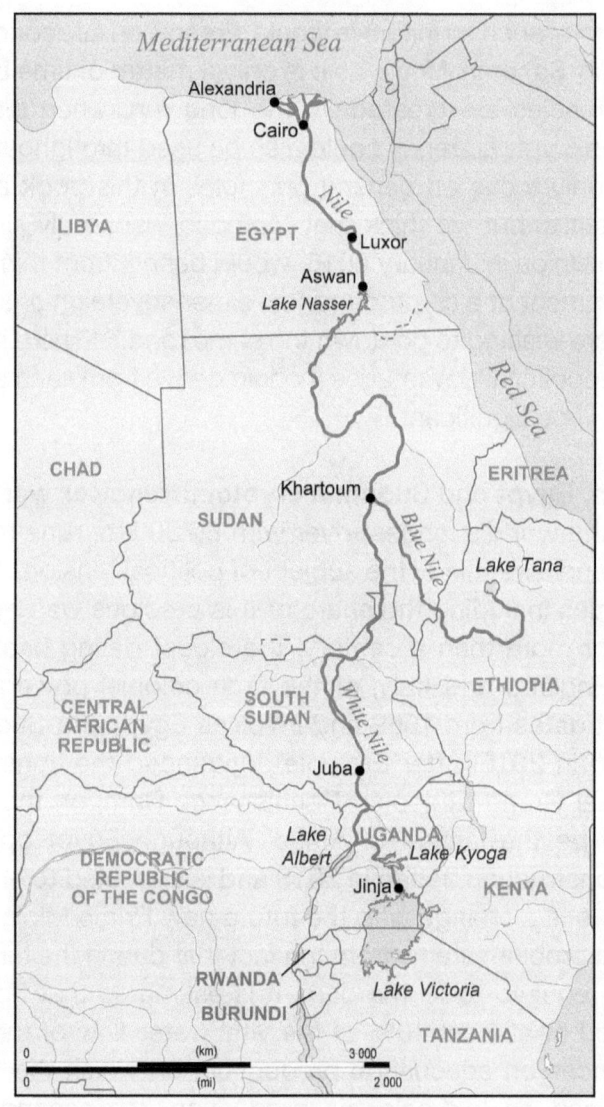

The Nile[255]

---
255. Author: Takasugi Shinji, Commons Wikimedia.

Various scenarios have already been discussed for some time, including an intervention by the Egyptian military to destroy the ongoing construction work. This would inevitably trigger war between two of the three most populous African countries behind Nigeria— about 102 million for Ethiopia and 96 million for Egypt—because the former would not give up its dam and the second would not be able to handle the impact, otherwise, the military could lose the country, despite the fact that all signs ara pointing to an easy reelection of President el-Sisi in March 2018. The conflict would be all the more likely to ignite regionally as Sudan has an economic interest in the Ethiopian project and supports it. If the situation degenerates, which other countries would get involved, if only to protect the Red Sea and the Suez Canal, through which most of the sea traffic between Europe and Asia passes, with incalculable consequences in case of blockage?

And if the creation of a cryptocurrency was the solution to prevent this apocalyptic scenario? It should involve at least Ethiopia and Egypt, and potentially Sudan. It would compensate Egyptian farmers and the state for the loss of hydroelectric power. It would also promote trade between the three countries.

It could be financed by a levy on electricity sold by Ethiopia to neighboring countries. We believe, however, that the economic parameters will not permit it, at least initially: on the one hand, Ethiopia must repay the huge financing of the work (at least $4 billion), and on the other hand, during the filling period of the dam, electricity production will not be at its maximum potential. In short, the principle of communicating vessels will not work: what Egypt will lose, Ethiopia will not gain (immediately). Hence the creation of a cryptocurrency— based on nothing—, to compensate for the loss of value.

Another solution is to use remittances; here are the figures for 2016 according to the World Bank:

Chapter 3

Data 2016 (USD)	Total (en millions)	Costs (8%)
Egypt	16,590	1,327
Ethiopia	772	62
Sudan	153	12
Total	**17,515**	**1,401**

Egypt is a big beneficiary, ranking seventh in the world (the figure for 2017 was even higher, exceeding $18.2 billion). Assuming 8% for transfer costs, we get a total of $1.4 billion. At least half of it, i.e. $700 million, could have been saved through a cryptocurrency and used to compensate agricultural and hydroelectric losses. With wheat at $191 per ton, over 3.6 million tons could be purchased—let us remember that Egypt is already the world's largest importer of wheat, with 12 million tons (estimate for 2017). In adding this 3.6 million tons to the daily consumption of wheat valued at 600 grams per Egyptian[256], the $700 million saved would feed about 16.7 million people, or more than 17% of the total population. So, is it worth looking into creating a cryptocurrency? These indications show that even if Egypt could not reach an agreement with Ethiopia and Sudan to create a common cryptocurrency, it should nonetheless seriously study the project (reminder: all calculations in this chapter are simplified to explain the basic principles.)

The question that arises however is: apart from the issuing countries, who will accept this cryptocurrency in payment? From the moment there are remittances, it means that there is an exchange of currencies: in fact, central banks will receive dollars, euros, etc. in exchange for the cryptocurrency units they sell and which will then be credited to the recipients' account. They will be able to pay for imports with these currencies. And they will receive the total amount of money in foreign currency, not just fees.

---

256. *Le blé en Méditerranée : sociétés, commerce et stratégies*, Sébastien Abis, CIHEAM, 2012.

To facilitate the creation of this common cryptocurrency, a third country could be partner, which would guarantee its solidity as well as the underlying peace process. The only state that can currently fulfill this role is Russia. For the following main reasons:

- It is on excellent terms with the three countries, Vladimir Putin having even received in November 2017 the Sudanese President Omar Al-Bechir, despite two international arrest warrants issued against him for war crimes, genocide and crimes against humanity. On this occasion, Al-Bechir called on Russia for help—or even rescue, given the country's catastrophic situation—from what he considered to be the "aggressive acts" of the United States.

- Russia is one of Egypt's leading wheat suppliers, but it also sells an increasing amount of weapons to the three countries (as well as other products). It could use the cryptocurrency received in several ways: for the payment of its imports of agricultural products; the payment of scholarships to the students of these three countries that it welcomes; by Russian tourism and investments in these countries which are in need of so many things.

- Russia is already in the process of developing its own cryptocurrency, so it will bring all its expertise to the project.

The creation of a cryptocurrency as a guarantee and source of peace, who can doubt that it is possible?

8) Qatar and Iran: a cryptocurrency, then war?

A priori, everything should irreconcilably oppose these two neighbors of the Persian Gulf: Arabs against Persians, Sunnis against Shiites, a monarchy against an Islamic republic. Yet it is not the case, especially since 2017 they share an uncomfortable situation: international sanctions. As a result, when Qatar went under a de facto embargo from 5 June at the behest of Saudi Arabia, followed by the United Arab Emirates and Bahrain, Iran was one of the first countries to fly to its rescue by delivering more than a thousand tons of fruit and vegetables every day by boat. The most important aid came from Turkey, which has a (small) military base there.

Chapter 3

Despite all that apparantly should oppose them, Iran and Qatar share an enormous resource: the largest natural gas field in the world, located in the territorial waters of both countries over nearly 10,000 km², of which 62% are on the Qatari side (name: North Dome) and 38% for the Iranians (South Pars).

It is so huge that the Qataris believe it could be exploited for a century. It has enabled them to become the world leader in LNG (liquefied natural gas) and among the first producers of helium, present in natural gas. Iran, victim of international sanctions, has been delayed in the exploitation of South Pars, but is currently making up for it.

South Pars and North Dome gas fields

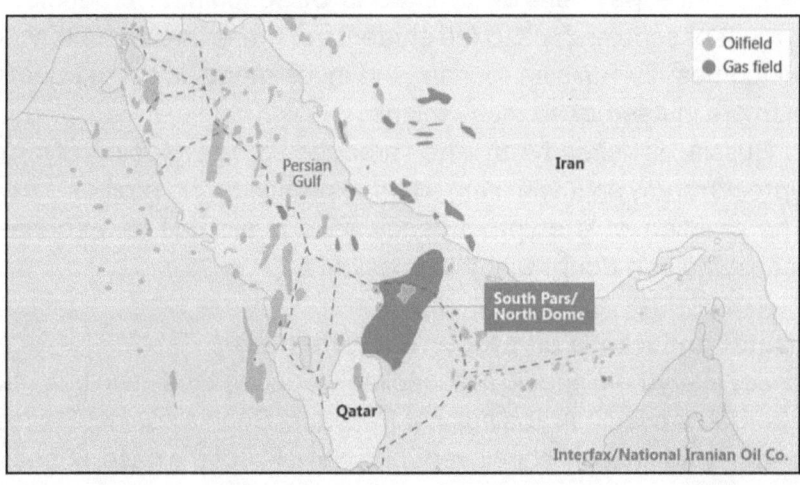

Geopolitics of Future Cryptocurrencies

Until June 2017, trade between both countries was low, since Iran represented only 0.26% of Qatar's imports in 2016, compared with, for example, 9.09% for the United Arab Emirates ($2.9 billion), ranked fourth, almost on par with Germany.[257] However, with the embargo and the necessary replacement of the United Arab Emirates, Iranian exports increased exponentially, almost quadrupling between June and August 2017:[258]

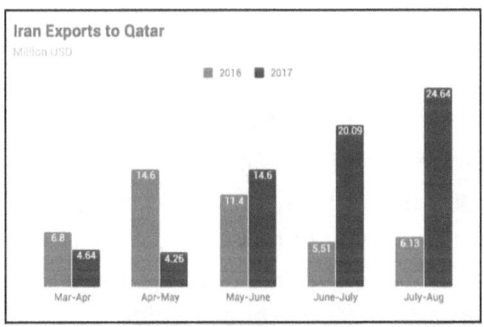

In order to facilitate trade between both countries, it might be useful to create a common cryptocurrency, at least for payments and compensations between the two central banks, which would save Iran's foreign exchange resources badly hurt by decades of sanctions. It could even be backed by a portion of the revenues from the North Dome and South Pars, before being gradually extended to companies and populations, and then to other partner countries.

It is, however, legitimate to think that such an initiative, given the stakes and positions of certain countries in the Middle East, would be considered by Qatar's Arab neighbors and their allies as a declaration of war. At a minimum, it should bring about regime change, especially as the United States has there its largest military base in the region. Who can believe that a (crypto)currency does not have geopolitical and strategic stakes?

---

257. Source: Wits (World Integrated Trade Solution), The World Bank.
258. *Iran Exports to Qatar UP 60%*, Sepehr Arefmanesh, *Financial Tribune*, 08/26/2017.

9) The Portuguese-speaking area

Portugal was a decisive maritime empire in the great discoveries that contributed to the Renaissance and the power of the West, with the navigators Fernando de Magellan, Vasco da Gama, Pedro Álvares Cabral, etc. The Portuguese-speaking community includes Brazil; in Africa, Cape Verde, Guinea-Bissau, Mozambique, Sao Tome and Principe; in Asia, Macau and East Timor. It must be added the diaspora present in many countries and Portuguese-speaking minorities among Brazil's neighbors, but also in India and Africa. In total, more than 240 million people have Portuguese as their native language, ranking it sixth in the world. Given Brazil's place in the world, it is a dynamic and growing language.

Since Portugal is part of the Eurozone, it cannot create a sovereign cryptocurrency. In order to promote the development of the Portuguese-speaking area, it could nevertheless think about launching a shared cryptocurrency, which would be distributed in cooperation projects. It would not be legal tender in Portugal, but nothing would prevent the population from holding it, including the large diaspora, as well as the Brazilians, even if their country decided not to participate directly.

10) The Turkish speaking area

Unlike the Portuguese-speaking world and Portugal, none of the countries that constitute it depend on an extra-national central bank. Made up of Turkey, Azerbaijan, Kazakhstan, Kyrgyzstan, Uzbekistan and Turkmenistan, the Turkish-speaking community extends to the Uyghurs of Xinjiang (China) and a large diaspora, such as the Turks in Iraq, in Germany, Bulgaria, the Netherlands, France, Cyprus (North), Azeris in Iran, immigrants in Russia, etc.

While at least two states are moving towards a national cryptocurrency (see Chapter 2), Turkey has not yet chosen this path. Moreover, the religious authorities, the Diyanet, declared in November 2017 that bitcoin is not compatible with Islam, which does not prevent a part of the population from possessing and speculating, confronted, among other problems, with the decrease of the Turkish lira and high inflation rates. However, "Turkish Central Bank Governor Murat Cetinkaya said in Istanbul earlier this month [November 2017] that cryptocurrencies can contribute to financial stability if well designed."[259]

Even if Turkey seems to have other priorities at the moment, the creation of a "pan-Turk" cryptocurrency, in cooperation with the countries of this extended linguistic area, would probably contribute to the increase of exchanges and thus to the improvement of the economic situation of the zone. It would also significantly reduce the costs of remittances, which many of these states depend on, and would facilitate investment by the Turkish-speaking diaspora.

Update: Mid-February 2018, Turkish Deputy Prime Minister Mehmet Simsek states that the country is studying the implementation of a sovereign cryptocurrency. A few days later, it is announced that Ahmet Kenan Tanrikulu, vice president of the Nationalist Movement Party (MHP), has prepared a report to propose a state-issued national cryptocurrency called "Turkcoin." Therefore the movement is also under way in Turkey.

11) Indonesia (Malaysia, Singapore, Papua New Guinea, Brunei, the Philippines)

In the largest Muslim country in the world, and the fourth most populous, after China, India and the United States, the main Indonesian exchange is bitcoin.co.id. It accounts for between 50% and two-thirds of national transactions, and claims nearly one million members. For now, cryptocurrency transactions are allowed, but not payments, only the rupee being legal tender (law No. 7/2011). In anticipation that Bank Indonesia (BI), the central bank, enacts in 2018 a regulation which could go as far as completely prohibiting any transactions, it asks merchants not to accept payments in cryptocurrencies.[260]

---

259. *What central banks say about cryptocurrencies*, David Kariuki, CryptoMorrow, 11/28/2017.
260. *Bank Indonesia to ban bitcoin transactions next year*, The Jakarta Post, 12/06/2017.

Chapter 3

On January 13, 2018, it publishes a new alert statement against cryptocurrencies and bitcoin in particular.[261] It concludes it by prohibiting all operators of bank and non-bank payment systems from processing transactions using these virtual currencies. In Bali, police intervention is even requested, especially at tourist sites, to ensure that only the rupee is used.[262]

On the other hand, there is no announcement of the creation of a national cryptocurrency, while Indonesia is one of the countries that would probably benefit the most, for the following main reasons:

- "It also has an enormous unbanked population, whereby as late as 2014 little more than a third of adults held bank accounts. And figures for the country's poorest point to only 20 percent having access to banking capital. The government in recent years has launched campaigns and initiatives to increase institutional financial literacy."[263] Results clearly show it is not enough.

- Indonesia is the world's fourteenth largest recipient of remittances, with more than $10 billion in 2015 (source: World Bank).

- With its more than 13,000 islands spanning nearly 2 million square kilometers, the cost of making and renewing banknotes and coins is a high burden.

- A cryptocurrency would have the advantage of fast and almost free transfers.

- Moreover, if it is shared with neighboring countries, it would reduce the use of the dollar, with Indonesia importing $132 billion and exporting $140 billion in 2016.

An obstacle to the success of this cryptocurrency would however be that the number of owners of a smartphone is estimated at 70 million for 2018, i.e. between a third and a quarter of the 265 million inhabitants, a rate obviously much higher if children are removed of the total. To support the deployment of its cryptocurrency,

---

261. *Bank Indonesia Warns All Parties Not to Sell, Buy, or Trade Virtual Currency*, Bank Indonesia, 01/13/2018.
262. *Bank Indonesia, police prevent bitcoin transactions in Bali*, The Jakarta Post, 01/15/2018.
263. *Indonesia Is Ripe For Cryptocurrency Disruption–Could It Be Asia's Next Bitcoin Hub?*, Sharon Lam, *Forbes*, 11/01/2017.

the government could ensure to increase the penetration of smartphones, all the more as its "Palapa Ring project, one of Indonesia's key infrastructure projects for the period 2016-2019, also plays a crucial role. By developing an undersea fiber-optic cable network that stretches across 13,000 kilometers as well as an onshore network of nearly 22,000 kilometers, the Palapa Ring project aims to provide fast broadband Internet to Indonesians in both the urban and rural areas."[264]

Indonesia could also share its cryptocurrency with its neighbors, Malaysia to begin with. Moreover, on December 11, 2017, the central banks of Indonesia, Malaysia and Thailand reached an agreement to trade with their national currencies rather than the dollar—for example, it represents 94% of exports and 78% of imports from Indonesia.[265]

Its links with Malaysia are important in many ways: the latter is Indonesia's sixth largest economic partner, the eighth largest for Malaysia (2016 figures); each country represents the second largest number of tourists to its neighbor; more than 300,000 Indonesians work in Malaysia; etc.

Admittedly, they still have some territorial disputes, especially on the oil-rich Ambalat Islands, but nothing that would prevent the creation of a common cryptocurrency, at least for exchanges between states. They should all the more be able to understand each other that they share two almost identical languages, Bahasa and Malay, and their respective history has been intertwined forever.

Gradually adding other countries in the area to the project, starting with Singapore, would give a first-rate economic and monetary package, with a population of 300 to more than 400 million people with the Philippines, or almost 500 million with Thailand.

Certainly, it is probably necessary to regulate transactions on bitcoin, but working on the creation of a cryptocurrency, at least a

---

264. *Internet & Smartphone Penetration in Indonesia Estimated to Grow Strongly*, Indonesia Investments, 07/2016.
265. *Indonesia, Malaysia and Thailand seek to boost local currency settlement*, Nilufar Rizki, Fransiska Nangoy, Reuters, 12/11/2017.

national one, would be a stake much more profitable for Indonesia. Not to mention that the blockchain technology would benefit many other areas, which would accelerate the development of the country.

12) CARICOM and OECS (map on p. 233)

Established in June 1981, the Organization of Eastern Caribbean States (OECS) comprises seven full members (Antigua and Barbuda, Dominica, Grenada, Montserrat, St. Kitts and Nevis, Saint Lucia, Saint Vincent and the Grenadines) and three associate members (Anguilla, the British Virgin Islands and Martinique). Among other objectives, it aims at economic harmonization and integration.

CARICOM, for "Caribbean Community," is composed of twenty members: the seven OECS members plus the Bahamas, Barbados, Belize, Guyana, Haiti, Jamaica, Suriname, and Trinidad and Tobago, and five associate members (Anguilla, Bermuda, the British Virgin Islands, the Cayman Islands, the Turks and Caicos Islands). Also known under the acronym CSME, for Caribbean Single Market and Economy, CARICOM has as a goal to deepen economic integration by moving towards a single market and strengthening links outside of it. On the monetary side:

- the seven members of the OECS plus Anguilla have adopted a common currency, the Eastern Caribbean Dollar, managed by the Central Bank of the Eastern Caribbean. It is linked to the US dollar at a fixed rate of 2.7 to 1 since 1976;
- the British Virgin Islands and the Turks and Caicos Islands use the US dollar;
- all other members emit their own currency.

Several of them are facing a threat that we have not yet encountered in the previous pages, to which one or more cryptocurrencies, or at least the blockchain technology, could provide a solution: "de-risking." When internationally a country is considered not to be fighting money laundering enough, it may become a victim of this phenomenon of de-risking, which means that foreign banks will gradually withdraw or no longer accept to be a correspondent to its local banks, which can definitively prevent them from carrying out financial operations with the outside world, including the transfer of funds, and automatically provoking the closing of bank accounts.

Faced with this threat, some of these island states have begun to focus on cryptocurrencies and blockchain, but also for the benefits they present. We will not list all their initiatives exhaustively, but one of the first came from the Central Bank of Barbados (CBB), which publishes on November 13, 2015 on its website a study entitled *Should Cryptocurrencies Be Included in the Portfolio of International Reserves Held by the Central Bank of Barbados?*[266] According to the authors, it is still too early for bitcoins to be included in the portfolio of central bank assets, but they nevertheless find that the blockchain would replace the SWIFT and RTGS systems (Real-Time Gross Settlement)[267], "given the effectiveness and unmatched speed of the blockchain protocol."

In February 2016, Bitt, a startup based in Barbados, announces the creation of a digital Barbadian dollar, which can be traded on its blockchain-based platform. The Bahamian dollar and the Aruban florin are expected to soon follow. Moreover, Aruba has developed the Smart Island Strategy (see the description of this ambitious sustainable project on the UN website[268]), employing the blockchain for different uses, including an online tourist reservation system and a cryptocurrency. A central bank representative said at the CoinDesk Consensus 2017 conference:

"We did a calculation for the economy of Aruba, and this could potentially lead to a 4-5% GDP growth. Now that, for a region that hasn't seen 0.5% growth in over two decades, is tremendous."[269]

---

266. *Should Cryptocurrencies Be Included in the Portfolio of International Reserves Held by the Central Bank of Barbados?*, Winston Moore, Jeremy Stephen, Central Bank of Barbados, 11/2015.
267. A Real-Time Gross Settlement system enables real-time bank-to-bank transactions. Transactions using the RTGS are generally large ones because the costs are high and made by central banks.
268. https://sustainabledevelopment.un.org/partnership/?p=514
269. *How a Tiny Island Could Give Cryptocurrency a Big Boost*, Noelle Acheson, CoinDesk, 30/05/2017.

The latest announcement is made by John Rolle, Governor of the Central Bank of the Bahamas, who declares on January 18, 2018 that they are considering the creation of a Bahamian digital dollar and are currently working on it.[270]

It seems obvious that the blockchain and a shared cryptocurrency would provide an economic boost to these states and territories, most of which have people living in poverty, without bank accounts, who depend on remittances. It is also recognized that the cost of transferring money between these different areas is expensive, especially for small transfers. In addition, the use of the blockchain would reduce or partially offset the consequences of de-risking.

Now all that remains is to consider how to create a common cryptocurrency, either within the framework of the OECS, with the Central Bank of the Eastern Caribbean, or within the CARICOM, with partnerships between members wishing to participate.

13) ALBA-TCP

"The Bolivarian Alliance for the Peoples of Our America—Peoples' Trade Treaty (ALBA-TCP) is an integration platform for the countries of Latin America and the Caribbean. It puts emphasis on **solidarity**, **complementarity**, **justice** and **cooperation**[271], which has the historical and fundamental purpose to join the capacities and strengths of the countries comprising it, in a view to producing the structural transformations and the relations system necessary to achieve the integral development, required for the continuity of our existence as sovereign and just nations. Additionally, it is a political, economic, and social alliance in defense of the independence, self-determination and the identity of the peoples comprising it.

Integration is for the countries of Latin America and the Caribbean, an indispensable condition to aspire to development in the middle of the increasing formation of huge regional blocs that occupy predominant positions in the world economy."[272]

---

270. *Central Bank eyeing digital version of Bahamian currency*, Xian Smith, *The Nassau Guardian*, 01/19/2018.
271. In bold in the original text.
272. www.alba-tcp.org

The ALBA-TCP currently comprises eleven members: Venezuela, Cuba, Bolivia, Nicaragua, Dominica, Ecuador, St. Vincent and the Grenadines, Antigua and Barbuda, St. Lucia, St. Christophe-and-Nevis, Grenada (in the order of accession)—many of them belong to OECS and CARICOM. Suriname has started the process to become the twelfth member; Honduras left it in 2010.

Given the objectives of the ALBA-TCP, a common cryptocurrency seems a project that would benefit everyone, even if the greatest disparity can be observed on this issue, between Ecuador, which is one of the first countries to have developed its own digital payment system, Bolivia, which formally has banned all cryptocurrencies and Venezuela, which is developing its own. Furthermore, there are huge differences in the economic, financial and geopolitical situations among the members.

This was nevertheless proposed on January 12, 2018 by Nicolás Maduro during the VII Extraordinary Meeting of the Political Council of Alba:

"I put on the table, brothers governments of the ALBA, the proposal of the cryptocurrency petro, for that we embrace it as one of the 21st century integration projects in a bold way, but also a creative one."[273]

The article continues:

"Maduro has ensured that the arrival of petro 'has launched all the most important cryptocurrencies with which trade is made in the world' and recalled that this new mechanism is 'under negotiation and marketing' and will come into circulation in the coming days."

This Extraordinary Meeting is held on January 12th; however, the Venezuelan Parliament declares the petro illegal on the 9th. Unless the declaration is not going to be taken into account—which will be the case—, how can it then be launched in the "coming days" and proposed to the other countries of the ALBA-TCP? The "brothers governments" response was not communicated.

Nevertheless, the proposal of N. Maduro is interesting, because it gives food for thought: is it better to create a cryptocurrency for the

---

273. *Maduro propone a los gobiernos del ALBA sumarse a la criptomoneda el petro*, Agencia EFE, 01/12/2018.

Chapter 3

countries concerned or use the one that belongs to one of them? No doubt this question will regularly be asked within the alliances that will be created.

14) Cuba, the anti-example?
As part of the Alba-TCP, Cuba is aware of the Venezuelan proposal to share the petro. Venezuela being its first economic partner, a common cryptocurrency would further increase trade and logically be profitable for both countries, especially since they suffer sanctions from the United States. Cuba has been under an economic, commercial and financial embargo since February 3, 1962 in violation of international law—Cubans even speak of "blockade." It is further strengthened in 1992 and 1996 by the Torricelli and Helms-Burton Acts.

Cuba's main source of foreign currencies is not tourism but the medical sector, with physicians working in sixty-two countries, including twenty-four in Latin America and the Caribbean and twenty-seven in sub-Saharan Africa, all generating an average annual income since 2011 of approximately $11.5 billion. A sovereign cryptocurrency would significantly reduce the cost of transfer fees.

However, what Cuba needs above all are foreign currencies to pay for imports. In a first analysis, a virtual currency seems to be contrary to its vital interests, because it would deprive it of receiving Brazilian reals, euros, etc. This situation is also illustrated by the new agreements signed on January 30, 2018 with Algeria, which will export 2.1 million barrels of oil a year in exchange for Cuban doctors. This barter makes it possible not to mobilize precious foreign currencies reserves.

In second analysis, a cryptocurrency could nevertheless be an asset. The government has two options: a national version or a shared one with one or more Alba countries. The first presents advantages, but the disadvantage is that, in international trade, who would want to be paid in Cuban money—except Venezuela, Bolivia, Russia, etc.—other than to have balanced trade exchanges? On the other hand, if Cuba participates in the creation of a common cryptocurrency, it would increase its value, since it would impact more countries, with which more trade would occur in this currency. In addition, Cuba would contribute to the economic weight and therefore to the value of that currency, which would ultimately amount to exporting (partially) its own currency. The government would then need less foreign currency sources.

As monetary policies generally tend to be linked to politics, it will probably be necessary to wait for the election of the new president of the Council of State on April 19, 2018, when Raúl Castro will officially announce his departure, to see positions evolve.

15) Alaska, California, Hawaii and Texas

We will end our world tour with the United States, which could see its borders shrink in the future. Talk of Texas claiming its independence has already gotten old, but the other three states have also seen their independence movements increasingly gain importance, especially since the subprime crisis of 2007, and the election of Donald Trump in the case of California—the situation has not been simplified in January 2018, with the project to create "New California," which wants to separate from California but remain a part of the United States, using Article 4 Section 3 of the Constitution.

Of course, these states are still far from secession, but, with the federal debt that continues to grow and exceed every new limit set by Congress, the increasing loss of the dollar's global preeminence as a reserve currency, derivatives in US banks exceeding $250 trillion, etc., who knows what political consequences may occur from a degenerating and uncontrollable financial crisis?

The impact would be even stronger as the Gramm-Leach-Bliley Act put in place by the Clinton administration in 1999 and repealing the 1933 Glass-Steagall Act that drew lessons from the Great Depression by banning banks to be at the same time commercial and investment banks, would accentuate the widespread collapse of the system, to such an extent that no Paulson plan—up to $700 billion in 2008 made available to save the banks thanks to taxpayers—could come to the rescue of those who are now presented as "too big to fail." Such a

Chapter 3

disaster scenario would probably result in the partial disintegration of the country. Independence at the end of a political process can not be excluded either, although it requires a lot of time, even if some progress had already been done, at various degrees.

Whatever the reasons, if this happens one day, the new state(s) will need their currency. The creation of a cryptocurrency seems to be the best solution. Using the existing ones, bitcoin, ether, etc. would also meet their needs, but it can only be temporary, unless one of them becomes a credible and reliable alternative.

Texas is one of the states, along with Nevada and New Hampshire, to have adopted the most favorable legislation on this issue, including legislation relating to taxation. An amendment to the Texas Constitution relating "to the right to own, hold, and use any mutually agreed upon medium of exchange" and expressly addressing cryptocurrencies, is even tabled on March 2, 2017 in the 85th Parliament, but it remains at the committee level.

California and Texas are two of the most populous states in the Union, with respectively 40 million and 28 million people, while Hawaii and Alaska are the opposite, with 1.4 and 0.7 million. One of the advantages of a cryptocurrency is that it can be created and used regardless of the size of the population, since it works even within a small community. If the four states gain their independence and decide to create a common cryptocurrency, it would also have the advantage of reducing the distances between them, while a fiduciary currency would pose logistical problems. It could even be accepted by neighboring countries, that is, Mexico, Canada, Russia—and the United States. Meanwhile, those who are pro secession are certainly already thinking of their cryptocurrency in their dreams of independence.

Will New York State be the first to have its own digital currency? On February 6, 2018, Assembly Member Clyde Vanel introduces Bill A9685, whose purpose is to create a task force to study the benefits of issuing a "NYcoin." A cryptocurrency before a future secession?

Common currency or shared parity?

To conclude this chapter, the following question arises: could a cryptocurrency between two or more states definitively replace their national currencies in the near future? Apart from Saudi Arabia and the United Arab Emirates, which are studying such a possibility, this seems unlikely in the short term, because a common cryptocurrency means a loss of sovereignty in monetary matters, and therefore a loss of sovereignty in general. Admittedly, there is the case of African monetary unions, which share the same fiduciary currency. Therefore, complementing or replacing it with a cryptocurrency should not pose insurmountable problems of governance, which would be the major source of difficulty in other situations.

The euro is probably a model of what should be avoided in terms of a common currency: Greece, for example, would not be in this catastrophic situation today if it had kept the drachma, because it would have devaluated it, thanks to what is called "competitive devaluations." This would have allowed it to keep its economy afloat.

Monetary institutions in the euro area have even contributed to the crisis the country is undergoing and proven that governance is always a fundamental problem of any alliance: who can still deny that the rescue plan to Greece was initially conceived to save first and foremost German banks, which had (too) largely invested in "peripheral countries"? The "rescue" of the country is anything but a rescue given the measures put in place against the population—in fact, it is a demonstration of the law of the strongest.

In fact, the European Central Bank (ECB) announces in October 2017 that its management of Greek government bonds between 2012 and 2016 under the SMP (Securities Market Purchase) has brought it €7.8 billion! These profits were then distributed to the nineteen national central banks in proportion to their participation in the ECB. It was initially decided that they would be returned to Greece, but Germany stops the procedure, for alleged tensions with the Syriza team, the party in office.

As a result, the country of Angela Merkel generates about €1.34 billion in profit to the detriment of Greeks, thanks to this crisis. Sacrificed on the altar of so-called "German virtues," how can the Greeks accept this and not speak of an "odious debt"?

As for Iceland, it has shown the way by refusing to transfer the private bank debt to the population. Admittedly, it suffers for three years, but the recovery has come, it is even higher than expected, with a 7.2% real growth of the economy in 2016, a rate that almost no country in the Eurozone could even dream of.

It seems preferable, therefore, that any creation of a cryptocurrency between two or more states should first be carried out in addition to their respective national currencies. This makes it possible, in particular, to vary the parities if needed and according to the evolution of the respective circumstances.

It also means accepting that two currencies can be legal tender in the same country, which is already the principle of those who are in the process of developing their own cryptocurrency when they also plan to keep their fiat money. The risk is that "the good currency chases away the bad one." However, there is nothing to presume a priori which will become the good one, a situation that can also be reversed over time. With the creation of a cryptocurrency, interstate or national, central banks enter a field of possibilities that seem limitless and look like a *terra incognita*. Let us start clearing the way in conclusion.

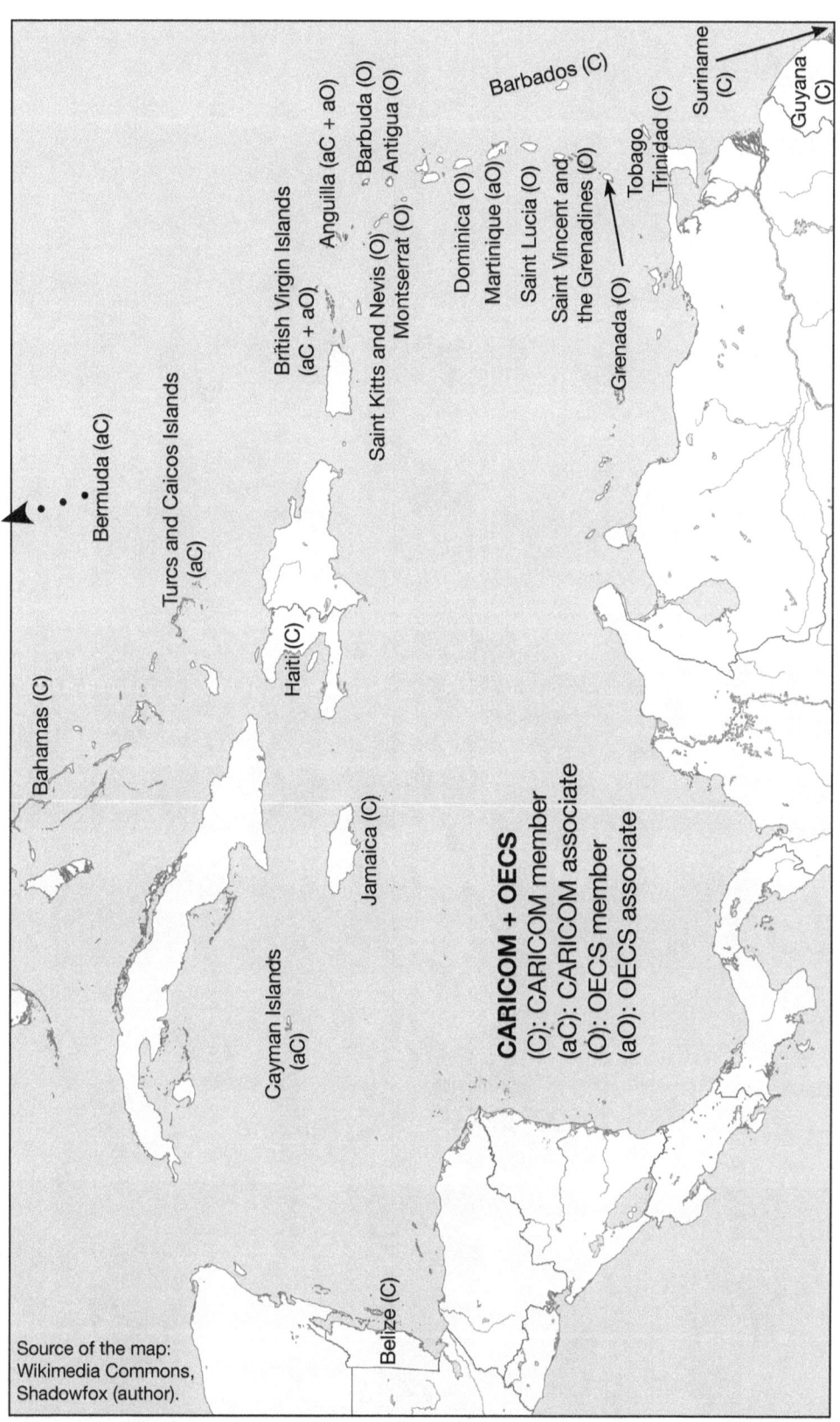

Conclusion

Two Opposing Futures

Here we are at the end of our world tour of cryptocurrencies. The reality is that the suppression of cash is accelerating, replaced with electronic payments, in different possible form. Whereas until recently the cards already appeared to be dealt, namely that all the money would be entrusted to only private banks, cryptocurrencies have come to reshuffle the stack, offering an alternative that did not even exist less than ten years ago and that has already shown far superior benefits. Let us compare, at least in a synthetic way, the main principles of each "world."

The old one, perfectly flawed
The monopoly of money creation belongs to the banks, be they central, public or private. In summary, here is what we can see:
- they have already made the world "collapsed" several times, the last time in 2007 with the subprime crisis, followed by the Paulson plan in the United States which has made up to $700 billion, taken from the taxpayer's pocket, available to the banks. How many schools, public infrastructure, healthcare, etc. could have been financed with such a sum?
- What will be the field of ruins left by the next banking crisis, that many experts expect to be cataclysmic compared to the last one? Let us recall that with the complicity of central banks and their unlimited printing machines or "quantitative easing," they are involved in a frenzied speculation, generating, among other things, derivatives that can prove fatal for the whole banking system, therefore for the whole "global community," because the total amount issued exceeds the imagination: it represents, at least, 1.2 million billion, or $1,200,000,000,000,000,000! In comparison, state debts seems almost ridiculous:

Conclusion

Categories	US$
Bank derivatives	1,200,000,000,000,000,000
Coins, notes and cash deposit accounts on the planet	81,000,000,000,000
Companies and entities listed on all global stock exchanges	70,000,000,000,000
Federal debt of the United States	20,000,000,000,000

Source: BFM TV[274]

- Even if central bankers keep claiming that cryptocurrencies contribute to the financing of terrorism and trafficking of all kinds, as we have already pointed out, is it bitcoin or the system that they are responsible for that in fact allows terror, drug traffickers, mafias, etc. to thrive for decades on every continent? Who can be made to believe that Daesh, al Qaeda, Boko Haram pay their jihadists in bitcoin or ether rather than in dollars, euros or pound sterlings? For the record, bitcoin did not exist on September 11, 2001. How else can we conclude that the banking system has proven a form of complicity, even if it may seem passive and unintentional? Not to mention banking and tax havens, which promote money laundering, tax evasion, corruption, etc. thanks to the "engineering" of the banks.

As a result, if cash disappears, who really wants all his money to go to commercial banks, who do not hesitate to falsify the banks' prime loan rate (Libor, Euribor scandals, etc.), loot the accounts of their clients (last major example: Wells Fargo), violate laws (between only 2009 and 2017, $345 billion in financial penalties were inflicted by the states to the eminent members of this corporation above all suspicion[275]), speculate on food and drive up the prices above what people can afford (Goldman Sachs ...), etc.?

---

274. *Les chiffres inimaginables du marché des produits dérivés*, Antoine Larigaudrie, BFM TV Trading Sat, 05/16/2016.
275. *Global Banking Recovery Stalls, as Risk and Regulatory Costs Bite*, Boston Consulting Group, 02/22/2018.

In the name of the so-called "too big to fail," banks can have whatever they want, including a law in the European Union that gives them the possibility to seize money from their customers with balances above €100,000, in case of difficulty, a system already tested in Cyprus. How can this not be considered as legalized theft?

We are not going to put the banks and their practices on trial here, which have the complicity and collusion of the central banks, the supervisory authorities and the governments, as it is not the subject, and one book would not be enough. Let us conclude, however, that this system has largely proved its limits and failures.

The New World
Let us start by confirming that we are not in favor of private cryptocurrencies as they exist today, at least for one essential reason: the principle that monetary creation belongs to individuals, commercial companies, anonymous organizations is unacceptable, since it is a sovereign right, vital for the people who depend on it. However, if they are thriving, it is because they profit from the shortcomings of a profit-based banking system and respond to a need that authorities have abandoned.

On the other hand, we encourage the creation of national or shared cryptocurrencies between several states, under the responsibility of central banks, although, for example, the Bank of England refuses to do so.

A) The credit, a false problem?

Among its arguments, it would be impossible to distribute the huge amount of credit needed by the economy as commercial banks do it. This seems to us more a pretext than a real reason. Indeed, what prevents an online loan application form from being set up and answered automatically according to criteria to be met, when such a technical possibility already exists with credit institutions?

Conclusion

Some may also argue that evaluating potential lenders' profiles could be an issue. Here again, this does not seem to be justified: if an individual requires a loan, the central bank would inevitably know the movements and balances since it holds his account, so monthly payments that his disposable income allows for repay could automatically be calculated, while adjusting their numbers according to the amount requested. The entire process, from when the online application for the loan is sent to the answer after the analysis, can then take place in less than a minute, 24/7. And it is no longer necessary to provide supporting documents, which, in any case, can be managed via smart contracts of blockchains.

The information system could include a feature that would calculate the monthly loan amount available for each account, updated every month. Then, the customer just has to write the amount required so that it is split between the number of monthly payments, and funds will be made immediately available.

The central bank could also provide insurance to cover everyday accidents, which keep people from meeting their payment deadlines. For the community, it would be cheaper and fairer than the current system, which is in the hands of commercial insurance companies who use it as a source of profit.

In the case of a temporary difficulty, it would again be easy to automate the system by allowing payments to be rescheduled or adjusted if disposable income decreases as a result of a life change or employment loss. As a result, having large litigation and recovery departments like commercial banks have today would no longer be necessary, because the central bank is not intended to make profits, so it can spread repayments over time, as long as necessary. In any case, this situation is already happening, with the example of the hundreds of thousands of pensioners in the United States who have not yet finished repaying their student loan, which proves the perverseness of the current system. With interest, penalties and fees, how many times have they repaid the amount of their student loan?

B) Guarantees—What guarantees?

The issue and processing of collaterals may also be presented as a cause for concern. This last point is not a problem either, since it is perfectly manageable, in an efficient and quick manner, and at a lower cost, by the blockchain technology, which banks are already experimenting with in various forms.

In any case, with a central bank cryptocurrency, it is no longer necessary to provide "guarantees," in the classic sense of the pawnbroker, who can cause problems if he is not repaid, as commercial banks tend to do. Indeed, monthly payments can be carried forward indefinitely, throughout the entire life of a person. On the other hand, difficulties to repay must exclude any new loan, unlike the current system, where it is possible to obtain additional credit to repay a loan, with a debt ratio that becomes unbearable and brings a rarely happy end.

This is not to say that the central bank should be lax, but it will not reach such extremes as commercial banks. Thus, not only would this system never have experienced a subprime crisis, but, moreover, there would not have been the immeasurable social cost of tens or even hundreds of thousands of American households being forced to live on the streets after being evicted from the house that they had not finished paying off, where many of them still "live" ten years later. In the meantime, stock markets keep breaking records and bank profits pile up.

C) Community versus the individual

In the event that a credit demand reaches the limit of the borrower's repayment capacity, regardless of the number of monthly payments, rather than asking for a cosigner, a third party can become the second borrower and partially cover payments or handle those that are unpaid. The computer system would manage it without difficulty. The blockchain even solves a problem that has no simple solution today: multi-borrowers. If twenty people want to collectively buy a property, it is almost impossible to take out a loan with so many signatories. The recommended solution then is to buy it through a property management or commercial company, which poses other problems. In the "new world," there would be as many co-borrowers as desired. Of course, it would be necessary to set the terms for cases where one (or more of the co-borrowers) has difficulties repaying: deferral of individual maturity, coverage by other co-borrowers, a mix of both. Smart contracts would allow groups to manage these types of rules and their execution.

It is clear that legislation will have to be adapted to this evolution, in particular civil laws and property laws, and legal safeguards to access account information will have to be created. What we are presenting is hardly a rough draft of the transformations that the creation of a central bank cryptocurrency and the use of blockchain technology will bring, as this is only the beginning, as we have already pointed out.

D) And businesses?

All of the above can be applied to any type of company. There will be variations in the rules: for newly created companies, for example, the central bank could wait for one year before allowing them credit. For all, the blockchain and smart contracts offer features, which allows companies to receive cash backed by their pending invoices.

Exporting can also be facilitated by simplifying the current system of letters of credit. The same applies for the management of foreign currencies, provided that convertibility is established between cryptocurrencies.

In summary, most of the services that a company needs can be handled by the blockchain. On the other hand, specific operations related to the investment banking, such as IPOs, capital raising, mergers and acquisitions, etc., could be left to investment banks or any structure that has the expertise to do it.

E) Panic on banks

Another argument the Bank of England uses to justify not developing a sovereign cryptocurrency is the supposed "bank run" it would cause: the population and businesses would rush into commercial banks to withdraw their assets and transfer them to their new account at the central bank. Of course, banks would not be able to cope with this situation, because everyone knows they do not keep their clients' deposits safe but use them to make money.

Again, this is a false problem, because this situation can be managed in different ways. One of them is that the central bank credits its new clients' account with the sums available on their commercial bank accounts, where they become temporarily "frozen," the time for operations in progress to be completed. At the end of it, the amount on the account at the central bank is adjusted to the actual balance. As for the commercial bank, which thus avoids the bank run, the "frozen" balance is transformed into debt vis-à-vis the central bank, and then it is up to them to set the repayment terms. If the balance is negative, the central bank is in debt to the commercial bank or banks—it can then be compensated with the receivables. It is up to the central bank then to recover the amount from its new client, according to the model above. It will also take over the loans previously contracted, with the same principles. This would divide the fees, and even the cost of credit, as we are about to see below.

F) Great benefits for the people

Basically, a commercial bank borrows money from the central bank at a certain interest rate, and in order to cover its expenses and also make a profit for its shareholders, it "resells" this credit to borrowers at a higher rate.

Let us look at the cost of this operation by taking, for example, a loan of 100,000—regardless of the currency, the demonstration is the same—at 5% interest rate over ten and twenty years:

Conclusion

Borrowed capital	Interest rate	Duration	Cost of credit	%
100,000	5%	10 years	27,279	27.28
100,000	5%	20 years	58,359	58.36

The cost of credit will respectively be at 27.3% and 58.4% of the amount borrowed. Let us compare with the cryptocurrency of a central bank, which does not have to borrow because it creates the currency itself, according to the mandate that a sovereign nation entrusted to it, or the nations, in a monetary union; and it does not have to pay dividends to shareholders because it is not a commercial bank. It is therefore no longer necessary to impose an interest rate, which allows a modest fixed cost, per step or not, for example 10 or 20 units per month, to cover operating costs.

Let us take the table above with, for example, a fixed cost of 10 (€, $, £...) per monthly payment:

Borrowed capital	Interest rate	Duration	Commercial banks		Central bank		Saving for the borrower
			Cost of credit	%	Cost of credit	%	
100,000	5%	10 years	27,279	27.3	10 x 120 monthly pay. = 1,200	1.2	26,079
100,000	5%	20 years	58,359	58.4	10 x 240 monthly pay. = 2,400	2.4	55,959

The result is obviously amazing: on a capital of 100,000, the borrower can save more than 55% once interest rates are suppressed, which suddenly resemble usury, whatever the interest rate retained.

G) Other unmatched advantages

Blockchain and central bank cryptocurrency have other incomparable advantages: monetary policy would be translated into facts without intermediaries and almost instantly; the data for the analysis would be available in real time, which would allow immediate adjustments; there would be no more logistical problems and the cost of fiduciary money.

Money would circulate much faster, which is a factor contributing to the wealth of economic agents, and at no cost. Thus, currently, almost two days a week are lost while the banks are closed, because they block transfers and part of the operations, which represents the immobilization of huge resources, whose cost to society is rarely mentioned.

Social benefits payments would be immediate and simpler to manage. Governments could take the opportunity to put in place innovative policies. In addition, laws that currently prevent states from refinancing with their central bank by requiring them to borrow from commercial banks and financial markets would be removed. Let us recall the example of France, which set up such a law in 1973, under a president of the Republic who had previously been the general manager of the Rothschild bank: it is estimated that during these forty-five years, it has cost the community more than €1.2 trillion in interest, with today an annual debt burden of around €46 billion (this amount represents only interests). As we have said before, how many schools, hospitals, roads, social benefits, and so on could have been financed with these huge sums instead of enriching commercial banks and speculators? This would not be the least of the benefits of a central bank cryptocurrency.

What to do with commercial banks?

We agree with the Bank of England that the implementation of a sovereign cryptocurrency would inevitably have an impact on the existence of commercial banks. This is probably the main reason why they back off on the issue. Admittedly, they have been indispensable until today—at what price, however, to the people?[276] But it is clear that the technology initiated by bitcoin and blockchain makes them useless in the context of this new world. It may seem inconceivable that commercial banks of today could disappear; it is also what the drivers and manufacturers of stagecoaches certainly thought in the nineteenth century, but it is what happened.

Some mention the possibility that commercial banks should continue to do scoring for the allocation of loans. We see neither the interest nor the utility, and we explained above why. For us, their future must be limited to investment banking and should no longer have any connection with the activity of deposits, like a sort of reinforced Glass-Steagall Act, which, let us remember, separated the two activities after the disaster of the Great Depression, which contributed to fascist parties coming to power in Europe, a direct cause of the Second World War.

It must also be used to clean up the system so that they can no longer speculate, as well as hedge funds and other vulture funds, against the currencies and the debts of states, and cause, for their sole profit, events like the Asian crisis, or the fall of the pound sterling, etc.

Abundance for tomorrow?
So, would implementing a central bank cryptocurrency be enough to lead to happiness and bliss? Of course not, especially since there are still many technical problems to solve, including security and transaction speed.

In any case, one should not expect, at least in the western hemisphere and among its allies, central banks to be the first to choose this direction, for various reasons. For example, in the United States, the Federal Reserve belongs to major banks. It will obviously not go against their interests.

Unless a banking crisis happens such that these central banks have no other solution, or there is a revolution, like in France a little over

---

276. *Banks, Two Centuries of Violence Against People*, Patrick Pasin, Talma Studios, 2019.

two centuries ago, the solutions will come first from other countries, a movement already in motion, as evidenced by *Geopolitics of Cryptocurrencies*. Meanwhile, the virtual world of cryptocurrencies is now a reality more than ever, and nothing can exclude that bitcoin, ether or an equivalent will one day replace the dollar, the euro and the pound sterling, and blockchains replace banks.

Whatever the final solution, central bank cryptocurrency or digital currency managed via commercial banks, we are witnessing the disappearance of a form of freedom that cash represents. If it is impossible to stop this evolution, we prefer, without hesitation, a sovereign cryptocurrency than to depend entirely on commercial banks that would have all the powers, including to continue speculating for their profit at our own risk. Unless a new path appears.

Paris, March 2018

Contents

Introduction ... 5

Chapter 1
General Overview of Cryptocurrencies

Concepts and definitions ... 11
Main cryptocurrencies ... 21
Highly speculative values ... 41
What can I buy with bitcoin? ... 46
Exchange Platforms ... 47
The role of exchanges in pricing ... 49
Pay attention to the electricity bill! ... 50
Geopolitics of vending machines ... 53
Attacks against exchanges ... 57
Beware, danger! ... 59
Beware, thieves! ... 60
When the United States misses out
on the deal of the century ... 64
Learning from one's mistakes ... 65
Finland and Bulgaria's turn ... 66
International regulation? ... 67
Are bitcoin transactions anonymous? ... 68
WannaCry and cryptocurrencies ... 70

Chapter 2
Sovereign Cryptocurrencies

Introduction: The Bitcoin Market Potential Index (BMPI) ... 75
I. When bitcoin becomes the safe haven of a country ... **77**
1) Cyprus, the first laboratory ... 77
2) In Zimbabwe, bitcoin saves the day ... 78
3) The United Kingdom like Zimbabwe? ... 80
4) Iran under sanctions and pressure ... 81
5) Afghanistan, hawala and bitcoin ... 85

II. Achievements and national projects — **88**
1) Iceland — 89
2) Scotland — 92
3) Ecuador — 95
4) Uruguay — 96
5) Canada — 96
6) The Netherlands — 97
7) The United Kingdom — 98
8) Poland — 100
9) Russia — 101
10) Abkhazia — 102
11) Kyrgyzstan — 103
12) Kazakhstan — 105
13) Singapore — 110
14) China — 110
15) Hong Kong — 113
16) India — 113
17) Dubai (United Arab Emirates) — 115
18) Saudi Arabia and the United Arab Emirates — 116
19) Israel — 117
20) Lebanon — 122
21) Tunisia — 122
22) Senegal, WAEMU and WAMU — 124
23) Nigeria — 128
24) South Africa — 129
25) Venezuela — 130
26) Marshall Islands (RMI) — 135

III. Other national situations — **138**
1) The United States — 138
2) Japan — 146
3) South Korea — 147
4) North Korea — 155
5) Cambodia — 158
6) Thailand — 159
7) Estonia, the European Union and the Eurozone — 160

8) Sweden	161
9) Belarus	166
10) Ukraine	170
11) Switzerland	172
12) Brazil	173
13) Mexico	175
14) Argentina	176
15) Colombia	178
16) Peru, Chile, Paraguay and others	178
17) Namibia	178
18) Swaziland	180
19) The East African Community (EAC)	180
20) Kenya	182
21) Mauritius	184
22) Australia	185
23) New Zealand	186
24) Vanuatu	187
IV. Countries where bitcoin is illegal	**190**
1) Egypt and the Muslim world	190
2) Morocco	192
3) Algeria	192
4) Bangladesh	193
5) Vietnam	195
6) Nepal	197
7) Bolivia	198

Chapter 3
Geopolitics of Future Cryptocurrencies

1) BRICS	203
2) The Russian-speaking area	204
3) Africa	206
4) The East African Community (EAC)	208
5) The Multilateral Monetary Area and Southern Africa	208
6) Western Sahara and the Arab Maghreb Union (AMU)	210
7) Ethiopia, Egypt and Sudan: a cryptocurrency or war?	213

8) Qatar and Iran: a cryptocurrency, then war?	217
9) The Portuguese-speaking area	220
10) The Turkish speaking area	220
11) Indonesia (Malaysia, Singapore, Papua New Guinea, Brunei, the Philippines)	221
12) CARICOM and OECS	224
13) ALBA-TCP	226
14) Cuba, the anti-example?	228
15) Alaska, California, Hawaii and Texas	229
Common currency or shared parity?	231

Conclusion
Two Opposing Futures

The old one, perfectly flawed	235
The New World	237
What to do with commercial banks?	243
Abundance for tomorrow?	244

Boxes

The Blockchain Against Hunger	13
PoW or PoS?	17
Cryptographic Hash Function	18
The NSA at the Origin of the Principle of Cryptocurrencies?	19
A Solar and Orbital Cryptocurrency	29
GAFA's Cryptocurrencies	36
Bitcoin, a Ponzi scheme?	44
The CoinHive Threat	62
How to Boost One's Stock Price?	73
Why Issue a Central Bank Digital Currency (CBDC)?	86
Costly Remittances	106
The CFA Franc	126
Catalonia—From Independence to Cryptocurrency?	137
The Fedcoin	142
Cryptocurrency Among the Sioux	143
Bitcoin, Inflation, GDP and Debt	153
Mining, the New Eldorado	163
The ForkLog Case in Ukraine	168
The Fabulous Success of Kenyan Mobile Payments	183
Evaluation and Taxation of Cryptocurrencies	189

www.ingramcontent.com/pod-product-compliance
Lightning Source LLC
LaVergne TN
LVHW042046070526
838201LV00077B/811